Cosmic History Chronicles

Volume V

Book of the Timespace

Time and Society: Envisioning the New Earth

The Relative Aspiring to the Absolute

Transmitted by Valum Votan—Jose Arguelles
Received by Red Queen—Stephanie South
"We are but the secretaries, the authors are in Eternity"

Blue Electric Storm Fifth Ray: Science and Harmony

Cosmic History Chronicles V – Book of the Timespace
Copyright © Galactic Research Institute

 Blue Electric Storm Year (2009)

ISBN 978-097859242-4
www.lawoftime.org

Original Graphics by Valum Votan (Jose Arguelles), Kin 11 and Red Queen (Stephanie South), Kin 185
Computer enhancement by Kelly Harding, Kin 240 and Jacob Wyatt, Kin 201
Book Design and Layout by Kelly Harding, Kin 240
Copy Edit by Forrest O'Farrell, Kin 140

Cosmic History Chronicles Volume V
Book of the Timespace
Time and Society: Envisioning the New Earth
The Relative Aspiring to the Absolute

Contents

Forward: Dreaming the Timespace

"…Throughout the world at this moment, without distinction of country, class, calling or creed, men (and women) are appearing who have begun to reason, to act and to pray in terms of the limitless and organic dimensions of Space-Time. To the outside observer such men (and women) may still seem isolated. But they are aware of one another among themselves, they recognize each other whenever their paths cross. They know that tomorrow, rejecting old concepts, divisions and forms, the whole world will see what they see and think as they do."

—Pierre Teilhard de Chardin, *Psyche*, Feb. 13, 1942

We are now slipping out of the historical framework that contains characters of the past—we are entering a new time where we are all being made into a new cast. We have been foretold in another time.

The *Book of the Timespace* occurs at a point when many preparations are being made in other dimensions and levels to assist us in this process. In this regard, *Tollan*, as described in this volume, serves as a focalizing point, sending down transmissions of Cosmic History to create specific programs that assist human evolution. These are wholeness and totality programs.

The full consciousness of the human planetary resonant field creates *the noosphere*, the planetary mind. In the timespace of the noosphere, we will no longer be fragmented or categorized, for we will have achieved the embodiment of the whole human, and in receiving the embodiment of the whole human we pass through to the mythic realm. We are leaving one time and entering another time through a shifting synchronic beam.

In the *Book of the Timespace*, chapters have turned into *channels*, thirteen in all. At any moment, we can tune into any of these channels and receive specific information anywhere from the *Galactic Beam* to *Telepathic Civilization*. This is an interactive process.

The *Book of the Timespace* is the fifth of a seven volume series. After completing the first four volumes, a cumulative impact of a perspective of Cosmic History was perceived—vaster than anything envisioned when we first began the process nearly seven years ago. This process has burgeoned and ballooned into a broad, kaleidoscopic, somewhat encyclopedic perspective, but from another dimension.

Book of the Timespace and all of the volumes of the *Cosmic History Chronicles*, are in preparation for the time when our lives will be immersed in the nature of telepathy and the creation of a new galactic cosmology according to the unified conscious cosmic field. With this fifth volume we are transitioning from the sensory quantum into the telepathic quantum in preparation of the noospheric consciousness in 2013 and beyond.

Cosmic History does not have a single author, but is rather the result of or production of a universal thought brought forth by a transmitting and receiving agent. In the process of creating this volume, the transmitting and receiving agents made a trip to Uluru, sacred site of the Australian aboriginal timespace. Soon after, on 5.13 (Electric Storm year), Kin 16, the Receiver had the following experience:

In the early morning of working on this text, the Receiver became very heavy and so closed her eyes. Immediately she began astral traveling through the cord of her solar plexus—Kuxan Suum. First she found herself floating through endless suburban neighborhoods taking note of the mental colorations along the way. Then she entered one of the homes, which at first appeared mundane, with a huge television monitor in the living room and dusty knickknacks scattered about the three-bedroom home. Continuing into what appeared to be an ordinary dining room, something caught her eye. Spread out over a large oak dining room table was a huge interplanetary "Telektonon" board with crystals set upon specific days and circuits. She heard a voice that said: "Pay attention to those circuits!"

Then, she received a telepathic message from the Transmitter indicating her to place her attention on it. She touched the crystal located on the externalizing circuit of Saturn and began to levitate, flying into a room in the back of the house. She entered through the door without opening it. The room was bathed in a soft, blue etheric light. In the corner sat the Transmitter at a large desk or drafting table working diligently on what appeared to be some type of codes.

On one wall she noticed a life-size star map and on another wall there was a terrestrial chart—a very detailed map of the Earth. As she studied the latter map she saw the Appalachian Mountains snow-capped in full view as if peering into a crystal ball projecting a hologram. The temperature in the room dropped dramatically.

The Transmitter then showed her a series of mathematical codes, subtle changes in the room began to occur; first sublime sensory effects, like the lighting began to soften and brighten, then the room's dimensions began to change; the ceiling got higher and the walls pulsed and then expanded. Different objects began to appear in the room while others disappeared. Every object in the room seemed to be shifting, altering, and morphing into ever greater creations, shapes and forms. Geometries began to appear. "These are the codes of the Timespace!"

She then floated out of this room into one of the smaller rooms in the seemingly mundane suburban home. This room was flashing in dimmed red and then brighter green coloring. There again, also, in this room sat the Transmitter wearing a large white and gold "shaman" hat. He was again sitting at a desk working on mathematical timespace codes. He said: "Hold on, I'm still working on it—the last one wasn't the final version."

Then she flew down a long hallway and opened the door to the third room only to see a large Chinese man eating a piece of fried chicken in a sterile looking room with subdued earthen tones. "Woops!" she said, "wrong door!" More journeys followed.

Before she returned to this third-dimensional reality, she woke several times into other realities, all lucid (meaning aware that you are in a dream). As she was trying to make her way back to this reality, she stumbled across many radio transmissions and began to receive various channels and crystal clear snippets of conversations.

Each snippet of conversation, which occurred in many languages, seemed to emanate from different dimensions. The channels would go static and fade, then new channels would come in, one of which spoke in pure mathematics and another which didn't speak at all but the transmission of the channel was felt and understood through vibration beyond words.

Once the Receiver came out of this prolonged astral travel, she inquired of the Transmitter what he had been working on during this time. As it turns out he had been mapping coordinates of the cosmic mind with corresponding mathematics coordinated in the underlying interdimensional substructure of the galactic whole, the matrix 441 and the holomind perceiver. While she had been on her astral journey, he had been receiving the Hunab Ku 21 archetypal substructures inclusive of tonal values, path, kin frequency, etc. (see *Channel 8*). This was all new information.

On the day of this occurrence the prominent telepathic frequency of these new codes was 108. It is the 108 or GM108X (Galactic Mayan mind transmission) that has been the guiding force of this entire series of the *Cosmic History Chronicles*. The Transmitter was tuning into and connecting mathematical frequencies that telepathically connected to all the different points and stages of the cosmic journey. In other words, he was absorbed in a transcendent reality that opened into many parallel realities, both subconscious and subliminal, simultaneously.

This parallel experience of Receiver and Transmitter was a sign of the new timespace and the synchronic order. All daily mappings of the synchronic order are applications of higher mental coordinates—this is the wiring of the noosphere.

Book of the Timespace is a quantum shift into a higher perspective and expanded cosmic perspective. Timespace is the context of the telepathic structure and order of reality. In terms of the cycle of the *Cosmic History Chronicles,* the fifth, sixth and seventh volumes create a mega telepathic quantum. We have left the sensory quantum of the first three volumes and have been catalyzed by the fourth. Now we are entering the telepathic realm. This is acute to the nature of timespace. This is an entirely new cosmology that ties into mathematical radiance and purity.

Welcome to the *Book of the Timespace*!

You have never been here before.

PART I
MAPPING THE TIMESPACE

CHANNEL 1

TIMESPACE EARTH

Between the cosmic Alpha and Omega lies the kaleidoscopic timespace. When we arrived on this planet, we entered a pre-organized timespace field or a stage set called Planet Earth. This is so basic that we take it for granted, but this is a highly complex organization of timespace that has evolved. Outside we see trees, mountains, clouds and sky; this is the organization of timespace. Inside we see tables, sinks, toilets and chairs. This is also the organization of timespace.

Timespace is like an empty theater with ever-evolving stage sets. Without timespace there would be no context in which to exist. Timespace is the most fundamental matrix of cosmic information. The most basic question we can ask ourselves is: What am I doing with my time in the space I have been granted?

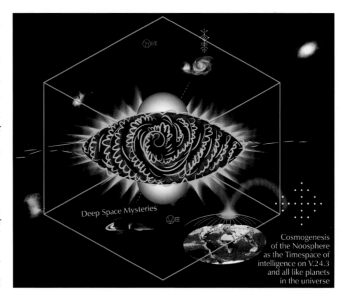

Deep Space Mysteries

Cosmogenesis of the Noosphere as the Timespace of intelligence on V.24.3 and all like planets in the universe

Look around you. Where do you now find yourself? What room are you in? What town are you in? What state or province are you in? What country are you in? What continent are you on? What planet are you on? What galaxy are you in? This is space. Space is an infinitely locatable point.

Look outside. Where is the sun in the sky? What day is it? What year is it? In what time are you living? How do you define it? Are you living in the end time? Are you living in the 21st century? How do you experience the passing of time? What purpose do you have in being in this time? This is time. Time is the universal factor of synchronization.

A timespace is a template of reality requiring organization of, by and for evolving intelligence. Any system of organization is an organization of a timespace. Timespace, as we know it, exists to accommodate a third-, and fourth-dimensional instrumentation called body. Timespace is the context in which matter and life evolve.

Timespace exists as a context that has meaning only when it is organized. How is your space organized? How is your time organized? Does your space synchronize with your time? Does the time you keep synchronize with your space?

A timespace is a context for the evolvement of cosmic life as it comes to be embodied into the human sensorium or form. The macrounity of this evolving context is the galaxy. Keep in mind that we have only recently become conscious of the existence of galaxies, via the telescope.

Earth is a Timespace Hologram

The Earth is a hologram of a particular timespace matrix; a type of training program. This timespace matrix is a function of a specific galactic beam, 5,125 years wide in diameter. As we move out of this beam in 2012, this particular timespace matrix dissolves and a new timespace phases in; the coming "Sixth Sun of Consciousness."

In order to understand the coming timespace, we must first understand how we construct our present timespace. Most people go through their entire life without considering the nature of the timespace they inhabit. Many think of timespace in terms of the third dimension, such as a room full of objects or a room arranged decoratively or artistically. Outside we might see through a window dividing inner from outer timespace, an arrangement of trees, bushes and grass and in the distance, mountains, sky and clouds.

In this present Earth reality, from which we are transiting, the foundation of understanding the timespace continuum began with Pythagoras who defined a triangle as $(a^2 + b^2 = c^2)$ where a, b, and c are the lengths of the sides of the triangle. This means that timespace could be organized as particular geometries of form. This train of thought continues with Einstein's theory of relativity, which states that neither time, length, nor mass remain constant additive quantities when approaching the speed of light. Einstein also said that time is the fourth dimension and left it at that—this is where the Law of Time factors in and the new timespace begins. But what is time? And what is space? And what is the relationship of mind and consciousness to time and space and of the third to the fourth dimension—are they inseparable?

If we stop thinking of time as having something before it and something behind it, then what is time? If we stop thinking of space as having something beside it, inside of it, or next to it, then what is space?

According to the Law of Time, time is radial. Space is infinite, or rather, an infinitely locatable point. Time is the fourth-dimension. Space is the third-dimension. Time is vertical. Space is horizontal. It is time, the fourth-dimensional order of reality that impresses and contains space, the third-dimensional order of reality. In this regard, timespace is the context of telepathic structures and orders of reality projected from the invisible fourth dimension to the visible third dimension. Earth, time and space form one inherent unity.

TIME AND SPACE

Time is the key in the reorientation of the mind. We have created a civilization that is space-oriented and space conscious—that is, it only focuses on what it can see, hear, taste, smell and touch. But now, with the advent of the Law of Time, time once again takes the forefront. Time is vertical. Time is invisible. Time is of the mind.

The primordial timespace is a telepathic context posited on the adage: the velocity of time is instantaneously infinite (N.A. Kozyrev). If we were to plot this on paper, it would look like a radial matrix with rays shooting out in all directions: This implies that time is generated, and that from any locus or point generating time, waves stream out radially in all directions. This is what is meant when physicists or esotericists say the past, future and present are one.

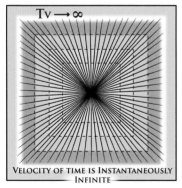

$T_V \longrightarrow \infty$

VELOCITY OF TIME IS INSTANTANEOUSLY INFINITE

Everything is happening simultaneously within one vast radial matrix of intersecting time waves. These time waves create interference patterns that condense into points of consciousness. Any point in this matrix is the central locus, no matter where it is located. This is an important point to keep in mind as we phase into a new timespace.

This self-existing radial matrix template is also what allows for the possibility of telepathy and time travel (which we will discuss more in-depth in later chapters). This description requires deep contemplation and meditation.

To further understand the radial nature of time, imagine a telepathic point of origin or a higher-dimensional thought moment. This thought moment radiates out from the fifth and fourth dimensions until it pierces third-dimensional reality, creating a massive volume of timespace. Within that radial matrix of timespace, the radiation of different thought moments of time are released. Each thought moment that radiates out creates a new radial matrix; each of these matrices is capable of creating a number of universes. This is an example of primordial time, and the simultaneously self-existing time wave thought moments that constitute all phases of cosmic evolution.

The timespace we find ourselves in can also be thought of as an alchemical vessel—a vehicle for transformation and evolution. The time of the 12:60 frequency represents an initiation of harmony through conflict; conflict with self and conflict with nature. At its root, this conflict was brought about and confirmed by an error in time.

Where are we going now? The Earth contains a series of layers or envelopes: the molten core, lithosphere, hydrosphere, atmosphere, biosphere stratosphere, and finally the magnetosphere. This creates an elaborate feedback system that maintains itself in a particular state of homeostasis, sometimes referred to as *Gaia*.

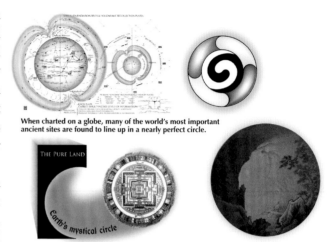

When charted on a globe, many of the world's most important ancient sites are found to line up in a nearly perfect circle.

THE PURE LAND

Earth's mystical circle

THE ROUND OF TIME IS THE FULFILLMENT OF SPACE
FROM THE POINT OF VIEW OF THE VELOCITY OF TIME, THE COSMOS IS CREATED; THIS IS A CONTINUOUS, CYCLICAL PROCESS.

When the homeostasis, which keeps everything in balance, is sufficiently disturbed, disruption or disorder occurs and the Earth enters into a new timespace. The present Earth is in its last stages of the *sixth day of creation*. At this stage, the Earth is a timespace capsule enveloped in the 12:60 machine frequency where money is the ruling force.

The whole Earth is encapsulated in this machine frequency brought forth by human free will. As the timespace shifts, some people work to unify and hold the balance, while others, out of self-interest, aid the disruptive forces in an attempt to halt the new world coming into being. The polarization between the two is the law of the system and only seeks to further the Plan. Within the Divine Plan, each individual has sealed in his/her heart a special duty to fulfill on behalf of the whole system. Many fulfill this unconsciously, while others choose to consciously fulfill it.

This 12:60 frequency creates the dissonance and ultimately a breaking of the homeostasis. If not curbed, it will result in a catastrophe (from the human point of view). However, even human disorder is a function of a higher order. Tipping the homeostatic balance in 2012 will trigger a pause in time, the *time quake*, when a massive timespace adjustment occurs, emanating from the tail of the magnetosphere.

From that timespace adjustment comes the creation of the next timespace or the next Earth for that timespace, the seventh Earth, the Earth of the seventh day of creation.

The Earth is currently passing out of a beam that is 5,125 years in diameter. The shift in timespace comes about once the Earth and its solar system are synchronized within the larger galactic community. This is the point of Galactic Synchronization of the Galactic Seed, July 26, 2013.

The universe is in a continuous process of creation and recreation. Most modern scientists agree that the beginning of the universe was 13.7 billion years ago. However, they are merely describing the

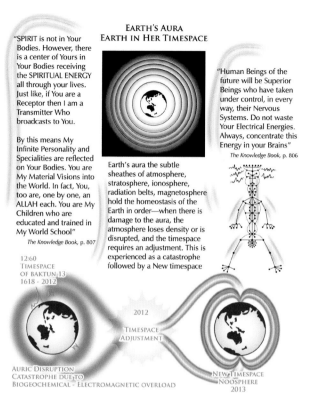

EARTH'S AURA
EARTH IN HER TIMESPACE

"SPIRIT is not in Your Bodies. However, there is a center of Yours in Your Bodies receiving the SPIRITUAL ENERGY all through your lives. Just like, if You are a Receptor then I am a Transmitter Who broadcasts to You.

By this means My Infinite Personality and Specialities are reflected on Your Bodies. You are My Material Visions into the World. In fact, You, too are, one by one, an ALLAH each. You are My Children who are educated and trained in My World School"

The Knowledge Book, p. 807

"Human Beings of the future will be Superior Beings who have taken under control, in every way, their Nervous Systems. Do not waste Your Electrical Energies. Always, concentrate this Energy in your Brains"

The Knowledge Book, p. 806

Earth's aura the subtle sheathes of atmosphere, stratosphere, ionosphere, radiation belts, magnetosphere hold the homeostasis of the Earth in order—when there is damage to the aura, the atmosphere loses density or is disrupted, and the timespace requires an adjustment. This is experienced as a catastrophe followed by a New timespace

12:60
TIMESPACE
OF BAKTUN 13
1618 - 2012

2012
TIMESPACE
ADJUSTMENT

AURIC DISRUPTION
CATASTROPHE DUE TO
BIOGEOCHEMICAL - ELECTROMAGNETIC OVERLOAD

NEW TIMESPACE
NOOSPHERE
2013

most recent cycle of the universe of matter. The telepathic universe is far more ancient than the mind can conceive. What we call timespace is actually a telepathic projection of an original template, known by the Maya as *Tollan*.

The primordial timespace exists in the higher-dimensional telepathic realms that are simultaneously aeons old and also exist in the present moment. This primordial timespace is organized by pure number; mathematical structures and geometries, etc.

Again, look around the room you are in and note what you see. Tables? Chairs? Computer? Or if you are outdoors, you might see some type of natural setting with trees, bushes, sky, etc. Reflect on what you see. Now reflect on what you don't see.

These objects are pure vibrational structures that exist in other dimensions simultaneously. These objects are actually manifestations of fourth-, fifth- and sixth-dimensional telepathic structures. What you see when you look at these objects or natural forms, is actually a reflection of a successful projection of form into the third dimension from the telepathic realms. Also keep in mind that everything has a particular vibration. Just think: You in your present form are a function of a telepathic infrastructure that is maintaining and projecting your form in this specific timespace from another dimension!

15

CHANNEL 2

NOOSPHERE, TIMESPACE AND MEMORY

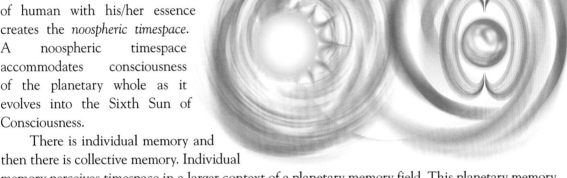

Timespaces alter according to the quality and clarity of the memory of the being, whether an individual or collective. The reconnection of human with his/her essence creates the *noospheric timespace*. A noospheric timespace accommodates consciousness of the planetary whole as it evolves into the Sixth Sun of Consciousness.

There is individual memory and then there is collective memory. Individual memory perceives timespace in a larger context of a planetary memory field. This planetary memory field holds the collective memory as well as the future vision of the planet or noosphere. The noosphere occupies a type of timespace that we have yet to fully encounter: a psycho-mental-solar timespace. The noosphere is too vast to conceptualize but can be experienced and absorbed psychomentally. The noosphere can also be experienced as an attribute of the timespace of the Sun.

We usually think of timespace in terms of the room we are sitting in or what it looks like outside the window. These are causal timespaces that are functions of highly conditioned optical terms. If this were all there was to timespace then there would not be much to contemplate.

The multi-leveled facets of timespace are vast and can be likened to the electromagnetic spectrum of light. Only a portion of this spectrum is visible light, where invisible colors contain infrared rays at the lower end of the spectrum, and ultraviolet rays at the higher end of the spectrum. Similarly, there is a sensory spectrum of timespace; and a non-tangible, infrared and an ultrasensory level.

There are timespaces beneath the level of our threshold of perception and there are timespaces beyond our threshold or level of perception. The ultrasensory timespace is represented by the noosphere or cosmic memory field; the infrasensory timespace is represented by the individual down to the atomic and subatomic levels.

THE NATURE OF MEMORY, THOUGHT AND TIMESPACE

What is memory? Memory occurs when there is a particular activation and configuration of analphs. An analph is an electro-sensory-conceptual storage unit. Therefore, memory is the activation of stored *analphs* triggered by stimulus of any variety of psychosensory impressions (see *CHC Vol. II*).

Memory is made of thought. Thought is an analphic engraving in a series. The act of thinking is the correct or incorrect manipulation of a series of analphic engravings. These analphs are projected and registered in a conscious area of the mind, based on knowledge previously acquired. If there is no previously acquired knowledge, then we try to establish correct thinking according to past engravings. New impressions are generally ignored in favor of what is already known. The only way new impressions can be absorbed is if the thinking process is suspended so that fresh engravings can penetrate the mind.

Where does memory take place? Is the analph like a hologram that, when activated, creates its whole timespace context? Where is the timespace of dream and daydream?

There are many types of physical timespaces, as well as numerous inner timespaces to explore. Let us define three examples of different levels of timespace:

1. **Spiritual timespace.** This includes the vast index of spiritual experiences or "awakenings". These experiences occur on subtle planes of reality within a construct that we refer to as "mind".

2. **Psychomythic timespace.** This is an inner timespace, best explained by: "Once upon a time there was a unicorn." Where was the unicorn? What did it look like? What did the garden it lived in look like? These are contemplations of the psychomythic timespace.

3. **Cosmo-physiological timespace.** Thoughtforms of this timespace include: "We came from the stars and the stars came from that galaxy which originated in this particular way. Then we constructed a cosmology of who we are, how we got here, what the whole system we are involved in is about."

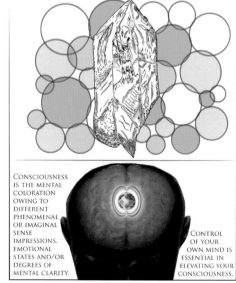

CONSCIOUSNESS IS THE MENTAL COLORATION OWING TO DIFFERENT PHENOMENAL OR IMAGINAL SENSE IMPRESSIONS, EMOTIONAL STATES AND/OR DEGREES OF MENTAL CLARITY.

CONTROL OF YOUR OWN MIND IS ESSENTIAL IN ELEVATING YOUR CONSCIOUSNESS.

Memory assists us by supplying us data in negotiating or navigating the evolving timespace. For example, the way we experience the passing of time is a function of our psychobiological continuum informed primarily by memory. Our psychobiology also equips our consciousness stream with an anchor or lens to view ourselves and to envision potential futures.

Two interesting questions to contemplate are: What isn't memory? What is habit and what is its relation to memory?

YOGA AND TIMESPACE: THREE LEVELS OF TIMESPACE PERCEPTION

Consider the following perceptions of timespace: biological, psychophysical and psychic/mental:

1. **Biological organization of timespace:** This refers to how our being is organized physically and how all of life represents a biological organization.
2. **Psychophysical/sensory organization of timespace:** This refers to our inner mental timespace as organized through sensory impressions combined with our interpretation. Interpretation varies according to our ever-shifting condition and level of consciousness. We generally think our interpretations correspond to something external, but it may or may not.
3. **Psychic/mental organization of timespace:** Refers to the index of dreams, memories and imaginings. In traditional yoga systems, these three levels are organized as five bodies.

HUMAN TIMESPACE: FIVE SHEATHES OF THE BODY

The human being has yet to fully explore the nature of timespace both within and without. The planetary human generally lives within a veiled awareness of him/herself. In classic yoga systems of India, the human, who is seen as the projector of all timespace as we know it, consists of five sheathes or bodies: 1). Anamayakosha—physical body or food sheathe; 2). Pranamayakosha—energy bodies, prana, subtle body; 3). Manomayakosha—Mental body, psychosensory; 4). Vijnanamayakosha—Body of discriminating intelligence; 5). Anandamayakosha—essence or bliss body.

1. **Anamayakosha (Physical body or food sheathe)**
   The physical body or *anamayakosha* refers to the way humans organize their timespaces so they can eat. In other words, human timespace is largely organized around food and feeding. This can be observed in the business district of virtually any city on the Planet. These business districts (timespaces) are largely organized around numerous eateries, cafes, restaurants, vendors and mini markets. Most people do not consider where the food from these eateries comes from. The point is that the majority of the social organization of timespace revolves around food and the feeding of the body.

TOLLAN ~ 5 SHEATHES ~ 7 CENTERS

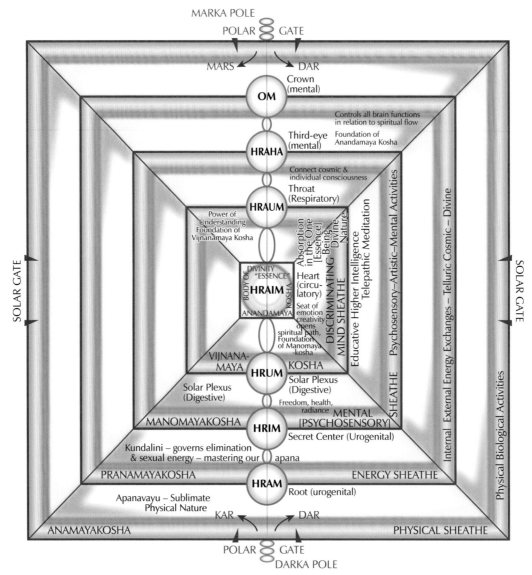

TOLLAN ~ THE CENTER OF SYNTROPIA
BRINGING ABOUT THE REALITY
OF THE UNIFIED HUMANITY

Contemplate how society is organized to satisfy the food sheathe or physical body. What happens if we change our eating habits and adopt a vegan or raw food diet? How does that affect our perception of timespace? How did our ancestors perceive food? Did it affect their timespace? Or was it so integrated into their timespace that it did not affect it at all? Now food is a very big deal. Most food is processed and relies on every aspect the technosphere to get it from an agricultural unit to our tables. This is an effect of the mechanization of timespace.

2. Pranamayakosha (Energy or Subtle Body)

Pranamayakosha refers to the energy body that takes in air and subtle nutrients—the prana and plasmas—that feeds the energy body inside. Most people breathe and don't think too much about it. The energy body has everything to do with the atmosphere of the Earth; it is inseparable from it. Do we understand the actual affects that polluting the atmosphere has upon the energy body?

The purpose of becoming conscious of our breath and practicing pranayams—yoga or discipline of breath—which assist in organizing the space of our internal system, is to cultivate greater cosmic perceptions. We cannot experience cosmic perceptions readily or systemically in a disciplined way unless we are working with the breath and energy body. How does control of breath bring new cosmic perceptions? Where is the base of those cosmic perceptions? Where do they come from, and where do they reside in our being? When we breathe consciously—pranayama—we are taking the akashic field into our lungs and energy body. The very act of breathing is a cosmic process that mimics the cycle of universal creation and annihilation. Through conscious breathing, our energy body becomes coextensive with the universal timespace field and the akashic energy field.

3. Manomayakosha (Mental Body)

Manomayakosha or mental body is the place in the psychophysical or psychosensory body where the data of the outer world enters through the senses. Most people do not think much about this. For most people, the inner sensory spatial organization is a jumble. Things are automatically or unconsciously sorted out according to how important they are to the ego. Manomayakosha also refers to the timespace psychosensory input, process and output unit. This includes the data storage and retrieval system, as well as the different mental spheres activated by and accounting for rapid fire sense impressions and conditioned response analphic firings. How this is connected to the noosphere is a topic of future investigation. By the practice of meditation we can begin to see the different impressions and workings of manomayakosha. We actually live in a wrap-around time sensorium where every element of our sense organs is constantly being addressed. Most of the input goes into "dead space" but a select amount is processed in order to maintain a particular orientation.

4. Vijnanamayakosha (Creative Mental Body)

Vijnanamayakosha or creative mental body is the discriminating, creatively active, discursive mental timespace that changes according to the nature of the ever-shifting mental constructs. These mental constructs are assembled by the "thinker," and are functions of the ego/self.

This is what we might call the timespace of ideas and concepts, conceptual, intellectual, ideational timespace. This is where we do our "head tripping", intentionally or otherwise. Vijnanamayakosha primarily corresponds to the third mental sphere (conscious) with input from the other mental spheres, either by random association, receptivity or intentionally. One of the purposes of meditation is to put an "Earth light" of awareness upon this sphere of mental activity to understand how it works and how it can be more focused and effective. This timespace is where our consciousness primarily resides. For this reason, it is important to keep it clear so we can perform everyday tasks which are dependent on correct use of logic, intellect and awareness, the essence of vijnanamayakosha.

5. Anandamayakosha (Body of Bliss)

Anandamayakosha or body of bliss refers to the timespace of our primal essence nature. This is a timespace that is essential to our evolutionary will, yet is the least known of our inner realms. When this timespace is activated it produces contact between our deepest essence and the Absolute, ultimate divine reality: the cosmic memory timespace itself. This contact is such a relief when it occurs that it produces a sensitivity called bliss that extends through the entire timespace by merging the sense of self and other into an experience of unitive ecstasy. This opens to cosmic timespace yielding an effect that is sometimes referred to as cosmic consciousness, or the Akashic records.

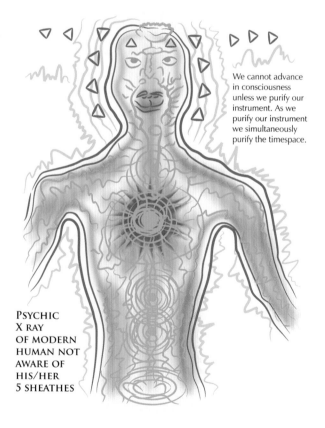

We cannot advance in consciousness unless we purify our instrument. As we purify our instrument we simultaneously purify the timespace.

PSYCHIC X RAY OF MODERN HUMAN NOT AWARE OF HIS/HER 5 SHEATHES

PRANIC-LUNAR CYCLE
OF STAGES OF BEING
& ACTION

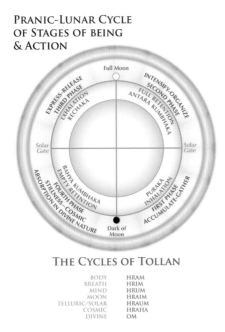

THE CYCLES OF TOLLAN

BODY	HRAM
BREATH	HRIM
MIND	HRUM
MOON	HRAIM
TELLURIC/SOLAR	HRAUM
COSMIC	HRAHA
DIVINE	OM

We also see this fourfold process in the synchronic order as input, store, process, output, matrix (see *CHC Vol. I*). Matrix refers to the whole field created by and accommodating this system as feedback. This is an example of timespace organization.

ORGANIZING TIMESPACE THROUGH BREATH—A SIMPLE EXERCISE

The temple part of the timespace that we inhabit (spatial) is organized as a four-fold process that can be understood through our breath. This can be experienced through a simple exercise.

Phase One—Inhale. This is the accumulation of cosmic energy. The cosmos inhales and is gathered from out of nowhere. Count to 4 as you inhale (input).

Phase Two—Intermediary. This is when the vital energy, the prana and plasmas go into the energy body to vitalize the whole system. Hold the breath 4 counts (retain, store, process).

Phase Three—Exhale. This is when the residue goes out with conscious intentions. Count to 4 as you exhale (output).

Phase Four—Total Stillness. This is the ripening of conscious where you are at one with the cosmic totality. Remain without breath for 4 counts (matrix).

As you do this exercise—at least seven times—keep your mind clear without fixating in a condition of intrinsic awareness. Feel the totality of the cosmos.

ORIGIN OF TIMESPACE

Where does timespace originate? Let's journey back further than the perceived Big Bang to consider what is behind our presently known timespace.

According to *The Knowledge Book*, three light universes preceded our current timespace. Each of these light universes was organized by the power of 49 (7 × 7), for a total power frequency of 147 (7 × 21). These light universes can be thought of as pure, abstract planes of reality. They consist of 1) the land of the loving ones, 2) the land of the sages and 3) the land of the preeminent ones. Before there was a physical universe, the primary existence was the layers within the light universes

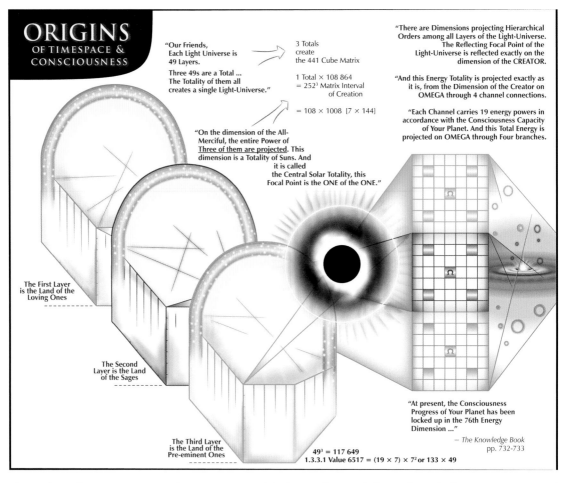

ORIGINS
OF TIMESPACE &
CONSCIOUSNESS

"Our Friends,
Each Light Universe is
49 Layers.

Three 49s are a Total ...
The Totality of them all
creates a single Light-Universe."

3 Totals
create
the 441 Cube Matrix

1 Total × 108 864
= 252³ Matrix Interval
of Creation

= 108 × 1008 [7 × 144]

"On the dimension of the All-
Merciful, the entire Power of
Three of them are projected. This
dimension is a Totality of Suns. And
it is called
the Central Solar Totality, this
Focal Point is the ONE of the ONE."

"There are Dimensions projecting Hierarchical
Orders among all Layers of the Light-Universe.
The Reflecting Focal Point of the
Light-Universe is reflected exactly on the
dimension of the CREATOR.

"And this Energy Totality is projected exactly as
it is, from the Dimension of the Creator on
OMEGA through 4 channel connections.

"Each Channel carries 19 energy powers in
accordance with the Consciousness Capacity
of Your Planet. And this Total Energy is
projected on OMEGA through Four branches.

"At present, the Consciousness
Progress of Your Planet has been
locked up in the 76th Energy
Dimension ..."
— The Knowledge Book
pp. 732-733

The First Layer
is the Land of the
Loving Ones

The Second
Layer is the Land
of the Sages

The Third Layer
is the Land of the
Pre-eminent Ones

49³ = 117 649
1.3.3.1 Value 6517 = (19 × 7) × 7² or 133 × 49

where these basic positive qualities pre-existed. The qualities of these three light universes are: 1) Love/compassion, 2) Wisdom and 3) Hierarchical Order.

From within the light dimensions came a projection on the totality of the solar dimensions. In the blueprint of cosmic creation exists the holographic template of every star, every sun, etc. In the template of the totality of suns is projected this light ray into the central solar totality. The focal point is the One of the One. In the center of each star lies the solar logos; the focal point of the One of the One. This is the focal point of the Hunab Ku, the One Giver of Movement and Measure. This seed is in every star, like a hologram of the total.

There are numerous dimensional totalities of different stars. There are 28 solar dimensions organized in four categories that create the projection of 112 hierarchical orders. Each order represents a totality, similar to what Michael Talbott referred to as the "holographic universe." Only the human mind divides. Everything naturally exists in a channel of wholeness.

There are three layers of 49 or 147 (49 × 3), one third of the 441 (21 × 21) cube matrix. This 441 cube matrix is created from the mathematical structure of the light universes; it is the primal multidimensional holographic fractal: 3 × 7 = 147; 3 × 147 = 441. This 441 cube matrix is evolved as a timespace cube enclosing the physical plane timespace cube.

41	40	39	38	37	36	35	34	33	32	31	30	29	28	27	26	25	24	23	22	21
42	117	116	115	114	113	112	111	110	109	108	107	106	105	104	103	102	101	100	99	20
43	118	185	184	183	182	181	180	179	178	177	176	175	174	173	172	171	170	169	98	19
44	119	186	245	244	243	242	241	240	239	238	237	236	235	234	233	232	231	168	97	18
45	120	187	246	297	296	295	294	293	292	291	290	289	288	287	286	285	230	167	96	17
46	121	188	247	298	341	340	339	338	337	336	335	334	333	332	331	284	229	166	95	16
47	122	189	248	299	342	377	376	375	374	373	372	371	370	369	330	283	228	165	94	15
48	123	190	249	300	343	378	405	404	403	402	401	400	399	368	329	282	227	164	93	14
49	124	191	250	301	344	379	406	425	424	423	422	421	398	367	328	281	226	163	92	13
50	125	192	251	302	345	380	407	426	437	436	435	420	397	366	327	280	225	162	91	12
51	126	193	252	303	346	381	408	427	438	441	434	419	396	365	326	279	224	161	90	11
52	127	194	253	304	347	382	409	428	439	440	433	418	395	364	325	278	223	160	89	10
53	128	195	254	305	348	383	410	429	430	431	432	417	394	363	324	277	222	159	88	9
54	129	196	255	306	349	384	411	412	413	414	415	416	393	362	323	276	221	158	87	8
55	130	197	256	307	350	385	386	387	388	389	390	391	392	361	322	275	220	157	86	7
56	131	198	257	308	351	352	353	354	355	356	357	358	359	360	321	274	219	156	85	6
57	132	199	258	309	310	311	312	313	314	315	316	317	318	319	320	273	218	155	84	5
58	133	200	259	260	261	262	263	264	265	266	267	268	269	270	271	272	217	154	83	4
59	134	201	202	203	204	205	206	207	208	209	210	211	212	213	214	215	216	153	82	3
60	135	136	137	138	139	140	141	142	143	144	145	146	147	148	149	150	151	152	81	2
61	62	63	64	65	66	67	68	69	70	71	72	73	74	75	76	77	78	79	80	1

The star, planet and galaxy all have a common resonance; the vibrating pulse of the original organization of the three primal light universes existing before the last big bang. The galaxy coordinates the star, and the star coordinates the planet, and the planet coordinates the human (noosphere). It is the star that creates the space of its system. It is the galaxy that creates the space of its system. It is the aggregate of the galaxy that creates the third/fourth-dimensional cosmic time space. This is the central solar totality that emanates to other totalities with the same program of totality.

There are also different solar dimensions according to different levels of evolution of energy. There are 28 solar dimensions, a key number in the formula of the Law of Time, 4:7 (= 28). What we call consciousness is a function of the planetary field. *Earth Ascending* describes a geomantic model of the holonomic brain.

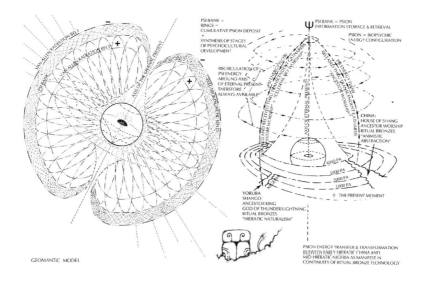

We can feel the quality of holonomic resonance by contemplating the construction of the Sun. The same process occurs in the brain, the mini holonomic field, and the solar and galactic fields. Once we apprehend what the higher levels of evolvement are then we can begin to organize our timespace accordingly to establish a holonomic timespace that accommodates the resonances of the noosphere and cosmic civilization.

PLANETARY TIMESPACE

Timespace gives the human a context to develop awareness and consciousness of itself as a member of a planetary totality. Totality is transmitted through the solar consciousness into the planetary field. The vast harmonic matrix of the 28 solar dimensions or totalities contains the whole range of hierarchical levels of organization of what we call the manifest and non-manifest multidimensional universe. The human being, through purification and integration, experiences the frequency coming through the planetary field into itself and begins to partake in the whole of totality.

This information is coming from a focalized point within the center of the Sun. Keep in mind that our Sun has a holonomic resonance with the totality of all suns. The center of totality of all suns then, has a resonance with the galaxy. It is from these centers that the information from the original hierarchical order is transmitted.

Stars create their own timespace field. Within this field, evolutionary currents take their place in different stages of evolvement. Within the myriad of galaxies of cosmic order there are innumerable different levels and stages of evolvement.

As *The Knowledge Book* defines it (p. 739), there are ultimately 28 primary solar dimensions that define the matrix of evolvement. In this 28-dimensional system there are four categories: 1) Solar systems; 2) Evolution dimension; 3) Energy dimensions; and 4) Solar dimensional (totalities). This defines 112 (4 × 28) categories of evolvement. This is only a small fraction or compendium of what exists in the universe.

The timespace is ever changing within the matrix of evolvement; in fact, it exists *for the purpose of evolvement*. Note: There are 28 Arabic letters with four ways of writing them whether the letter is alone, in the front, in the middle or at the end of a word for a total of 112 characters.

Because we are the focalizers of the Milky Way, our planet itself is also known as the Milky Way galaxy. Tollan, the archetypal, interdimensional source of our psychocultural planetary timespace is located within the Milky Way galaxy.

The galaxy coordinates the star, and the star coordinates the planet, and the planet coordinates the human (noosphere).

TABLE OF WORLD EVOLUTION ENERGY DIMENSIONS
SYSTEM OF 28 – 4 CHANNELS – HARMONIC STANDARD

$$2523 \div 28 = 144 \times 441 \times 9$$

Timespace occurs only in the first seven stages. Cube System Hypertime governs next 9 stages to OMEGA.

Left-margin vertical labels: **ONE TOTAL** — Terrestrial Knowledge (7)(49), Celestial Knowledge (7)(49), Universal Knowledge (7)(49) — **ORDINANCES OF ALL TYPES OF SPIRITUAL POSSIBILITIES** — **POST-HUMAN SUPRAMENTAL / HIGHER ENLIGHTENMENT / PURE DOMAIN OF HUNAB KU**

Solar System/Frequency	Evolution Dimension	Energy Dimension	Solar Dimension (Totalities)	(Description)
0 Frequency (V.24.3)	3rd Biophysical V.24.3	12 = The Temple	1st Solar D. V.24.3 Milkyway Totality	Milky Way Galaxy, 1st Step Evolution of Knowledge
1 " V.24.3	4th Astral-Mental-Spiritual Terrestrial Knowledge (7)	16 (4^2) Entry Gate to Karena *reincarnation comes*	2nd Solar D. V.24.3 *to an end here*	Dimension of Heaven
2 "	5th Dimension "Higher Self"	20	3rd Solar D.	*NOOSPHERE* Hyperorganic higher-dimensional supramental evolution
3 "	6th Dimension of Ascension "Immortality"	24 Exit Gate from Karena	4th Solar D.	
(4) " 4:7 Reflecting Gamma Principle	(7th) Dimension of Evolutionary Perfection	(28) Final Manifestation Boundary of Humanity	5th Solar D. *preparing evolution for 14th solar system*	
5 " Reflective focal point of 15th Solar System	8th 1st Step of Spiritual dimension	32 Crystal Dimension *first of nine steps - final*	6th step = Path of Golden Light	1st Stage post-terrestrial spiritual dimension
6 " **NEW TESTAMENT** Reflective focal point of 16th Solar System	9th Quran Lordly dimension	36 Dimension of Manifestation of Sacred Texts	7th "	
7 Entrance to Medium of Unity	10th Transition to CUBE SYSTEM	40 Cube System *development of supramental faculties*	8th "	Supramental Evolution: Medium of Unity
8	11th Dimension of Central Channel. 441 Cube Matrix	44 Prepares for Evolvement to 118th Dim. Alion	9th "	
9	12th	48	10th "	Cube System
10	(13th) Dimension ordinance of Cosmic Cycles	52 Sirius B Codes Law of Time	11th "	
11	14th Elimination of Religious Consciousness	56	12th "	Average level of Consciousness Attainment *V.24.3 at this moment (12-12)*
12	15th	60	13th "	
13 Frequency of Cosmic Wave Cycle	16th The Mighty Dimension	64 Energy of Universal DNA Codes	14th " 1st hemicycle of 28 dimension complete	Last 5 Steps 9-step Spiritual dimension
14 GAMMA	17th Reflections made to 7th dimension	68 Frequency of Intergalactic Navigation	15th "	
15 *Dimension in which*	18th Quran was prepared 18-dimensional universe	72 Reflection made to 8th dim. 18.72–2012 Codes Prepared	16th " 1st Step Ω Dim. *Mass preparation program for Omega dimension*	
Ω 16 OMEGA: Point of projection of Hierarchical Orders	19th 9 Layers of Omega dim. Final evolution of V.24.3	76 1st Evolvement Step Dim. of Salvation KNOWLEDGE BOOK	17th " Golden Light	Final Super Human evolutionary step
17	20th	80	18th "	
18 Frequency of 18 Dimensional Universe	21st Focalization dimension of Hunab Ku *21st solar system*	84 Dimension of Dharma Codes	19th " Domain of Direct	Domain of Post-human Supramental Solar Entities
19	22nd	88	20th " Ordinance of Hunab Ku	
20 Frequency of Totality Hunab Ku as manifest form	23rd Frequency of solar sunspot cycle	92	21st " Preparation for "Star Masters"	
21 Frequency of Hunab Ku Focalization point of all Cosmoses	24th Dimension of Radiant Return to Source	96	22nd "	"Those who come to Your Planet from the Energy Dimensions beyond the (20)th Solar System are the Missionaries of the Galaxies. They are the Prophets - Saints - Sages and the Solar Teachers." —The Knowledge Book p. 740
22	25th	100	23rd "	
23	26th	104	24th "	
24 Frequency of Return Cycle	27th Dimension of Heart of Nine	108 Energy of Templates of Star Mind for Avataric Projection	25th " Totality of Fifth Force as Star Master Matrix	
25	28th	112	26th "	Beyond the 20th Solar System is the 21st frequency of Hunab Ku, indescribable generation of the Core of all galaxies governing universal spin, form, number and stages of evolvement.
26	29th	116 Alion Planet =	27th " Alion System of Sixes established	
27 "Heart of Nine" 3^3 System of Nines	30th	120 118th Dim = =6.0 1 Mirror Neptune Entrance	28th " Harmonic Standard	

EXIT TO PURE LIGHT UNIVERSES

Harmonic Matrix accommodates all stages of Cosmic Evolution potential within the vastness of Allah's Totality. It is simply a system for the registration of the variety of Soul Experiences in a certain self-defined experimental domain.

Tollan is one of the star bases that projects the hierarchical orders to our Sun and then through our Sun into the planetary field.

From Tollan as a focalizing point, there are two main energy streams that affect our understanding of timespace. The first energy stream emanates from the cube system located within the eleventh energy dimension and beyond. The second energy stream is focalized through the Sirius B-52 system located within the thirteenth energy dimension. These two energy streams are significant for the evolvement of timespace on this Planet.

Tollan also serves as a blueprint for all higher social organization including temples, urban sites, etc. To contemplate and articulate timespace requires a stepping down from the light universe to a solar focal point of the totality of all suns, and then to the physical plane suns, and finally to the planetary levels.

At first, it might seem overwhelming to contemplate the different systems and levels of timespace organization. At the third-dimensional biophysical, spiritual/astral level, we can perceive the physical organization of timespace as different objects or planetary bodies and stars, etc. From these observations we make star maps of varying degrees of sophistication, but these are never wholly satisfying. Even at the third-dimensional level the cosmic timespace is nothing less than overwhelming, dynamic and ever-changing.

To summarize: The timespace is a system for the registration of the variety of soul experiences that are self-defined at a very early stage of this matrix. The timespace provides the context that includes evolvement of soul material from 1) the third and fourth plane of reality; 2) the material etheric dimension; and 3) the fifth to the seventh dimensions. This develops the noospheric plane of reality. These planes always exist and can be activated through self-reflective consciousness. Once this is in place we can experience, as an evolving mass, soul travel and beyond.

A VIEW OF DISTANT TOLLAN - "STAR BASE" - COMMUNICATION AND ENERGY CENTER

CHANNEL 3

TIMESPACE IN METAMORPHOSIS

We are now at the end of the sixth day of creation; the seventh Earth of the seventh day of creation will begin to emerge after December 21, 2012. This New Earth will be fully manifest by the Galactic Synchronization date of the Galactic Seed, July 26, 2013. The metamorphosis of the timespace of the whole of reality augured by this moment is without precedent.

As the old structures erode and create more disillusionment, some people go into fear, anger or panic, while for others who are more conscious, the fading away of structures represents the potentiality for heightened telepathic comprehension and understanding. This is the function of the noosphere: to maximize telepathic understanding so that when we reach the critical juncture, we will stabilize into a higher-dimensional norm.

The Quran says that God created seven universes and the same number of earths, then He commands the flow of information among them; God is omnipotent and is fully aware of all things. (Sura 65:12)

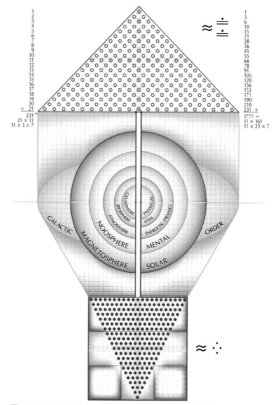

TIMESPACE MATHEMATICS OF THE NOOSPHERE

What does it mean that God created seven universes? And seven earths? Do these earths exist on different alternative or parallel universe dimensions simultaneously? Or do these earths refer to a succession or dynasty of earths that exist or have existed in different timespaces?

Different thought matrices are created when the pulsations of time radiate out from a particular point of origin and pierce the wall of fourth- dimensional reality. This process is also coincident with telepathy. We conclude that there were seven primordial creation matrices known on Earth as the *seven days of creation.*

These seven days of creation are related to the mysteries of the seven generations referred to in the Chilam Balam prophetic texts as the Book of the Seven Generations. A similar reference is found in the *Documents of Takenouchi, a*n ancient tradition in Japan that refers to the seven generations of the divine era, a nonmanifest era of duration of billions of years before the present universe. So we have the 7 divine generations, 7 generations, 7 days of creation, 7 tribes brought by "Votan" from across the sea, and also the Book of Seven Generations. These all refer to primordial stages of creation.

The first "seven days" of the seven divine generations presented in the document of Takenouchi exist in a pure telepathic realm, a fractal ratio of seven that is the basis of the *interval of lost time in eternity*. This is a theme put forth most notably by Sufi master Qadi Saiid al-Qummi (see *CHC Vol. I*), which says that the primal cosmos was a perfect sphere that then was somehow fractured. The *interval or fracture*, then, represents the first manifestation of time from within cosmos, in which there is "no time".

We have to think the unimaginable: a flawless featureless (to us) cosmic sphere of untold scale—beyond time and space. These are like the light universes present in *The Knowledge Book* or the "Night of Brahman" in the Hindu tradition. A perturbation occurs from within; a fracture that shatters, projecting a resonant frequency intrinsic to itself—a self-born ratio with a frequency of seven.

The lost interval ratio of seven is the holographic memory (akashic field) from which the entire timespace and universe arises.

This interval ratio 7 is stepped down, as the seven divine generations, the archetype of the seven primal generations, and then the seven days of creation, thence establishing lower dimensions until it reaches the seventh, sixth and fifth dimensions. At this point, the electronic structures that organize the underlying patterns of phenomenal reality of the third and fourth-dimensional timespace manifest according to the primordial mathematical structures of reality.

This lost interval of time corresponds to the role of seven in the primary and self-intrinsic ratio of the Law of Time: 4:7::7:13. This is the prime frequency ratio of creation. Any time a frequency ratio is set there occurs the interaction of different frequencies set up at intervals. The relation of intervals to each other is what creates number. Number is the grammar and vocabulary of telepathy. Number and telepathy generate the ever-evolving timespace continuum as an etheric or akashic medium capable of transmitting information and energy telecosmically.

Most modern scientists agree that the age of the universe is 13.7 billion years. At this point the manifestation

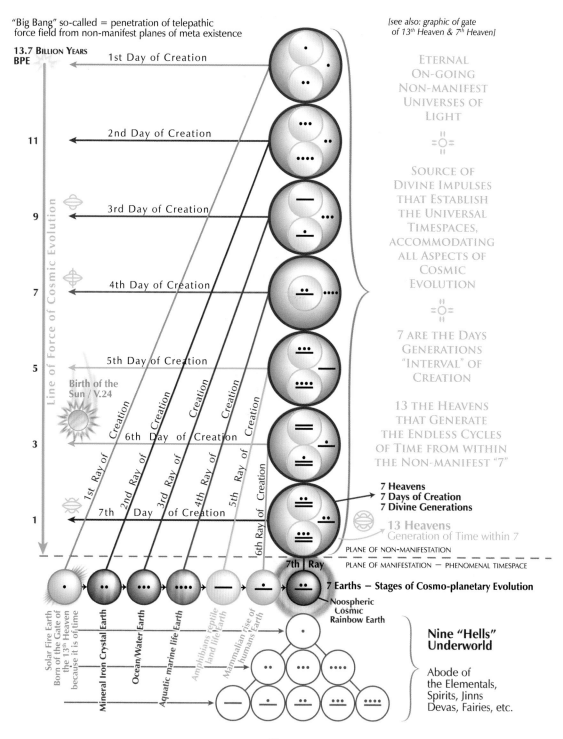

"Big Bang" so-called = penetration of telepathic
force field from non-manifest planes of meta existence

[see also: graphic of gate
of 13ᵗʰ Heaven & 7ᵗʰ Heaven]

13.7 Billion Years BPE

1st Day of Creation

2nd Day of Creation

3rd Day of Creation

4th Day of Creation

5th Day of Creation

Birth of the
Sun / V.24

6th Day of Creation

7th Day of Creation

11

9

7

5

3

1

Line of Force of Cosmic Evolution

1st Ray of Creation
2nd Ray of Creation
3rd Ray of Creation
4th Ray of Creation
5th Ray of Creation
6th Ray of Creation

7th Ray

ETERNAL
ON-GOING
NON-MANIFEST
UNIVERSES OF
LIGHT

SOURCE OF
DIVINE IMPULSES
THAT ESTABLISH
THE UNIVERSAL
TIMESPACES,
ACCOMMODATING
ALL ASPECTS OF
COSMIC
EVOLUTION

7 ARE THE DAYS
GENERATIONS
"INTERVAL" OF
CREATION

13 THE HEAVENS
THAT GENERATE
THE ENDLESS CYCLES
OF TIME FROM WITHIN
THE NON-MANIFEST "7"

7 Heavens
7 Days of Creation
7 Divine Generations

13 Heavens
Generation of Time within 7

PLANE OF NON-MANIFESTATION

PLANE OF MANIFESTATION — PHENOMENAL TIMESPACE

7 Earths — Stages of Cosmo-planetary Evolution

Noospheric
Cosmic
Rainbow Earth

Solar Fire Earth
Born of the Gate of
the 13ᵗʰ Heaven
because it is of time

Mineral Iron Crystal Earth

Ocean/Water Earth

Aquatic marine life Earth

Amphibians reptile
land life Earth

Mammalian rise of
humans Earth

**Nine "Hells"
Underworld**

Abode of
the Elementals,
Spirits, Jinns
Devas, Fairies, etc.

enters from the non-manifest light universes and causes a Big Bang! Or the RANG! as Cosmic Science describes it. The *RANG!* is what created the disassociation of two inharmonic fields of force within the ether enabling the dynamic of cosmic evolution to commence.

Ether (akasha) is the constant gravitational inert force existing in the cosmos. Because of the RANG, the ether shattered piercing through to the veil of dimension of this loaded , highly charged and embryonic structure of the holographic totality of cosmic reality. As this cosmic reality pops through, it then blasts off as the origin point of the instantaneously infinite time waves creating the cosmic show.

From this point the physical universe began to rapidly take form. This includes the formation of telepathic structures and dimensional "kingdoms". These higher dimensions are slowly stepped down until they finally appear in this physical plane. What we call the "seven heavens" signifies, first of all, the seven primordial generations in the non-manifest realm. The seven earth's refer to the succession of states of manifestation—seven days of creation—as well as the seven earths from the time of the creation of the primal Earth some 9 billion years after that beginning point 13.7 billion years ago!

FRACTAL CYCLES

Cosmic History is a matrix derived from the primal fractal ratio of seven. The lost interval ratio of seven is the holographic memory (akashic field) from which the entire timespace and universe arises; it is constructed, or rather projected, into existence as a whole template that contains the entirety of the process of cosmic evolution.

To understand this, we must further consider the creation formulation of the Law of Time: 4:7::7:13. Just as 4 is the center of a sequence of 1-7, so 7 is the center of a sequence of 1-13. To understand the universe timespace matrix structure, we have to understand that the 13 is generated from the seven. While the seven represents the form fractal of creation, the 13 represents the momentum of that form ratio through endless fractal cycles of creation. The 7 and 13 create a whole of 20 equal parts each of 18 degrees arc of a circle = 360 degrees.

The Earth that we inhabit corresponds to a pattern of seven earths as fractals contained in the interval ratio of lost time and the primal non-manifest seven generations. These creation programs were loaded into the orbital structure of the Earth, which is hooked into all conceivable numerical frequencies. This is the meaning of the *solar ring*. From this point, we can consider the six days of creation and how each of the six days creates another earth as being reposited within the memory of the Earth.

While there are 7 heavens of the seven days to creation, there are also 13 heavens in the tradition of the Galactic Maya; through the gate of the seventh heaven comes the descent of the 13 heavens. This refers to thirteen different heavens coming down to the dimension of manifestation. While the seven heavens refer to stages of creation, the 13 heavens refer to the guiding celestial forces that accompany the cycles of universal existence or cosmic time.

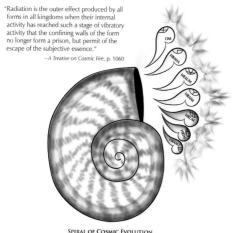

"Radiation is the outer effect produced by all forms in all kingdoms when their internal activity has reached such a stage of vibratory activity that the confining walls of the form no longer form a prison, but permit the escape of the subjective essence."

—A Treatise on Cosmic Fire, p. 1060

SPIRAL OF COSMIC EVOLUTION
SOUNDING THE SEVEN TONES
OF THE SOLAR LOGOS
EACH IN TURN EMITTING THE RADIATIVE FORCE
TO MAGNETIZE DIFFERENT PROTOTYPES
OF MANIFESTATION
EVENTUALLY EVOLVING INTO THE SEVEN
ETHERIC CENTERS OF SPECTRUM HUMAN-SUPERHUMAN
SO THAT THIS EVOLVED TYPE MIGHT ALSO MANIFEST
AND PROJECT THE RADIATIVE FORCE AS
BOTH INDIVIDUAL AND THE PLANETARY
RAINBOW BODY

THIRTEENTH GATE, SEVEN HEAVENS AND SEVEN EARTHS.

The first Earth (fire), the second Earth (ice), the third Earth (water), the fourth Earth (aquatic life), the fifth Earth (life on land), the sixth Earth (human), and the rise of the seventh Earth (the psychic noosphere Earth).

Sun or stars are born from the thirteenth gate. They give birth to the primordial form and structure of the planets. This is the gate of the thirteenth time and of the primordial Earth in its primordial solar timespace. The 13 baktuns are likewise a reflection of the principle of the 13 heavens, as the Earth of the seventh day of creation will be born from the thirteenth baktun. It is important to grasp the holographic nature of these primary frequencies and the notion of ongoing cosmogenesis.

Likewise, there are nine underworlds or "hells". These are storehouses of the succession of manifestations of time and destiny as they affect the sixth and seventh earths of the sixth and seventh days of creation. The Sun, for instance, is born out of the thirteenth gate of heaven and the emerging feminine principle, and from the Sun is born the succession of the seven earths.

The timespace is the function of different creation matrices that can be mathematically and geometrically postulated. The logarithmic spiral, for instance, is well known to underlie many configurations of nature as well as many facets of human art and skill. Its intrinsic system of proportions defines spatial relations occurring throughout nature. This numerical sequence is credited to Leonardo Fibonacci (1170–1240 CE). Fibonacci called this series the Golden Ratio or phi because the interval ratio between all numbers is 1.618 or phi. In the Fibonacci series, each new number is the sum of the two previous numbers, beginning with zero:

0:1:1:2:3:5:8:13:21:34:55:89:144:233:377:610:987.

These numbers define the measure of evolution of whole systems unfolding as a galactic timespace spiral.

Another key point to grasp—and this is fundamental to the entire perception of cosmic history—is that *number, as its own dimension of intelligence, is the coordinating means of a vast system of telepathic knowing.* This is how, for instance, the akashic field could be a cosmic memory template.

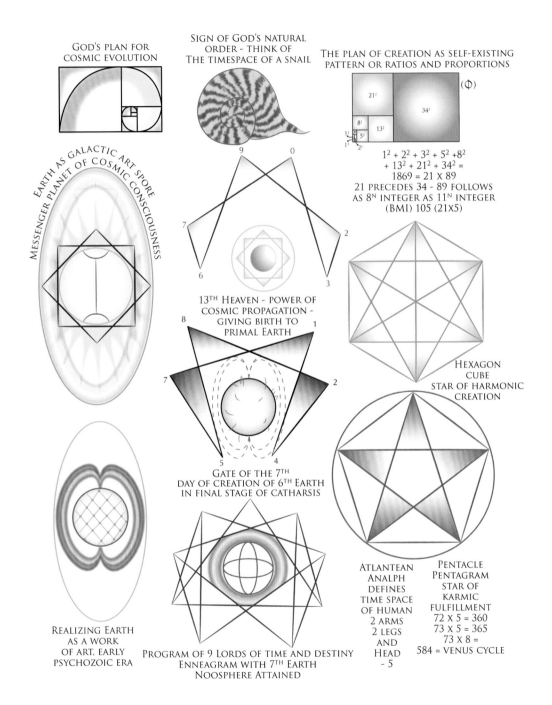

GOD'S PLAN FOR
COSMIC EVOLUTION

SIGN OF GOD'S NATURAL
ORDER - THINK OF
THE TIMESPACE OF A SNAIL

THE PLAN OF CREATION AS SELF-EXISTING
PATTERN OR RATIOS AND PROPORTIONS

21^2

34^2

8^2

13^2

5^2

(ϕ)

$1^2 + 2^2 + 3^2 + 5^2 + 8^2$
$+ 13^2 + 21^2 + 34^2 =$
$1869 = 21 \times 89$
21 PRECEDES 34 - 89 FOLLOWS
AS 8^N INTEGER AS 11^N INTEGER
(BMI) 105 (21X5)

MESSENGER PLANET OF COSMIC CONSCIOUSNESS
EARTH AS GALACTIC ART SPORE

13TH HEAVEN - POWER OF
COSMIC PROPAGATION -
GIVING BIRTH TO
PRIMAL EARTH

HEXAGON
CUBE
STAR OF HARMONIC
CREATION

GATE OF THE 7TH
DAY OF CREATION OF 6TH EARTH
IN FINAL STAGE OF CATHARSIS

REALIZING EARTH
AS A WORK
OF ART, EARLY
PSYCHOZOIC ERA

PROGRAM OF 9 LORDS OF TIME AND DESTINY
ENNEAGRAM WITH 7TH EARTH
NOOSPHERE ATTAINED

ATLANTEAN
ANALPH
DEFINES
TIME SPACE
OF HUMAN
2 ARMS
2 LEGS
AND
HEAD
- 5

PENTACLE
PENTAGRAM
STAR OF
KARMIC
FULFILLMENT
72 X 5 = 360
73 X 5 = 365
73 X 8 =
584 = VENUS CYCLE

This is the perception of infinite radiation of the instantaneous thought moment that punctures through and creates the big bang and cosmos. Different phases of that thought moment create different matrices of possibility. These matrices of possibility give rise to all the different stages of the trajectory of cosmic evolution. At one point, world systems are created. Each matrix that is created by the radially pulsating, instantaneously infinite time beams creates different time waves or infinity waves. From those infinite waves endless successions of interference patterns occur from which world systems are formed.

LEMURIA AND ATLANTIS: STEPPING DOWN OF CREATION

What we know of Cosmic History on Earth is very limited. Our world, our Earth, and our present root races are preceded by vast world systems, most of which are remembered only as mythic archetypal worlds. And even these are only remembered by a few. Of the most familiar of these worlds are Lemuria and Atlantis.

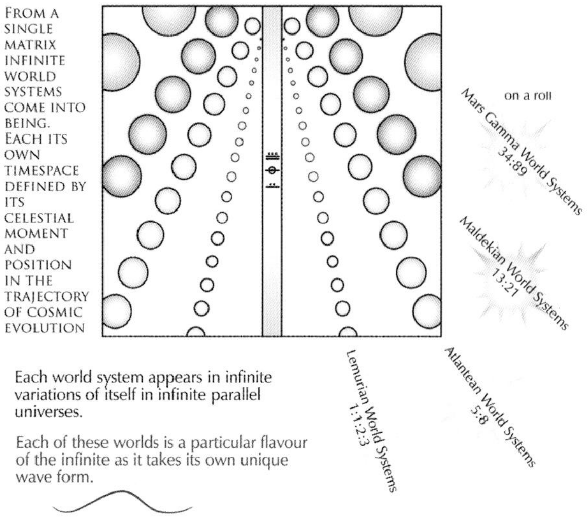

In the graphic the green represents the Lemurian worlds. These are the world systems where there is a stage called "Lemuria", a primal stage where the beings have their own order of life, their own reality, but are still living largely in the unconscious. They live in a number of other dimensions just as much as the physical plane. They are highly multidimensional, plastic or elastic types of beings.

FROM A SINGLE MATRIX INFINITE WORLD SYSTEMS COME INTO BEING. EACH ITS OWN TIMESPACE DEFINED BY ITS CELESTIAL MOMENT AND POSITION IN THE TRAJECTORY OF COSMIC EVOLUTION

on a roll

Mars Gamma World Systems 34:89

Maldekian World Systems 13:21

Atlantean World Systems 5:8

Lemurian World Systems 1:1,2:3

Each world system appears in infinite variations of itself in infinite parallel universes.

Each of these worlds is a particular flavour of the infinite as it takes its own unique wave form.

In the graphic, the blue represents the Atlantean worlds. These are the primordial worlds that merge into the oceanic unconscious (the Lemurian worlds are almost preconscious). These Atlantean beings live in a hyperdimensional reality that creates forms of what we call "culture". The Atlanteans are highly advanced forms compared with the Lemurian as far as the creation of a culture. This does not mean Lemurian is unintelligent, for their powers of telepathy and transference of telepathy is highly evolved, making them highly elusive.

The Atlanteans represent the evolutionary stage of the primordial cradle of civilization focalized on language and tool making or artefacts. These are world systems that exist in many different galaxies, orders and dimensions of reality.

MALDEK AND MARS

While Atlantis and Lemuria represent archetypal places on numerous planets, Maldek and Mars are planets unto themselves. In the graphic on page 37, red represents Maldek and orange, Mars. Maldek is the planet that exploded, self-destructed or was destroyed by jealous gods on Jupiter, according to Dreamspell cosmology. On Mars there was also much evidence of a civilization whose biosphere was wiped out. Similar states evolved on Maldek.

It is interesting to note that early mappers of Mars named one area Lemuria and another Atlantis. From our perspective today, Lemuria, Maldek, Mars and Atlantis represent mythic archetypes of a timespace gone by. Nonetheless, the location in consciousness of these distant archetypal timespaces can be mathematically mapped according to the logarithmic spiral.

LOGARITHMIC SPIRAL

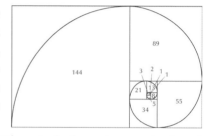

The mathematical process of creation is based on the logarithmic spiral, the living structure of reality. This logarithmic spiral can be seen in all types of shells; snail shells, sea shells, and even in your clenched fist. The logarithmic spiral is the mathematical order of reality. It can also be thought of as the projection of the telepathic order of evolving consciousness into a manifest reality.

Within the logarithmic spiral is God's plan for evolution. The spiral of creation can be found anywhere in nature, from a pine cone to a coiled up snake, to the curve of the still-forming human and animal fetuses. In modern civilization, this spiral can be found in basket weavings, scrolls, and toilet paper rolls, or in anything that is coiled or rolled up. Next time you see a shell think of the creature that inhabits it; what kind of timespace does it experiences? It must be highly cosmic living in a spiral timespace.

As a plan of cosmic evolution, the logarithmic spiral shows the proportions and ratios for the stages of evolution of any given timespace on any world system. The movement of frequency ratio intervals represents different quantum shifts in the conscious order of previous stages of the evolution of cosmic civilization. For example, the Lemurian system is 1:1:2:3. The Atlantean world system is 5:8, which create the 13, encompassing a whole chromatic octave of reality. This is why the Atlanteans encompass civilization as a whole. However, it is still an early stage. Note: Lemuria 1:1:2:3 = 7, Atlantis 5:8 = 13.

The Maldekian world system is represented by 13:21. So we have the cosmic power of 13 to 21, which creates the *Hunab Ku 21* (see Channel 7). The Maldekian frequency culminates in the 28. This frequency contains the registration of the power of 13 and 7 (× 3 = 21, × 4 = 28). Maldek, in many ways, was a more evolved planetary system than the Atlantean system. The Martian or

Mars gamma world system is 34:55:89—a very complex system and civilization that sets the stage for the reality of Earth.

Note: In the spiral of creation, everything is a function of a primary order of number and structure. We see again how Lemuria (2:3) is a primary structure whereas Atlantis (5:8) creates an overtone (5) fifth and a diatonic eight-tone octave that then is able to establish the chromatic octave, 13.

The Maldekian frequency, with the 13:21 ratio creates the whole chromatic structure of the cosmic cycle being affected by Hunab Ku 21. The Martian frequency is even more evolved and developed and represents the ratio 34:55:89. Then we get to Earth with the 144:233:377. This Earth

DIAGRAM OF SPIRITUAL POWER OF THE WORD THAT RETURNS TO ITS ORIGIN

KEY

1. Truth
2. A
3. WA
4. U
5. Deductive Method
6. 7th Dim.
7. 6th Dim.
8. 5th Dim.
9. 4th Dim.
10. 3rd Dim.
11. 2nd Dim.
12. Universe
13. The Whole Universe
14. 7th Dim.
15. 6th Dim.
16. 5th Dim.
17. 4th Dim.
18. 3rd Dim.

19. Great Origin
20. Soul Origin of the Great God–Moto Ohkamitama
21. Sphere
22. Sphere–Center–Truth–Creation
23-24-25-26-27. Power of Creation
28. Center of the Universe
29. God of Amatarasu–Pillar of A. Triple lower strata, multidimensional axis, runs through all dimensions, Pillar of ???

30. Center of Divine Spiritual World
31. Great God Kunitoko-tachi
32. Sphere
33. Sphere of Totality
34. All Phenomena
35. All Physical Matter
36. All Physical Bodies–God incarnate Sumera Mikoto

37. Center of the Earth
38. Absolute Bottom
39. } Humanity
40. }
41. Words [Kotonoha]
42. All Existing Matter–Energy Forces Natural Resources
43. Kotodama–Spiritual Essence of Words

SPIRITUAL POWER OF OUR RETURN TO SOURCE

We start with time as a pre-existing structure telepathically coordinated at one point. Then comes the Big Bang or RANG that results in the creation of the physical universe, which is a very small unit.

In this graphic of the multidimensional universe sphere derived from the Documents of Takenouchi, the physical universe is miniscule compared with all other dimensions of the nonphysical universe. At this stage, the immensity of the nonphysical universe is almost incomprehensible to us. The dimensions represent different patterns and layers of thought, and possibilities of potentiating life forms and things we might invent.

All potential first exists in the non-manifest. A central axis runs through it all: the axis of the eternal present. Even though we are "down here" in this physical universe, the smallest and bottom-most sphere of manifest being, there still exists the possibility of channelling the telepathic potentiality of other dimensions. In this way, we can train our mind to ascend vertically through this channel. This is the job of Tomorrow.

cycle tops off at 377 (13 × 29); 13 is the cosmic cyclic function (Maldek) and 29 (28 + 1) is the cosmic constant. Earth vibrates at a very high frequency representing an advanced stage on the spiral of cosmic evolution. Within all the proportions and ratios on the spiral each stage subsumes the previous stage. This means that all the different stages are included in the previous stage: Lemurian, Atlantean, Martian, etc.

Then we can take the squares of the different major units, up to 34. If we add those squares together they equal 21 × 89, the maximum of the Martian frequency multiplied by the maximum of the Maldekian frequency.

Squares
1 = 1
2 = 4
3 = 9
5 = 25
8 = 64
13 = 169
21 = 441
34 = 1156
= 1869 = 34 × 21 (all squares added together).

> When we come to understand the timespace of Earth, we see that creation is a function of primary whole numbers of the spiral of creation and the 441 matrix.

MATHEMATICAL ORDERS OF CREATION

The logarithmic spiral represents the proportions and ratios of cosmic creation that extend beyond the Earth. We can safely assume that other advanced orders exist throughout the universe, like the order that goes from 610 to 987 to 1597 (17th unit) the stage of genuine galactic civilization; or the higher levels of cosmic civilization that starts at 2584 (18th unit), and on and up the logarithmic spiral until we reach the point 21 units up or 10946, the maximum number ratio necessary for evolution. From this level, we then reach the frequency of 17711 (22nd unit) which takes us proportionately beyond this universe.

In Earth civilization, we have the base 144 and are working with the 233 (the 13th unit), but we have yet to reach the frequency of 377, 13 × 29—just to stabilize the noosphere. Even to reach this frequency is light years beyond the Lemurian frequency—how much more advanced then is that of the frequency 17711, especially if we think of each of these units as gates of consciousness. For instance the different between our maximum and 17711 is 17334, representing a phenomenal "distance" of conscious evolution.

GATE OF THE SEVENTH DAY OF CREATION

The logarithmic spiral defines and informs the cycle of the galactic evolution of consciousness. Within the greater context of Cosmic History, there are also geometric codes that define the seven days of creation and the 13 heavens. The elegance of the simple geometries of the gate of the seventh day of creation and gate of the thirteenth heaven owe to a common method. Both geometric constructions are based on 1) dividing a circle into ten 36 degree arcs, numbered 0 -9; and 2) making a figure that connects in order the digits in the reciprocal numbers of seven and 13. A reciprocal is a number that corresponds to 1 divided by a specific number, i.e. 1/7 = 1 divided by 7 = 0142857 = whole number equivalent, 142857.

TIMESPACE IS CONTEXT FOR TELEPATHIC ORDER & STRUCTURES OF REALITY
PRIMARY LEVEL ORGANIZER SHOWN AS NUMBER
PHYSICAL WORLD IS MANIFEST PROJECTION OF TELEPATHIC STRUCTURES OF KNOWING

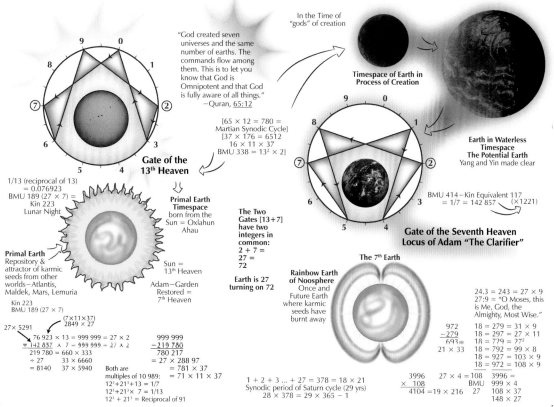

13 = 1/13 = 1 divided by 13 = 0.076923 = Whole number equivalent 76923. On two circles divided into 10 parts each, numbered 1 – 0 (10), for gate of 7 connect in one circle sequence: 1-4-2-8-5-7; for gate of 13 on the other circle connect in sequence: 0-7-6-9-2-3.

SEVEN EARTHS

While the 13 heavens are born from the seven days of creation, the seven earths are evolved from the 13 heavens. The seven earths refer to timespace matrices evolved from these higher dimensional telepathic geometries. Since everything is by the power of seven, the seven earths in their cumulative increase correspond to the recombinant factors of the reciprocal of seven. This number 142 857 is the supreme recombinant cyclic number; the product of its factors 1 – 6 are all variations of the same sequence 142 857.

These mathematical codes summarize the differences in the timespace of the seven earths:

1. $142\ 857 \times 1 = 142\ 857 =$ first earth – Solar earth
2. $142\ 857 \times 2 = 285\ 714 =$ second earth – Molten rock
3. $142\ 857 \times 3 = 428\ 571 =$ third earth – Water earth, aquatic life
4. $142\ 857 \times 4 = 571\ 428 =$ fourth earth – Reptilian life, amphibian
5. $142\ 857 \times 5 = 714\ 285 =$ fifth earth – Land life, mammalian, and birds (aviary).
6. $142\ 857 \times 6 = 857\ 142 =$ sixth earth – Human life

Note: the sixth earth reverses the original order of the two sets of three digits, it completes the evolutionary cycle of the sixth day of creation. Then comes the seventh, a complete quantum shift, $142\ 857 \times 7 = 999999$!! (Noospheric Human).

The first day of Earth is the first creation of Earth from fire. Through the succession of the eons, different earths represent different stages of timespace and cosmic evolution. For a long time, Earth was like the solar Earth, hot and molten giving off light and radiation. When this cooled, then appeared the second earth that looks like the Moon, or planet Mercury. As the Earth further cools, the next stage of creation emerged—water and life (see *Wavespell of Creation, CHC Vol. II*).

This is the point where the water is formed on the third earth. How did that water get formed? Earth is well over two-thirds ocean. How did that form? If Earth was molten rock and then it was cold rock, how did that much water form from that? Was it from a massive condensation of H_2O as steam given off by hot rocks? Was that water part of a planetary engineering project projected from a great distance that then created the right chemical solution and Presto! Zap! And the Earth was covered with ocean? Think of the immensity of that single ocean and the amount of water in it! From the ocean emerge life forms. What a fascinating contemplation. It is thought that this occurred about 500 million years ago.

With the creation of oceanic life comes the fourth day of earth, then amphibious life, followed by reptilian life, while the mammalian life represents the fifth earth. Finally comes the sixth day of creation which is the stage set for the human, the main character of the sixth earth.

Through the gate of the seventh heaven, the sixth earth is transformed and becomes the seventh earth. This is the phase that is now heating up and going through its karmic wrinkles which gives birth to the seventh earth—the noosphere. Each of these earths has its particular timespace represented by the recombinant product of 142857, multiplied by numbers 1-6. But the seventh earth 142857 = 999999 means that by this analogy it will be like nothing that preceded it.

We are in an unprecedented timespace in metamorphosis. If we trace the different stages of earth, we could find at least seven different major stages. Each stage is punctuated by a magnetic flip or catastrophe.

We are now at the tail end of the sixth day of creation, the thirteenth and final baktun, and about to enter the seventh day of creation, with the frequency 999999 ($7 \times 1/7$). The structure of the thirteenth heaven is very different from that of the seventh day of creation, and from the gateway of the nine lords of time and destiny which contains the Earth as the seventh day of creation. Through these primary patterns we can see the structures of different timespaces that we pass through.

TIME SHIFT—WHAT WILL HAPPEN?

We are actually leaving a particular timespace and entering a new one—this is a quantum shift, mind shift, global shift; Worldshift 2012 (as Ervin Laszlo phrases it). At this point everything comes down to zero and a cosmic pause occurs. Within this pause comes the dissolution of the previous hologram of the sixth day of creation, followed by the imprinting of the structures of the new timespace hologram of the seventh day of creation.

This imprinting informs us that we are shifting into a new evolutionary stage—the noosphere—also known as the Second Creation. As this occurs, there is a break in the electromagnetic field, creating a pause—a shift—that then resumes in another frequency. If we are awake and attuned, we will realize our divine nature.

At this stage many different potentialities occur. As toxic structures dissolve, we may feel the presence of higher intelligences, moderating the timespace adjustment to a hyper telepathic Earth. These are potential event moments of heightened consciousness that can occur at this time.

The logarithmic spiral defines and informs the cycle of the galactic evolution of consciousness.

Everything is a function of the incremental increase of waves of the primordial telepathic time of the lost interval of eternity as it is continuously beamed through the universe. World systems themselves are functions of different waves. The wave builds up to a crest, followed by a descent, crash, and build up to a different wave. Waves also criss-cross and create interference patterns.

The small mind is focused on the crashing wave of the sixth day of creation. The crashing is viewed as apocalyptic only to the degree that ego attachments are involved. For some, this particular point at the end of the sixth day of creation may seem horrendous or apocalyptic only because they have grown accustomed to a certain way of existence. Spiritual teachers and masters appear to remind people that there is a higher plan than reported by their senses. In this Plan it is beneficial to cultivate faith, flexibility and supreme trust in the Plan of the Creator.

At this point in time, the karmic ripening accelerates. The amount and intensity of the accumulated karma intensifies tremendously as the wave is coming down and crashes. The net effect is the wiping away of the karma. When it crashes then that particular wave is over. This is followed by a pause as the cosmic memory plate is washed clean, giving way to a purified memory structure. Then a new wave starts to build again. This is what is set to occur 21-12-2012.

Following the Rhythmic Moon 9 solstice (December 21) 2012, is the sequence of the final seven moons, the expression of the renewed creative power of seven. These seven "mystic" moons from the Resonant Moon through the Cosmic Moon of 2013 represents the beginning crescendo of the timespace of the next cycle. These waves are massive in their duration.

Each of the seven mystic moons recapitulates the frequency build-up of the seven days of creation and of the seven earths based on the reciprocal of seven, 142 857 and its first seven factors. Within each of the moons, mini waves may occur. By the end of the seventh mystic moon, we reach the point of Galactic Synchronization, where the creative power of 7 and the telepathic powers of the cosmic 13 will be totally understood and felt. Our minds will integrate into sets of telepathic frequencies knowable by a distinct self-contained set of numbers and permutations.

Purification of mind and body

is essential in order to receive

the elevated telepathy that

electronically saturates the

timespace.

Note: *There are exactly 216 days, 6 cubed, primal cube frequency—between Rhythmic Solstice 2012 and Day out of Time, 2013—eve of galactic synchronization. We shall be mystically cubed on Galactic Synchronization.*

These number permutations will be the actual patterns we will utilize to enact different phases of the cosmic second creation. This will phase in at the Galactic Seed of 2013. These are important points to understand. We really are in this process of moving into another timespace, so right now there is the beginning of a feeling of heightened telepathy.

Preparing for the New — Transmission of Electricity Freeing up the Blog Jam of Babylon

The underlying vibrancy of any timespace is infused by an all pervasive self-existing quality of electricity; this is where cosmic science begins. What is comic electricity? The partons and plasmas underlie and permeate the whole of the timespace. This is what makes the akashic medium of the timespace so alive.

> *"Human beings of the future will be superior beings who have taken under control in every way their nervous systems. Do not waste your electrical energies. Always concentrate this energy in your brains. In other words the brain and nervous system are the conductors of electrical energy in the nervous system."*
> —The Knowledge Book, p. 807

The electricity of the universal timespace is accessed through the wiring of the brain and nervous system. The electricity of the timespace carries within it unconscious patterns of whole systems of communication. The only telepathic communication we need is in the air we breathe and in the world we live in. Purification of mind and body is essential in order to receive the elevated telepathy that electronically saturates the timespace—this is the cosmic purpose of the present timespace metamorphosis.

The present timespace perceptual field is being purged so that the timespace can be purified and regenerated. The pure electric plasmic saturations contain the record of all telepathic communications. When the slates are wiped clear, this is all that will exist.—ourselves and great intergalactic ethers of the akashic timespace beaming the next unfolding of the primal hologram of the interval of lost time. At this point, we will no longer need radio or internet. We will understand everything through our own wiring and its neuro-electrical system. This marks the opening of the next timespace: The timespace of the seventh day of creation—the noosphere—the rainbow Earth.

SEVEN AND THIRTEEN

The seventh Fibonacci power is 13. The seven and thirteen, the most magical and mysterious of numbers, are functions of the primal Law of Time, 4:7::7:13. 4 × 7 = 28, the triangular of 7 = 28. A triangular of a number is the presentation of the number by a pyramid of units where the top unit is one, the second unit is two, etc, to the seventh unit for a sum of 28 units, in this case, the triangular of the number 7:

$$1 + 2 + 3 + 4 + 5 + 6 + 7 = 28 = (4 \times 7).$$

(Note: the number 7 is repeated 28 times in the Quran). The triangular of 13 = 1 + 2 + ... + 13 = 91 = 7 × 13, the square of 7 = 49. Whereas the square of 13 = 169. However, the reciprocals are equally fascinating, the reciprocal of 7 = .0142857 = whole number fractal 142857. The reciprocal of 13 = .0769236 = whole number fractal = 76923.

Note: 142857 is not divisible by 7, nor is 769236 divisible by 13, but 142857 divided by 13 = 10989, and 76 923 divided by 7 = 10989! This is because 10989 = reciprocal of 91 = 0109890. All these reciprocals are products of 37 and 27.

3861 × 37 = 142857; 5291 × 27 = 142857 = 13 × 11 × 999 = 142857; 2849 × 27 = 76923; 2079 × 37 = 76923 = 7 × 11 × 999; 407 × 27 = 10989; 297 × 37 = 10989 × 91 = 999999.

BABYLON TO BLOG

Word, number and sound are a unity. The more evolved a timespace is, the more it is consciously impacted by telepathic configurations of number.

Originally, every word was understood to hold a specific vibration or sound of power, but over time, the relation between number, word and the creation of language was lost.

The tower of Babel (babble) is created when words are disconnected from the root power of sound and number that informs the word. This creates the cycle of history from Babylon to blog. Blog is the final form of the tower of Babel where everyone is babbling simultaneously to everyone and anyone who will listen. Everyone is rehearsing their opinions to everyone else. This is the disconnection. But who is really listening? And what do they hear? What does it mean that everyone is expressing their opinions all at once?

The power of the word comes from the vibration frequency of the sound. Aum....there is a resonance to that. When you hear it, it stops the mind and you enter the sacred world of sound. Underlying the creation of sound and number is a vibrational frequency called telepathy. Entering the

Om: The highest frequency power that a terrestrial thought can attain at the terrestrial dimension without help.

—*The Knowledge Book*

seventh day of creation, we will understand once again the intrinsic power of the word as a telepathic order of sound and number. We will experience and understand and learn through resonant telepathic frequencies expressed as sound and number.

TIME, NUMBER, MIND AND NATURE

The propagation of the universal timespace is a function of the dimension of time, number, mind, and nature. This cosmic propagation emanates from the thirteenth heaven contained within the vertical seven heavens. The Earth in all of its evolution of timespaces is *ordained by mathematical programs, principally the power of seven.*

The logarithmic spiral, the succession of squares and the generation of primary geometries and solids form the cube—and from the cube are derived the star, the hexagram, the pentacle, etc. The pentacle describes Earth's orbit ($73 \times 5 = 365$), which is also the frequency (73) that encodes a Venusian synodic cycle, 584 days = 73×8. Hence Earth: Venusian ratio = 5:8, same as logarithmic Atlantis ratio. These are structures that encode the order of time. As we go through the annual cycle, we are creating a pentagram of enlightenment.

When the Earth is evolving as a noospheric work of art then it forms into a type of cosmic egg. This cosmic egg is now in an aura of protection by the higher galactic guardians as it is being evolved into a galactic art spore. Once Earth reaches this stage, it creates a hyperconscious level—represented by the octagonal structure that informs all harmonic orders of art as the subtlety of music, or any frequency that has this artistic function. When the noosphere becomes a giant galactic rainbow and the Earth within it is transformed into a full galactic art spore—this a whole other timespace story.

PART II
TIMESPACE AND THE NEW COSMOS

CHANNEL 4

TEMPLATES OF ORDER AND DISORDER

A society is a reflection of the time it keeps. A timekeeping device is how timespace is organized. Everyone lives in a space; a program of time moves through that space so people coordinate their lives to that time. The rituals of civilized life are actually functions of different programs coded into timekeeping devices.

For the Ancients, timekeeping was primarily associated with the relationship of the patterns of stars in the sky, the seasons and the Moon. The need for a count of weeks or years might not have existed, though it appears they were aware of the passing of the 13 moons a year.

The Lakota Sioux Indians tracked moon cycles on buffalo skins and Neanderthal or early homosapiens in cave cultures marked the lunation cycles on deer, ox and cow horns. When we reach the stage of civilization, with the creation of urban centers, and the proliferation of matter, then the organization of life requires greater order.

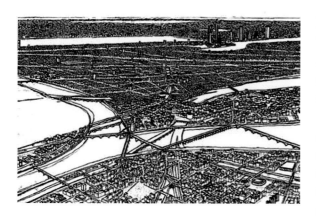

Civilization means living in cities. Modern cities, by nature, are highly chaotic. The chaos of the city is a result of urban zones sprawling out of control, showing a lack of planning. The spiral of the soul within matter creates greater and greater disorder.

City maps contain a hodgepodge of streets that create different neighborhoods strung together by freeways, railroad lines and subway trains. The primary purpose of these systems of transport is the movement of people in and out of the city to participate in the cycle of the seven-day work week. In this cycle, humans earn money for selling their body and soul to artificial time, usually eight hours a day, five days a week. The week is often spent in anticipation of the weekend when the human has two days of "free time."

What is the essence of civilization today? By means of mechanical transport for five days in a row, more and more humans jam into high-rise buildings to work at machines to earn money. At set periods, the buildings disgorge the humans who rush to places to eat and then rush back. Less people occupy the city on Saturdays and Sundays than on work "week" days. Work days in the central business district of any major metropolis are frantic.

This mechanized process represents "chaotic order" or entropy that highlights the final stage of the Babylonian template governing civilization. Babylonian time runs against the grain of natural time. But even here, in this final stage of mechanized disorder, is the fulfilment of a cosmic pattern.

Within the cosmic timespace allotted to it, living matter follows a general pattern of development: From an original crystallization that holds a specific pattern of life in place, to the final chaos that results in dissipative structures. The pattern of civilization is no exception. Why do civilizations rise and fall?

Civilizations, as we know them, rise and fall because historical consciousness no longer comprehends timespace as an Absolute Matrix of Order. As the memory of the Absolute escapes human civilization, so does the memory that life is meant to be lived according to larger cyclic orders that govern universal life.

How could this be different? How can we, as a species, return to natural order? Is there another template of time that we could apply? Is there a primal template of order?

Plato distinctly stated that everything visible was created or evolved out of vision and eternal will. He says that our heaven was produced according to the eternal pattern of the "Ideal World," contained, like everything else, in the dodecahedron (*Timaeus*, 28). This insinuates that there is a primal template of order. What creates this template of order, and what is the quality of a timespace?

The timespace is a medium that exists for the organization of intelligent life and forms. In this regard, the timespace establishes a living order and context that allows us to re-establish communities attuned to the One, the Source. The primal blueprint or template of order is referred as *Tollan* (Tulan) or Tula. Derived from a Nahuatl word that means "place of cat-tails", Tollan also refers to a place of reeds. When people gathered in Tollan it was as if they were reeds clustered around a lake. In the Mayan language *Tollan* sometimes refers to a palace or large house.

Tollan is the place of primal order, the archetypal city of the Absolute. Civilizations rise and fall but the archetype of Tollan endures. Tollan is a recurring theme in the legends of Mexico

In the Book of Daniel in the Old Testament, it says that God shall set up a kingdom which will not be destroyed and that will stand forever (2.44).

and Mesoamerica; there are different Tulas or Tollans, just as there are different versions of Quetzalcoatl.

This notion of an archetypal city of the Absolute occurs in many traditions, including the beginning stages of Chinese civilization where there are structures built as a reflection of the temple of heaven. An example of this is seen in the Forbidden City in Beijing where a temple was constructed in the fifteenth century by Emperor Yuan of the Mongol Dynasty, to reflect the temple of heaven.

The archetype of Tollan also occurs in Mesopotamia at the beginning of civilization where the city represents a crossroads that goes in four directions: a black road, a red road, a white road and a blue-green or yellow road. It is at this crossroads that the city is established.

Tollan is an example of one complete cycle of organization and timespace; people leave Tollan and then return. Leaving Tollan symbolizes the departure to history and the return to Tollan symbolizes the return to sacred order. So there is a Tollan *before* history; a Tollan *of* history; and a Tollan *beyond* history. In the *Book of Daniel* in the Old Testament, it says that God shall set up a kingdom which will not be destroyed and that will stand forever (2.44). This represents Tollan beyond history.

In the original description of the seven major Arcanum, the fifth is Timespace/Tollan or the template of the Absolute of pure hieratic reflection.

TOLLAN AND BABYLON

As an archetype, Tollan is at one pole and Babylon is at the other: Babylon represents the city as the symbol of the beginning of disorder. Babylon is the city of history and Tollan is the city of atemporal history or the city that transcends history. It is the city that is in the flux and flow of civilization.

BABYLON   TOLLAN

Babylon is the materialist counterpoint to Tollan in the old world. Tollan is the order that contains the archetypal templates of the Absolute

53

TOLLAN AND NEW JERUSALEM

In the *Popol Vuh* and other Mayan texts relating to Quetzalcoatl, Tollan represents the paradigmatic kingdom and the world of enlightened government. Every culture has its version of Tollan. In the Western tradition, Tollan relates to the heavenly city or city of New Jerusalem as foretold in the *Book of Revelations*.

New Jerusalem represents the regeneration of the human soul and mind that occurs at the end of history, after the judgment. New Jerusalem and Tollan are similar in meaning. Tollan also represents the primordial city. The *Popol Vuh* states that Tollan was the city across the sea, the place from where all early texts were brought.

According to the mysterious text, *From Distant Tulan*, the mythic people of Tollan came to Earth from the star Tau Ceti in the constellation Cetus (whale). Heavenly Tollan is an archetypal template reflecting hieratic purity of the Absolute. This template was projected through a time beam or time lens to the mind of Earth.

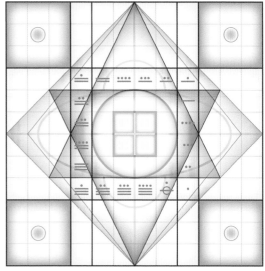

TEMPLATE OF THE STAR BORN TOLLAN WITHIN NEW JERUSALEM

GALACTIC TEMPLATE GENERATED FROM COSMIC FORCE OF 72ND ENERGY DIMENSION

Timespace Establishes Cosmos as Basis of Cosmic Consciousness
UR Harmonic 72 ~ 72nd Energy Dimension, 18th Evolution Dimension

$72+36=108$ ~ $144-36=108$, Star Mind Frequency,
108th Energy Dimension, 27th Evolution Dimension
$36=$ 4th Power of Nine ~ $108=$ 12th Power of Nine
$144=$ 4th Power of 4th Power of Nine

The radiogenetic codes projected through this template seeded the culture and mindset of the Galactic Mayans at the time of their earthly incarnation. The memory of Tollan was imprinted into the DNA codes of the psi bank program, so that, by attunement, the image and reflection of Tollan was always with them.

As we mentioned earlier, the ancient texts also have their coded origin at Tollan. These texts, codices or metaphorical inscriptions carried within their coded language a primal message for the Mayan/Toltec people; wherever they settled the imprint of Tollan was stamped in them informing their timespace creation. The impetus for civilization is projected from these images to build cities, urban centers and ritual ceremonial centers. This is how the blueprint of Tollan was incarnated radiogenetically in the DNA of the Mayan and the Toltec people, the Nahuatl.

The *Popol Vuh* says Tollan is the place where the gods appeared. This indicates the destiny of the journey toward this primal Tollan, where the people travel onward until they reach Tollan-

Zuvuya, as it is sometimes referred. There, the gods gave them knowledge as described in the *Annals of the Cakchiquels.*

"...from the other side of the sea we came to the place called Tulan ... From four places the people came to Tulan. In the east is one Tulan; another in Xibalbay; another in the west from where we came ourselves, and another is where God is; therefore there were four Tulans. And setting out we arrived at the gates of Tulan. Only a bat guarded the gates of Tulan ... Then we were commanded by our mothers and fathers to come, we the thirteen clans of the seven tribes, the 13 clans of warriors ..."

This is a rich, mythic text in which we see at least four archetypal Tulans. We also see the two principle numbers of the cosmic timespace matrix, 7 (tribes) and 13 (clans). Similarly, in the ancient tales, the one known as "Votan" is described as arriving with the seven clans or the seven families, corresponding to the image of the people arriving in Tollan endowed with the creative power of seven (see *CHC, Vol. IV*). This was to become the basis of the *Book of Seven Generations.*

The *Popol Vuh* says that the people leave Tollan in the night looking for the first dawn. They are led by the four elders or star prophets, the *Balam Quitze*. When they arrive at the four crossroads: the red road, the white road, the black road and the blue-green road, they each take one of these roads and are each appointed a different direction.

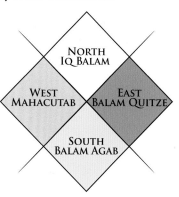

The Balam take the people looking for the first dawn. When the dawn arrives, Tollan is reduced to memory. The *Popol Vuh* says "the people shall return to Tollan." This belief is echoed in the myth and stories of Quetzalcoatl.

Quetzalcoatl

Following an archetypal life-pattern, Tollan (Tula), with its fourfold palace and fourfold gates, was erected by Quetzalcoatl, the mythic culture-bringer. In the same pattern, Quetzalcoatl experiences the "fall", when he is deceived, gets intoxicated, and sleeps with his sister. He then leaves the city in shame.

This is a metaphor of the inevitable degeneration that comes with the creation of civilization; the passage from crystalline order to dissipative structures. Rather than stay with disorder, Quetzalcoatl chose to leave, just like the four star elders, or Lord Buddha when he left his palace, or like Muhammad who left Mecca for Medina.

Before his journey's end, Quetzalcoatl re-establishes Tollan at Chichen Itza in 987, where he revivifies Mayan culture. This had been prophesied after Chichen Itza was abandoned in 692. *Note:* 692 is also the time of the dedication of the Temple of Inscriptions in Palenque, Chiapas.

We can see that Tollan plays multiple roles, 1) Tollan the archetypal four-fold city, the reflection of the Absolute, which is also the reflection of the primal star born Tollan; and 2) the earthly Tollan as a pattern which occurs in different ways and places: With the Quiche Maya and Tollan-Zuvuya; and then with 3) the historic Quetzalcoatl who founds the city of Tollan (Tula) in the present state of Hidalgo, Mexico, as the place for him to fulfill his archetypal role.

When a social center is established in Mesoamerica, that center becomes another Tollan or cosmic template. Teotihuacan, with its supreme degree of order, was but another Tollan. French writer, Laurette Sejourne, said that Quetzalcoatl was possessed by the vision of an eternal reality in order to dominate time with intentional acts. His eternity was nothing more than a succession of consciousnesses, each level engendering the next.

AT HIS JOURNEY'S END, QUETZALCOATL ACQUIRES WISDOM, UNITES HIS HEART WITH THE MORNING STAR, VENUS, AND ASCENDS INTO THE SKY, MERGING WITH THE SUN'S BRILLIANCE.

TEOTIHUACAN AS ARCHETYPE OF TOLLAN

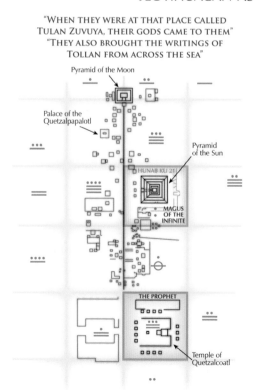

"WHEN THEY WERE AT THAT PLACE CALLED TULAN ZUVUYA, THEIR GODS CAME TO THEM"
"THEY ALSO BROUGHT THE WRITINGS OF TOLLAN FROM ACROSS THE SEA"

Pyramid of the Moon

Palace of the Quetzalpapalotl

Pyramid of the Sun

HUNAB KU 21

MAGUS OF THE INFINITE

THE PROPHET

Temple of Quetzalcoatl

Teotihuacan is a master archetype of Tollan that emerges from the culture and mindset of Mesoamerica. The city was at its height 400 years after Christ and had a vast cultural influence that spread throughout Mesoamerica. Its influence was particularly strong upon the Maya, especially at Tikal where evidence of the Teotihuacan style is most prominent. Quetzalcoatl's Tula was also based on this master template.

The design of the city is based on a highly majestic sense of order that spreads over many square kilometers. Even the aerial mapping of the city reveals that it was designed as an absolute whole. Unlike Mesopotamia (literally between the rivers), Mesoamerica has no principle rivers or waterways. However, at Teotihuacan, there are underground rivers that may have been created as irrigation canals from the nearby Lake Texcoco, which is now dried up.

Located on a high, arid plane, surrounded by mountains, no one today would likely build a city where Teotihuacan arose in all of its glory. There were lakes nearby, but they have all but evaporated. Though it might have been built at a crossroads, the city of Teotihuacan was clearly designed for cosmic purposes.

MAGICAL PYRAMID

Teotihuacan is a storehouse of magical knowledge. In primal times, shamans gathered at the underground grotto beneath the Temple of the Sun. If we draw a 7 × 7 km. grid of the city, we see that the Pyramid of the Sun is at the center. This is the space of channelling Hunab Ku or Source. This channelling would then be directed at the temple atop the Pyramid of the Sun.

Teotihuacan is built on a flat plain, with buildings that reflect the cosmic order distinguished by the Pleiades, and the North star (this is why it is oriented slightly 15 degrees north precisely at the pole star). It is a geomantic gathering point where the image of the heavenly city could be reflected. At this place the main pyramid served as a focalizing point of the cosmic showers or analphs of the lost planets that were projected here.

At Teotihuacan, we find the psychomythic locus engendering the Fifth Sun or fifth root race. This magical city is comparable to Mecca, Lhasa or the Forbidden City, and provides the perfect place to channel the information from the heavenly Tollan. The city is saturated in cosmic showers that communicated or transmitted various star memories making Teotihuacan the most cosmic city on Earth—a veritable Tollan.

TOLTEC AND TOLLAN

Tollan is also related to the word *Toltec*, master builder or artist, the genius behind Teotihuacan. Toltecs created a society with an original vision of the Absolute expressed through the creation of master art works. The highest value of Toltec society was artistic expression. They created spaces that merged the temporal succession of the flow of time with the eternal reflection of the absolute. This is what invested their ceremonies with meaning and the whole of the city with value. In Toltec society, the purpose of life was "flowers and song."

We are here to create beauty and art, to be as the flowers. This is what the vision of the primal order reveals. All the cities of Mesoamerica were abandoned and left behind. The elements we associate with history were already coded into the unconscious planetary noosphere program of the entire race that adopted an urban way of life. Those Babylonian analphs also saturated the field in Mesoamerica, particularly in the races that had embarked on living in cities. By the eighth century, Tollan/Teotihuacan succumbed as well.

Tollan is the order that contains the archetypal templates of the absolute within the evolutionary spiral. Hunab Ku is also represented by a spiral. In the cosmic journey there is an evolution that always spirals from the template of absolute order into matter in which spirit spirals "downward." As an involution into the proliferation of matter seeking always to express itself from its imprisoned material state, spirit in matter finally becomes urbanized. The urbanization of matter is epitomized by Babylon.

Matrix of Disorder

While Tollan is an archetype that ever seeks to emulate the Absolute, Babylon is the restless desire of spirit to explore matter. Thus, in the cosmic evolutionary stage of Babylon, a different type of order enters the picture. This is the order based on the seven-day week. Where did this come from? Keep in mind that Tollan, in its primal state, is organized as a reflection of the Absolute; as a mandala moved by the power of 13, whereas Babylon is based on the matrix of the seven-day week.

Seven
Seven is a fundamental number; it is the fractal of the primal measure of eternity. Seven refers to the lost time in eternity. Seven is the middle point of measure between one and thirteen. Hence, 7 tribes and 13 clans. Within the 13, seven has a unique power, but apart from 13, seven is limited.

In Babylon, the cycle of city-life is based on seven as the operational measure of the power of time, whereas, 13 is a supreme and comprehensive measure that invests the seven with its cosmic significance. This order of time based on 7 apart from 13, has become utterly established throughout the entire civilized world. In the Babylon template, the seven-day week corresponds to the seven "planets" or heavenly bodies as the rulers of human destiny, while the 13 is regarded with supreme superstition. The myth of the unlucky 13 can be traced back to the Babylonian Code of Hammurabit (1780 BC).

Instead of life lived as the reflection of a pattern in eternity, or cosmic cycles, the measure of life is based on the seven-day structure imprinted by an ever-repeating, astro-psychology as the time allotted to "earn one's bread." This represents a type of planetary timespace coordination of human activities into constellations called cities.

The Hebrew word for Saturn is *sabbat* or Sabbath. In the Jewish religion, Saturday is the Sabbath or holy day related to Saturn. Saturn goes in 378-day synodic loops ($21 \times 18 = 378$). These loops create a whole sequence; 28 of them occur precisely every 29 years. Jupiter and Saturn are the largest and main planets visible in the sky, making Thursday (Jupiter) and Saturday (Saturn) the "power" days in the Babylonian work week.

Originally, the Babylonian "week-end" was Sun-day and Moon-day, while the days of the planets made up the work week. But in modern Judeo/Christian times Saturn is the Hebrew holy day and Sunday is the Christian holy day. The weekend is a confused amalgam of Babylonian, Jewish and Christian holy days.

Seven is also related to the phases of the Moon. What is important in the phases of the Moon is not the number of days in that phase but the phase itself. For example in the 13 Moon calendar, the week, which is organized by red, white, blue or yellow, reflects the patterns of the phases of the Moon: Red initiates (corresponds to 7 days after the New Moon), white refines (corresponds to the second phase, half Moon to full Moon), blue transforms (corresponds to the seven days after the full Moon), and yellow ripens (corresponds to the final seven days of the waning Moon).

The emphasis on the quality of the week, then, is a stage in a four-phase cycle of 28 days or four seven-day weeks, hence "lunar month." These cycles relate back to a cosmic order of the four stages of evolution.

The Babylonian seven-day week emphasizes the rapidly rotating succession of days that make up the astrologically based work-week. The week is actually the measure of time in the 12:60 order where every week repeats a superstitious program. So we have the succession of the two-day weekend and five-day workweek, ad infinitum. These are controlled by two factors: money and astrology.

All modern cities have newspapers and all newspapers have an astrology section. The seven days of the week all have astrological significance. If we study the meanings of the days of the week that we follow without question, we find they are associated with planets and violent mythologies covered over by agrarian myths and deities. Why would we want to perpetuate these programs?

13:20 NATURAL TIME, 12:60 ARTIFICIAL TIME

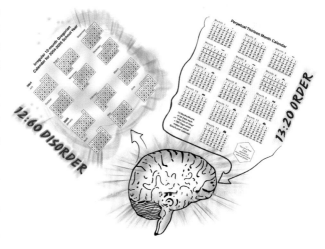

The Babylonian city is a template of organized disorder; Tollan, by contrast, is a primal template of cosmo-harmonic order. What timekeeping device was Teotihuacan governed by? It was governed by *Tonalpohualli*, the (Tzolkin) or 13:20 matrix, as well as lunar and solar calendars. The Babylonian city consists of the seven-day week. Since 13 had been superstitiously banished, 12 came to dominate; the 12 astrological constellations and 12 houses of the zodiac, etc. Later came the 12 month civil Julian/Gregorian calendar, which is not an even or a natural measure.

Then there is the lunar calendar, which is still utilized in places such as China, Iran and Israel. Now, even these countries are overridden by the Gregorian calendar: the 12 month lunar and civil calendars and the 60 minute hour—12:60 reigns all over the world. In the Quran it says 12 is the number of months ordained by God; this refers to the 12 lunar months of the 354-day lunar cycle.

As we know, the sidereal cycle, based on the same place where the Moon actually reappears in the sky, is 27.3 days. However, all Moon (lunar) calendars are based on the synodic cycle of 29.5 days. This means the synodic calendrical lunar cycle measures the length of one day on the Moon! When people follow this cycle they are actually living moon days. There are 12 moon days per year. Every three years there is an extra moon day to catch up with. In a 19 year Metonic cycle there are 235 moon days and 247 28-day moons that synchronize.

From the template of Tollan—the Absolute—to the template of Babylon there occurred a degeneration of order into chaotic disorder. This is experienced in the modern world as a governing template—the seven-day work week that repeats incessantly—based on irregularity and breeding perpetual dissatisfaction. The Vatican has declared that it is a crime against God to break the succession of the seven-day week. And as noted, 13 is considered unlucky—the unluckiest day being Friday the 13th, a superstition embedded in the Gregorian calendar mind-set.

A calendar is a timespace template regulating cycles of human social function and activity over different periods of time.

OUTWORN ARCHETYPES

Through the Babylonian historical process, also comes a degeneration of archetypes. At the beginning of history people played out certain archetypal roles. The sense of individualism was not very marked at the beginning of history and certainly not in the aboriginal societies where everyone lived out a role within a matrix of communal equality.

In the contemporary world instead of having archetypal heroes like Quetzalcoatl or Ulysses, and the different myths of legendary emperors, ladies of Camelot, etc, we have sensational magazines where the same set of celebrities are elevated to mythic stature generally based on a manipulation of images that are projected onto the mass mind. To the average person reading about these people's lives, it is a fairy tale compared to their own lives. In the Babylonian history we see a degeneration of archetypes, mythic, hero and heroine, into soap opera sensationalism. This is an example of the final stage of the devolution of the archetypal order.

Tabloid and fashion magazines are everywhere, from Thailand, Japan, India, and even in the United Arab Emirate states. In these magazines, no matter what country, we see the faces of same people continuously in most every grocery store. This tabloid fascination transcends language and race, creating a universal set of sensationalist archetypes that correspond only dimly to characters remembered from a forgotten past. Usually in the focussing of archetypes in this way, there is always an inevitable collapse or fall.

TEMPLATES OF ORDER

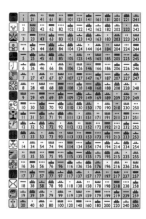

What is a template of order and how can we experience it? Let us examine a few different systems of order. For example, in the Tzolkin 13:20 matrix we can see a definite pattern of order. From 13 numbers that repeat 20 times emerges a pattern of 52 galactic activation portals. The tones (numbers) of which every four of the radial sets always add up to 28 and so on. This demonstrates the harmony of the template of the 13 Moon/28-day template.

The 13 Moon/28-day calendar has been used since ancient times by Polynesians, Native Americans, Egyptians, Druids, Inca, Chinese and the Essenes.

BALINESE WUKU CALENDAR

The 30-week Balinese Wuku calendar is another example of a template of order. This calendar is highly complex and has a five-day week, a seven-day week and also a calendar of one-to-ten day weeks. This calendar displays tremendous order and synchronization. In the Tzolkin and Wuku calendars the emphasis is based on recognizing junctures of synchronization where different patterns of order and time occur. These synchronizations are key moments provided for numerous ceremonial events.

Because the Balinese operate principally on five-day and seven-day weeks, every 35th day is significant; this is when the five-day and the seven-day cycles synchronize. In the 30-week calendar this occurs on the seventh day of weeks 2, 7, 12, 17, 22 and 27. These days mark special event points coordinated with the lunar cycles. For the Balinese, life is a vast ritual filled with ceremony, art and a high degree of synchronization.

The 13 Moon calendar consists of a 28-day template that repeats every 13 moons. Each week is coded by one of four colors that signify different qualities of actions, styles of activity and functions. The 13 tone wavespell also accommodates the 28-day cycle where each position is the equivalent of

WUKU — 210-DAY CEREMONIAL CALENDAR OF BALI

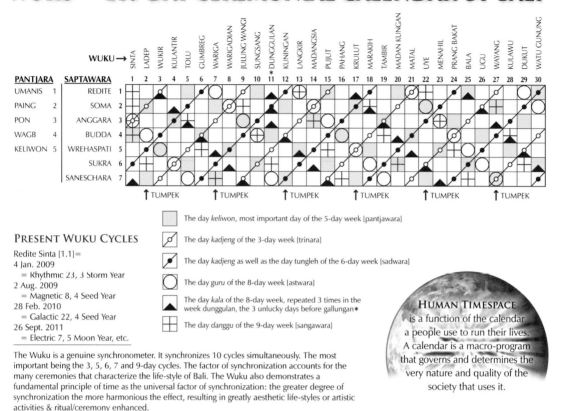

| PANTJARA | SAPTAWARA | ↑ TUMPEK | ↑ TUMPEK | ↑ TUMPEK | ↑ TUMPEK | ↑ TUMPEK | ↑ TUMPEK |

PRESENT WUKU CYCLES

Redite Sinta [1.1]=
4 Jan. 2009
= Rhythmic 23, 3 Storm Year
2 Aug. 2009
= Magnetic 8, 4 Seed Year
28 Feb. 2010
= Galactic 22, 4 Seed Year
26 Sept. 2011
= Electric 7, 5 Moon Year, etc.

The day *keliwon*, most important day of the 5-day week [pantjawara]

The day *kadjeng* of the 3-day week [trinara]

The day *kadjeng* as well as the day tungleh of the 6-day week [sadwara]

The day *guru* of the 8-day week [astwara]

The day *kala* of the 8-day week, repeated 3 times in the week dunggulan, the 3 unlucky days before gallungan*

The day *danggu* of the 9-day week [sangawara]

HUMAN TIMESPACE
is a function of the calendar
a people use to run their lives.
A calendar is a macro-program
that governs and determines the
very nature and quality of the
society that uses it.

The Wuku is a genuine synchronometer. It synchronizes 10 cycles simultaneously. The most important being the 3, 5, 6, 7 and 9-day cycles. The factor of synchronization accounts for the many ceremonies that characterize the life-style of Bali. The Wuku also demonstrates a fundamental principle of time as the universal factor of synchronization: the greater degree of synchronization the more harmonious the effect, resulting in greatly aesthetic life-styles or artistic activities & ritual/ceremony enhanced.

28 days or one Moon. This has its own cosmic cyclical form. This pattern creates a specific social organization based on moving patterns within the 260-unit Tzolkin matrix weaving through the 28-day template.

Both the Tzolkin and Wuku templates create a specific type of social organization that emphasizes synchronization. Synchronization occurs when there are intermeshing cycles set within an order. This order is ultimately a reflection of the Absolute.

The Absolute is coordinated at the relative plane by the recognition and synchronization and recurrence of different cycles. We can observe this, to some degree, in the astrological cycle with the Saturn return every 29 years. This occurs when there are twenty-eight 378-day synodic loops that Saturn makes around the Earth.

The Gregorian calendar provides all banks with timing. In the postal bank calendar of Australia there are 7-day weeks but no synchronization with the months. Every year the months and days of the week change. Then there is a list of official holidays programmed into the calendar: pension check, taxes, weekends, etc.

THERE IS ONLY DAY AND NIGHT ON A PLANET BODY TURNING ON ITS AXIS GOING AROUND A STAR. SUCH A PHENOMENON DOES NOT EXIST FOR A STAR.
A DAY-NIGHT = 1 ROTATION

TZOLKIN AS THE HARMONIC MODULE

260-day cycle presents a radial matrix with a high degree of synchronization; meshes with 13 Moon Calendar to create perfectly harmonized 52-year cycles.

Perpetual 13-Moon Calendar
Total cyclic & periodic order. Harmonic synchronization; every 28-day cycle the same, 13 times per year. 364+1 day orbital measure

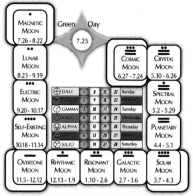

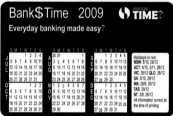

GREGORIAN CALENDAR 2009 YEAR
Note that there is little cyclic or periodic order. Minimal synchronization

A CALENDAR (SO-CALLED) IS ACTUALLY A TIMESPACE TEMPLATE OF ORDER (OR DISORDER) REGULATING THE CYCLES OF HUMAN SOCIAL FUNCTION & ACTIVITY OVER DIFFERING PERIODS OF TIME. IT IS A PROGRAMMING DEVICE WHEREBY THE SOCIETY THAT USES IT CREATES ITS PSYCHIC FIELD OF INFLUENCE AND ORGANIZES ITS COLLECTIVE LIFE.

BALINESE WUKU
Total cyclic and periodic order, like the Tzolkin, synchronizes with 2, 3, 4, 5, 6, 7, 8, 9 & 10-day cycles.

Balinese society: highly ceremonial timespace

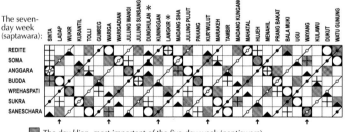

The seven-day week (saptawara):
REDITE
SOMA
ANGGARA
BUDDA
WREHASPATI
SUKRA
SANESCHARA

The day klion, most important of the five-day week (pantjawara)
The day kadjeng of the three-day week (triwara)
Also indicates the day kedjeng, as well as the day tungleh of the six-day week (sadwara)
The day guru of the eight-day week (astawara)
The day kala, also of the eight-day week. This is repeated three times in the week of dunggulan, the three unlucky days before galunggan (*)
The day danggu of the nine-day week (sangawara)

Every time that the day klion falls on kadjeng the day, kadjeng-klion, is propitious for offerings, especially to evil spirits. This occurs every fifteen days.

When klion falls on saneschara, it is tumpak, an extremely lucky day. It occurs every thirty-five days (↑)

Other lucky days propitious for offering are anggara-kaseh, when klion falls on anggara; and budda-chemang, when budda falls on wagé.

TIKA, Key to Understanding 30 week WUKU Ceremonial Calendar of Bali

In the Gregorian calendar there is very little cyclic or periodic order. Months are uneven, the length of month does not correlate with number of seven-day weeks that exist, and the numbers change every month. There is no cyclic or periodic order; this is why civilization is a chaotic disorder.

The order of civilization is based on the clock and everything has to conform to the clock—a non-human, non-organic machine device—which creates a very frantic running around to comply with this. The governing order of the modern world is the eight-hour day, 9-5 workweek. In the macroprogram of the calendar there is no order so that a mechanized confusion is the (dis) order that governs civilization.

Once again, simply put: A calendar is a timespace template regulating cycles of human social function and activity over different periods of time. In the modern world, you have to have a calendar on the wall to know when the month is going to end. Because that's pay day and the day you have to pay. It is the programming device of the society who uses it. The calendar creates a psychic field of influence and organizes its collective life. In those examples we see what kinds of societies are created by following different calendars.

The Balinese calendar creates a highly ceremonial ritualized society. The Tzolkin 13 Moon calendar also creates a society with a high degree of synchronization, something like the Balinese but with a much more cosmically oriented sense of cycle and order.

All order begins with a macroprogram, ultimately a galactic template. (The Hunab Ku 21 is the template of that order. The module of that template is a 21-unit pattern set within the whole, which is a 21 × 21-unit matrix. In the pattern you can see the order of the 21 archetypes of Hunab Ku 21 as well as the purely symmetrical order that organizes the center and the cross—the pure archetypal template.)

Then there is the extending radial order that corresponds to the four limbs of the human body that create 13 more units. The central unit represents both 13 and 21; this is absolute order. From this order comes the organization of all the cycles of time. These cycles can be organized in conformity to the reflection of a higher template of order. We are all capable of channeling a new template of order. We can witness this in the early Mayan genotypes that incarnated on earth and received the reflection of the absolute image of Tollan—and embodied that image.

Quetzalcoatl leaves only to return to Tollan. Tollan existed before history, during history and after history. Babylon is the template of disorder and in the end when Babylon is wiped away; way down beneath you will find the template of Tollan and the New Jerusalem: the template of the new order. In this order we find the reflection of the higher level cosmic principles of timespace that govern the manifestation of all evolved states of consciousness that accommodate both the absolute and the relative expressions of the cycles of time.

CHANNEL 5

SOLAR RING AND THE COMING SIXTH WORLD

All of life depends on the Sun. The Sun is the source of everything that exists in this world, and is the creator of all possibility of life yet to come on our Planet. This Sun is not the only sun. According to the ancient prophecies, our Sun is the fifth sun. The prophecy of the Aztec Sunstone reveals that the Fifth Sun will soon give way to the Sixth Sun: the Sixth Sun of Consciousness. Mayan prophecies speak of 2012 as the coming solar age—this is the same as the Sixth Sun.

The Sun is the coordinator of consciousness. The Sun is the brain, heart and root of the entire solar system. The coming Solar Age is the participation in the consciousness of the Sun itself. The historical disconnection of consciousness from the Sun is what accounts for our remnant personalities and fragmented memory loads. This is all a function of the Fifth Sun.

The Aztec prophecy, representing the tradition of the Toltecs, says that we are living in the Age of the Fifth Sun, the sun of the shaking earth. The birth of the Fifth Sun is equivalent to the fifth world or fifth root race in Western esoteric traditions. According to cosmic history, the birth or origins of the fifth root race and Fifth Sun is commemorated at Teotihuacan, Mexico.

Teotihuacan provides a focal point on Earth for the planetary logos, the solar logos, and the cosmic logos. The inheritors of Teotihuacan, the Aztecs, were the last civilization and last people of ancient Mexico. For this reason, they carried the prophecy and teachings of the five worlds or the five Suns into our present time.

"Celestial" Transmitter
TOLLAN
Place of the Primal Order of the "Star Elders"

"Distant Tollan" Established in the Template of the Galactic Matrix Hunab Ku 21/441, Set in Master Focalizing Time Lens–432.

"Archetypal Tollan" Cultivated by the 21 Archetypes of Hunab Ku Fifth Force Codes.

"Cosmic Showers" including lost planet analphs meant to ripen during last 60 years of 13 Baktun Cycle [1952-2012]

"Descent of Cosmic Knowledge" 60-year cycle 1952-2012 / 1953-2013 Pre-coded by Cosmic Foundation Galactic Maya Toltec Tollan.

Inter-dimensional Focalizing Point, Sirius B

Flow of channeled information to code Teotihuacan as a time release terrestrial information module. Central Program: Prepare fifth root race for coming Sixth Sun of Consciousness, 2013-13

Palace of the Quetzalpapalotl

Pyramid of the Moon

Terrestrial Receptor
TEOTIHUACAN
Place Where the Gods Touch the Earth, activator of the memory grid of Hunab Ku 21 Vulom Magnetic Template

AVENUE OF THE MILKY WAY

Pyramid of the Sun subterranean cavern of serpent initiates. "Birth" of 5th Root Race

Citadel & Pyramid of Quetzalcoatl

Road to 2012

> ### THE FIVE SUNS
>
> The first Sun was the Sun of the Jaguar that ended on 4 Jaguar; the second Sun was the Sun of the Wind that ended on 4 Wind; the third Sun was the Sun of the Storm that ended on 4 Storm; and the fourth Sun was the Sun of the Water that ended on 4 Moon. Now we are in the fifth Sun, Nahui Ollin, 4 Earth which is soon ending. Then we shall phase into the Sixth Sun of Consciousness, leading us into spiritual illumination.

The Pyramid of the Sun at Teotihuacan synthesizes the previous five suns and commemorates the coming Sixth Sun. The five levels and platforms that form the Pyramid of the Sun correspond to the completion of the human being as a total sensory organism during the first five suns. The lowest platform of the base foundation corresponds to the sense of touch, followed by taste, smell, hearing, sight, and then the opening above the platform at the top to the *Sixth Sun of Consciousness.* All knowledge of this world and previous worlds is encoded in the Pyramid of the Sun and is awaiting the moment of transfer from the fifth to the sixth order of cosmic reality.

In the Sixth Sun, mind will open to the Absolute. During this era we will see the development of the mind as the science of telepathy. The Sixth Sun of Consciousness completes the human being and integrates the senses as we move into the Age of Harmony.

> ### TIMESPACE TOLLAN
>
> The mythic order of timespace Tollan refers to successions of improvisation of psychic states of archetypal consciousness. In the Toltec Mayan cosmo-vision the primal city was meant to be a reflection of the Eternal Reality, a reflection of the Absolute. Teotihuacan is a prime example of this. Teotihuacan is so majestic and spectacular that it is out of this world.

THE SOLAR RING

"The 260-day count, the sacred calendar of Middle America is a great deal more than a time calendar, it is a way of life, a constant reminder of the ever-present gods, (it also) predicts the future and recalls the past. It is perfect as nature is perfect, it is an endless circle without a real beginning or end."

—Tony Shearer

The Harmonic Module and the Aztec Sunstone are the two main calendrical instruments that represent the 13:20 time science of ancient Mexico. The Sunstone was dedicated near the end of the civilization of the earthly Tollan in Mesoamerica (1479). The two images are completed by the image of the Moon going around the Earth 13 times as the Earth goes around the Sun once.

At the center of the Sunstone is an eagle bowl representing our Sun; the four glyphs around the center circle represent the four past worlds: 4 Jaguar, 4 Wind, 4 Water, 4 Rain. 4 Earthquake

(*Caban, Earth*) is Nahui Ollin, the symbol that contains the whole form of the central core of the Sunstone, showing that the present world contains the previous four worlds. The four directions are within a stylized cross—the circle of the Universe, the cross of the winds.

The circle and the cross were a universal sign among the American Indians—a symbol of light within the universe of life. Not only does the eagle bowl represent the future and recall the past, but also predicts the utter destruction of human life and gives the date 4 earthquake (Self-Existing Earth) which is the same as Nahui Ollin—only the gods know when that day will come. The Nahui Ollin is the summation of all previous world catastrophes.

As we saw in the previous chapter, Tollan is the archetype or blueprint of the original civilization; the basis of Tollan is the *solar ring*. The Sunstone is the application of the solar ring.

On Nahui Ollin of 2000 (May 5), eight planets were lined up on one side of the Sun, with the Earth on the other side. Much has changed from this time. War, terrorism and natural disasters that we are now experiencing on our Planet *is* the shaking of the Earth. Many people do not realize that the apocalypse is happening now, in slow motion.

CIVILIZATIONS RISE AND FALL, BUT THE ARCHETYPAL TEMPLATE TOLLAN ENDURES. HOW IS THIS SO?

Tollan: The Paradigmatic Kingdom and the Metaphor of wise government like Plato's Ideal Republic or perhaps even Atlantis.

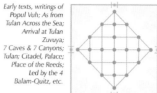

Early texts, writings of Popul Vuh; As from Tulan Across the Sea; Arrival at Tulan Zuvuya; 7 Caves & 7 Canyons; Tulan; Citadel, Palace; Place of the Reeds; Led by the 4 Balam-Quitz, etc.

Tulan is Order,

Babylon, the Beginning of Disorder

In leasing Tulan, language became different languages.

They left Tulan to seek for the Dawn

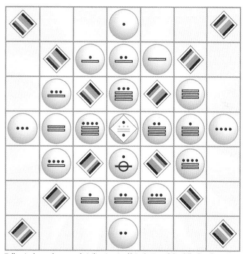

Tollan is the archetype of civilization itself, inclusive of the fall of civilization and the journey it precipitates and redeems. The history of civilization in the New World corresponds to all those different archetypes.

NAHUI OLLIN

The final Nahui Ollin of the 13 Moon Dreamspell cycle will occur on Crystal Moon 16, 6 Wizard year (June 14, 2012). On the long count, the last Nahui Ollin will occur on Magnetic Moon 6 (July 31, 2012) of the Resonant Storm year. The shaking of the Earth is expected to peak during this time.

The shaking Earth is at the center of the solar ring. The root of Cosmic History is the solar ring; without the solar ring there is no Cosmic History. The solar ring establishes the possibility of cosmic order. Whether humans are aware of it or not, the Earth is going around the Sun and its orbit makes a solar ring. This is an actual path or circuit that Earth invariably follows. With the accurate measure of 13 moons, each with 28 days, the solar ring can be made conscious and harmonically normalized.

Without the solar ring there is no cosmic perception. The solar ring carries prophecy. The solar ring on the Sunstone is depicted as two fire serpents going in opposite directions. There are 11 fire symbols on each side, separated by four bands on each side. The 13 Moon/28-day cycle is correlated at the top of the Sunstone and shows that it is the actual solar ring of the Earth.

The orbit of each planet carries a particular frequency. The frequencies of the planets in relationship to each other accounts for the creation of different stages or aspects of consciousness. The planetary orbits and solar system represent different qualities or aspects of consciousness. These five circuits of consciousness represent the five worlds: metaconsciousness, instinctual-telepathic consciousness, biotelepathic consciousness, internalizing and externaling consciousness.

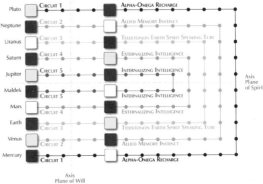

The internalizing (where sense perceptions are internalized—corresponds to circuits of Maldek and Jupiter); and externalizing (where interior perceptions are externalized—corresponds to the circuits of Mars and Jupiter). The disruption of these planets is why we have such a difficult time in our psychology.

WE ARE SOLAR BEINGS. WE ARE SOLAR BROTHERS AND SISTERS. WE ARE CHILDREN OF THE SUN. THE SUN IS NOT ONLY THE AUTHOR OF LIGHT AND LIFE ON THIS EARTH BUT ALSO OF CONSCIOUSNESS.

Earth and Uranus hold the third circuit of consciousness: the biotelepathic circuit. The biological life that flourishes on Earth is meant to be telepathically wired and hooked up to Uranus through the flux tubes. Presently, the internalizing and externalizing circuits are disconnected. This is what is meant by "hooking up the noosphere." The next circuit is the allied-memory instinct circuit held by Neptune and Venus. The final circuit is the metaconscious circuit held by Mercury and Pluto—it is the higher consciousness that comes from the galaxy and connects with the Sun.

PLANETARY KARMA

We are now completing a phase of karmic cleansing that traces to the destruction of civilizations on Maldek and Mars. Karmic residues from these two planets was transferred to Earth, where we are now on a clean-up mission. This is a whole solar system—Kinich Ahau—karmic cleansing. Once it is complete, the wiring will be reestablished—then will occur the critical hookup between Earth and Uranus, which will establish a unity between the internal and externalizing circuits. This will create the biosolar-telepathic circuit to establish the noosphere or Sixth Sun of Consciousness.

Note the Bode frequency numbers for Mars (16), Maldek (28), Jupiter (52) and Saturn (100) equal 196, the Bode frequency of Uranus. The Earth being re-connected to Uranus reactivates the entire zone of consciousness that has been out of commission during the historical cycle.

The Cube of the Law integrates the Martian orbital frequency, 16. The 13 Moon/28-day calendar reestablishes the Maldekian frequency (28). 13:28 coordinates a perfect 52-week cycle; 52 is the Bode number of Jupiter. Saturn holds Bode number 100, the basis of the monetary system. By reestablishing the connection of all frequencies, the monetary system runs out of steam and dissipates. These are examples of subfunctions of higher solar consciousness.

Planetary Bode Numbers:

Pluto	388
Neptune	300
Uranus	196
Saturn	100
Jupiter	52
Maldek	28
Mars	16
Earth	10
Venus	7
Mercury	4

Unconscious	Conscious	Continuing Conscious	Superconscious
Cube 7 Hand Accomplishment	Cube 6 Worldbridger Death	Cube 5 Serpent Sex	Cube 4 Seed Flowering
DAY 13	DAY 12	DAY 11	DAY 10
Cube 8 Star Art	Cube 15 Eagle Vision	Cube 14 Wizard Timelessness	Cube 3 Night Abundance
DAY 14	DAY 21	DAY 20	DAY 9
Cube 9 Moon Purification	Cube 16 Warrior Intelligence	Cube 13 Skywalker Prophecy	Cube 2 Wind Spirit
DAY 15	DAY 22	DAY 19	DAY 8
Cube 10 Dog Love	Cube 11 Monkey Magic	Cube 12 Human Free Will	Cube 1 Dragon Memory
DAY 16	DAY 17	DAY 18	DAY 7

16-Unit Cube of the Law
Days 7-22 of every 28-day Moon
on the 13 Moon Calendar

When we refer to the coming Solar Age and the Aztec Sunstone, the Sun should not be confused with God—the Sun is the basis of life on Earth as a whole system. Until we fully understand this system we will not understand life on Earth. The Sun is God's instrument to establish a zone of stellar consciousness. In this way the Sun is merely an instrument to maintain the order of life in this part of the galaxy, an infinitesimally small part of the whole.

The Sun is the coordinating consciousness and mind of the solar system. The ancient Mayans were attuned to and in resonance with this solar consciousness. This is what is meant by the Sixth Sun of Consciousness, the coming Solar Age—this is only possible through a time change.

13 Moons and the Solar Ring

The function of the 13 Moon/28-day calendar matrix is not only to calibrate the cycle of this solar ring but also to make conscious what is already encoded into it. In this system, the Sun functions as an energy transmitter, beaming different levels of information, plasmas and radiation to Earth and to the entire solar system. Each planet receives a certain amount of beams and plasmas depending on its size and position.

The 13 Moon/28-day cycle locks into the harmonic frequency knowledge of the solar ring that precipitates a heightened awareness or consciousness previously unknown. By following the 13 Moon/28-day cycle, in one year's time, our consciousness will bring the orbital frequencies into proper alignment with the human mind. This would unlock the stored orbital frequencies interfacing with the psi bank as well as the Sun. Attuning with this solar frequency will result in an amping of consciousness—this is the evolutionary trip switch that enters us into heightened consciousness.

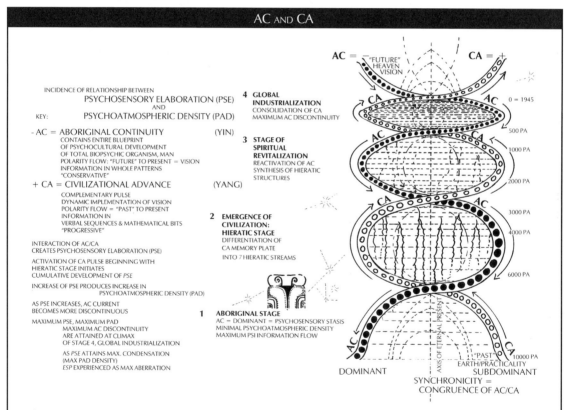

Without awareness of the solar ring through its precise measure of the 13 Moon/28-day cycle, then there can be no continuing consciousness of cosmic perception. (Note: This is why in Earth Ascending the AC as the Aboriginal Continuity is meant to become Absolute Conservation, and the CA as the Civilizational Advance is meant to become Cosmic Awareness).

Cosmic Awareness is the direct result of the solar ring made conscious. AC refers to Absolute Conservation of energy, which is the Earth itself. Russian scientist, Vladimir Vernadsky, has demonstrated through his investigation of the biosphere that the biomass remains constant—this is AC. The interaction of the different cycles of Earth (photosynthesis, oxygen, carbon dioxide, etc.) maintain an absolute conservation of energy or homeostasis, while through the biogenic migration of atoms there is a continuous process of mutation and evolution.

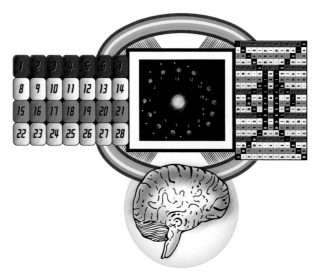

The civilization of Tollan is rooted in this solar ring as a balance of AC and CA—Absolute Conservation and Cosmic Awareness. When history began in Babylonia, Sumeria and the Middle East it forfeited knowledge of the solar ring in favor of the synodic lunar cycle, which has little to do with the solar ring based on 13. So instead of Cosmic Awareness there is *Civilizational Advance*. Cosmic Awareness can only be realized with a measure that corresponds to the actual orbital frequency of Earth, which is 13:28. Before history, consciousness was naturally entrained in the 13:28 cycle.

Where the Earth is in the universe is in relation to a star. The Earth goes around the star once in 365 days (= 13 × 28 + 1 day). If we limit our measure strictly from New Moon to New Moon then we decapitate Cosmic Awareness on the spot. By forfeiting the correct standard of the measure of the solar ring, Cosmic Awareness is lost and is replaced by Civilizational Advance—as civilization advances the energy meant to be conserved by Aboriginal Continuity is expended, exploited and depleted.

The principle of Aboriginal Continuity has been totally overturned in the last 260 years, disrupting the absolute conservation of energy. With the rise of industrialization, toxic energies hitherto not in the biosphere are released into it in great amounts. Cosmic Awareness does not expend energy, but expands energy and is rotated on the solar ring. This is why we say that the civilization of Tollan is rooted in the solar ring; Maya-Toltec knowledge of ancient Mexico was based on the knowledge of the solar ring. They were completely interfaced with that solar orbit, whence came their knowledge. This is the meaning of solar consciousness.

During the conquest of New World civilization, the Babylonians attempted to destroy all knowledge of the calendar that contained knowledge of the solar ring. By destroying this knowledge they also destroyed the basis of cosmic perceptions, setting the mass human consciousness on an irrevocably downward spiral. This is a root point of the calendar change and closing the cycle—the restoration of cosmic awareness as a natural, every day condition.

Once we experience one solar ring by means of the erroneous and irregularly measured knowledge (12:60), and then that is repeated year after year without questioning it, we are further entrained into a disharmonic frequency that has nothing to do with experiencing the harmonies of the solar orbit as the cosmic path laid out for Earth in its journey around the Sun. This dims the mind and leads society into a hopeless situation of decreasing harmony.

No matter how great certain points in civilization may appear, they are also filled with problems, vice and evil. Since the program of civilization adheres purely to the lunar calendar in combination, finally, with a false or inaccurate solar measure, each stage of civilization increasingly worsens straying farther from the perfection of original order.

The meaning of the closing of the cycle is the reintegration of human consciousness into the solar ring through the application of the correct standard of measure.

Since the calendar creates the template of civilization, using an irregular standard of measure limits consciousness and creates a society that accepts certain idiosyncrasies and norms. This program is repeated daily, weekly, monthly and yearly creating a continuous feedback loop that predisposes the mind to further irregularities. This system has nothing to do with natural order. So here we are today at an apocalyptic stage—it is a beast gone insane due to the forfeiture of cosmic awareness.

The Babylonian inheritors traveled across the globe on little boats and destroyed the civilizations of the New World. Since the Earth is one single sphere and the human species is a single organism its like saying, "that part of our brain isn't any good let's cut it out." This is a metaphor for the effects of having destroyed the knowledge base that existed in the New World. For this reason different prophecies exist: the Nahui Ollin prophecy, the 13 Heavens and 9 Hells prophecy, and the Telektonon prophecy.

These prophecies exist because Cosmic Awareness was decapitated by the forfeiture of correct knowledge of the solar ring for the lunar or 12-month standard which doesn't measure the solar ring. The 20-day Haab cycle works within the 13:28 but is based on the 20 and the 9 (18) rather than 7 and 13. The Haab actually defines a circle (tun) plus five days.

The accurate cosmic standard of measure of the solar ring is the 13 moon/ 28-day count. However, because the Haab, the 360 (+5) day cycle, is based on the 20-count it is integrated with the 260-day count, and consequently within the 13 moon, 28-day cycle. Nonetheless, the Haab is a 365-day count, as is the 13 Moon count. They are both solar measures integrated with the 260-day cycle every 52 years.

The 360 tun cycle upon which the Haab is based coincides with the 260- and 365 (364 + 1) day cycles precisely only every 3744 years. 3744 years = 1366560 days (kin) which in the long count occurs only once in the 13 baktun cycle—AD 631—the moment of Pacal Votan's coming into his avataric power and the triumphant reentry of Muhammad into Mecca (360 × 3796 = 260 × 5556 = 365 × 3744, etc.)

Civilizational Advance closes humans off from the possibility of cosmic reality. By the time of modern civilization there was no proper measure of the solar ring. The Christians called Mayan time knowledge the work of the devil because they knew if they gave it credibility, it would undermine their system. This intolerant mind-set contributes to the state of our world today.

Divine intervention appears the only solution—this is the purpose of prophecy. The Prophecy of Pacal Votan is a true form of divine intervention with a far reaching world impact. This prophecy enables us to analyze the world situation from a cosmic perspective above the whole Earth. The principle of the ancient knowledge formulated as the Law of Time and 13 Moon calendar was revived through the Telektonon prophecy. When we discover the principle, then we can universalize knowledge into a context that transcends the local context.

Through the Law of Time and the 13 Moon/28-day calendar, the Telektonon prophecy universalizes the principle of terma (hidden knowledge) and the Mayan knowledge base that was destroyed during the conquest. Through this prophecy, the error in time is rectified and the solar ring made conscious. With the solar-lunar calendar, the Moon going around the Earth is like the minute hand and the Earth going around the Sun is like the hour hand. This is the principle that was lost and glossed over by Babylonian mechanization. Following only a lunar calendar is like only focusing on minutes and not hours.

The meaning of the closing of the cycle is the reintegration of human consciousness into the solar ring through the application of the correct standard of measure. The cycle that is being closed is the cycle of the Earth in relationship with the Sun that occurs every 365 days. When the correct harmonic standard is applied then a resonance is created with human consciousness that seals the orbit. Because the cycle closes, it becomes endless. It cannot do that unless the correct knowledge and instrument is brought into the forefront of human consciousness once again.

The perpetual 13 Moon/28-day calendar is the basis of ending the drama on Earth—bringing the human consciousness into the correct frequency with the solar ring so the Civilizational Advance can be erased and Cosmic Awareness can be restored. This is why the work we are doing is so urgent because it says in the prophecy that if by 2012 human consciousness is operating by Cosmic Awareness and not Civilizational Advance then there is a renewal of the intelligent life cycle on Earth. But if human consciousness is still operating on Civilizational Advance then…

COSMIC AWARENESS AND THE NEW PROGRAM

It takes a four-year cycle to establish Cosmic Awareness or a Seed-Storm year bundle—this is so because it takes the 4-year cycle for the solstices and equinoxes to balance out in the North and South. (This is why there are 4 psi plates). If we make it to 2012 in Cosmic Awareness it means we have successfully erased the old tapes. But if we fail to make this switch, then the human Earth and the solar frequency will not match—then the humans Earth program gets vaporized. If we are in Cosmic Awareness at that point it will only be because the correct instrument was applied.

The closing of the cycle is pivoted on bringing the Earth into the correct frequency range with the Sun in the solar ring. Knowing how to close the ring is the function of the knowledge brought forth by the GM108X transmission. The key lies in the frequency of registration between human consciousness engaged with the solar ring and the solar registration. This has everything to do with solar frequencies engaging the Earth's orbit through human consciousness reengaged in the proper instrument of measure bringing it into a heightened state of consciousness.

Our principle aim is returning the Earth within the solar ring—this brings us back to the principle of Absolute Conservation of energy—now we are in absolute depletion. When Cosmic Awareness replaces Civilizational Advance there will be a regeneration and restoration of the AC function as well. The Earth already represents the supreme form of the absolute conservation of energy—we just need to balance and then expand the energy through cosmic awareness; this is the lift off of Timeship Earth and the entry into the new timespace.

13:20 TIMING FREQUENCY

Once the human mind is established in the 13:20 timing frequency then the frequency locks will open. These frequencies are now stored in the underground cave that connects the top of the Pyramid of the Sun to the center of the earth, and to the higher guiding forces outside: The "watchers". This is all part of an ancient meditation held for aeons by seers who are now in other dimensions, watching this vision and holding this vibration.

The vision of the fifth world, the fifth planet of consciousness was foreseen from the time of the destruction of Maldek. When Maldek was destroyed there emerged the creation of an etheric cosmic egg. In the center of the cosmic egg was the vision of the nexus point of the planetary logos as the Pyramid of the Sun. This nexus point contains five layers that correspond to the power of the fifth root race—serpent initiate of wisdom. The pyramids were built so well that their structure and frequency range are still standing now at the end of the cycle. We are now in the stage of the purification of the five senses—the 12:60 world of materialism is the biggest hindrance to purifying our sense organs.

The activation of the noosphere is dependent on the release from the 12:60 mental field and the establishment of a new collective mental house. This represents the collectivization of the human imagination and mind and the planetization of consciousness. The research of Russian scientist, Alexei Dmietriev, demonstrates that the Sun has been undergoing incredible changes especially in the last 15 years with the last solar sunspot cycle. Another cycle will peak in 2012-2013—this will be the final sunspot cycle of the 13 baktuns of history.

Since we are the Sun and life depends on the Sun, then changes in the Sun will result in the reorganization of life on Earth. All of this is part of the coming Sixth Sun of Consciousness. This involves what some might call an apocalyptic shakedown of the old order based on illusions strung together on the notion of artificial time and artificial means of Exchange, primarily money. This shakedown is experienced as apocalyptic to the degree in which there is dependency on the technosphere.

This has all been foretold in many prophecies including Mayan, Christian and Native American. Apocalyptic shakedown has to occur for purification to be complete. Knowledge of the solar ring and the 13-moon, 28 day calendar is the salvation of Planet Earth; it is a cosmic mechanism that creates a frequency that matches the solar frequency. The 13:28 frequency locks in perfectly with the 13:20 frequency to create a 52-year solar galactic loop, the measure of Sirius B in its orbit around Sirius A.

The ending of the ninth hell in 1987 was the beginning of the time of prophecy: 1987-2012. This is the time allotted for the human beings to get their act together. The timing of the prophecy is very precise and accurate. This has to be done by means of the human paranormal potential which depends upon the right use of power. The right use of power is to exert in a way that is increasingly magical in its applications and effects so that we can assist humanity over the bridge into the next timespace. All the forces are gathering for this. When we establish the solar ring, Tollan can be returned and the new timespace will emerge in all its glory.

CHANNEL 6

GALACTIC BEAM

Entry into the new timespace has everything to do with a galactic beam—a higher frequency time wave that is emanated from the galactic core. All of history is condensed within a galactic beam that we are now passing out of. This particular type is a 5,125-year beam; its purpose is to accelerate human activity around the planet. This acceleration is called recorded history. This 5,125-year beam is nested within a 26,000 year beam, which is nested in a 104,000-year beam. These all climax in the Harmonic Convergence of 2012.

Beams are resonant frequency waves. Like radio waves, these beams are not like plasma, photons or meson waves or gamma or alpha or beta waves. The beams are actual radio waves generated from the galactic core, and mediated through the Sun. These very high frequency radio waves are coded with holographic information of an epoch of a whole cosmic era or cosmic aeons of evolution.

Our solar system is actually a star system within a constellation of other star systems, one of many within a single galaxy system. We are operating in a larger galactic field that contains many energy beams that influence the different constellations. Physicists call these beams "density waves" that continuously sweep through the cosmos affecting the stages of evolution with life programs coded as different frequency configurations.

The Mayan Factor states that the time beams are emitted from the Hunab Ku, the galactic core, and even more specifically, from the black hole which is close to the galactic center. A black hole is the point at which the gravitational field of a star or galaxy becomes so intense that it draws into it everything in its immediate range. Then everything caves in, sucking in all the light.

On the other side of the black hole is another universe. Inside the black hole is a dense core. This dense core, a collapsed gravity field of imploded light, is a synthesized information unit of everything that the particular star system or universal order represented. This synthesized information unit is then condensed into a force that is emitted as a higher frequency wave—a time wave. This is similar to what astrophysicist Kozyrev spoke of as "time beams", where time is emitted from stellar cores of different celestial bodies. This is where the time beams, including the 5,125-year acceleration synchronization beam, originate.

The beam that we are passing through contains the entire hologram of all that has ever occurred and that will still occur in human history. As a wave harmonic of an event-continuum, all information and patterns of events that have unfolded since 3113 BC are encoded in a hologram contained within that time beam. This is why it is called a *synchronization beam*. The program of the total hologram of the time beam synchronizes with the actuality of events playing out within third-dimensional matter as it is or has unfolded to create the wave harmonic of history.

The galactic beam information forms the basic premise of *The Mayan Factor*, particularly the 5,125-year/13 baktun cycle or the wave harmonic of history. According to *The Mayan Factor*, the (long count) measure of 1,872,000 days, 13 baktuns, 260 katuns, 5,125 years 5200 tuns, is actually the measure of a particular synchronization beam. This Great cycle is the measurement of this planetary passage through a time beam that is 5,125 years wide.

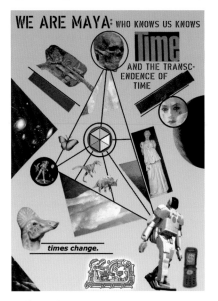

HARMONIC RESONANCE

For the Galactic Maya the measurement of time is a function of harmonic resonance. Days are actually tones, called kin, represented by numbers; sequences of days (kin) create harmonic cycles, called vinal (20 days), tun (360 days), katuns (20 years), baktuns (144,000 days), and so forth. All the different kin, katun cycles, etc., constitute the harmonic calibration of Earth's passage through the beam. The different calendars are used to mark synchronization points within the beam's passage. The principle synchronization cycles are the 260-, 360- and 365-day cycles.

The galactic Mayan time engineers calibrated the beam with precise information, particularly the carving in stone of different long count dates, usually in and 5-, 10-, 15-, 20-year cycles. They made calibrations about the larger organic order, such as the harmonic pattern of Earth in relation to the Sun, the galaxy and beyond. In these meticulous trackings were recorded the calibrations of the beam at its time of maximum harmonic attainment. The maximum harmonic frequency calibrations occur in the 52-year cycle between 631 AD and 683 AD; marking the 52-year time of power of Pacal Votan.

The year 631 marks 3744 years and 3796 tun since 3113 BC, while the year 683 is 3796 years since that beginning date, making 631–683 AD the precise harmonic span of Pacal Votan's cycle of power. There are precisely 52 years from his ascension to power to his death.

As noted the 3744-year cycle is the principle point at which the three key cycles come together, the 260, 360, 365. That is why this point in time 631 was so remarkable. It is the only point during the entire 13 baktun cycle that these three calibrators synchronize with so many other factors. For instance, 3744 also corresponds with a number of (36 × 104 years) Venus cycles.

The maximum period of the calibration of the beam was between the 3796 tun (AD 631) and the 3796 year (AD 683) markers—this is the harmonic cycle or frequency that marked the 73rd solar-galactic 52-year cycle since 3113 BC. Seventy-three is the key number of the biomass constant. The magic correlate number of all the cycles is 1366560.

The main Mayan time science centers, from which the beam was calibrated, were Palenque (Nah Chan), Copan and Quirigua. The Mayan time engineers knew there would be a pivotal date marking the heliacal rising of Sirius on 16 July (Julian) (26 July Gregorian) in 692, precisely 1320 solar Earth years until this 13 baktun cycle closed in 2012. They could calibrate the mathematics of the increasing complexification of the frequencies of the beam as they maximized out into baktun 12. They knew that at the culmination of baktun 12 a perfect harmonic frequency of 1, 728,000 kin (days) is attained.

FRACTAL NOTE
1728 is the root fractal base of 12 cubed, 12 × 12 × 12 or 144 × 12 = 1728. 144,000 days of the 12 baktun cycles is complete. This is the cube of the perfect 144 frequency. This occurred in 1618 AD. Note on the Telektonon playing board Uranus circuit 8 is comprised of units 17 – 28, while Earth is 1 – 12 (1728 = 12 cubed).

The Galactic Maya knew that in baktun 13 would occur the phenomenal acceleration and velocity of human existence or the climax of matter: the cube of 12 plus one. At this stage there is a quantum shift into a greatly accelerated, high frequency civilization. This is a complete departure from everything that went before. How could this be? Because this is the first time in all of history that earthly civilization is living within an encapsulated artificial bubble of Babylonian time—the 12:60 frequency. The potential for this frequency was established in 3113 when this particular time beam hit.

When the Earth phases out of the beam at the end of 2012, humans have the opportunity to create a unified global civilization living in harmony with nature in anticipation of the next evolutionary cycle: Timeship Earth 2013.

High Frequency Radio Waves

The galactic beam is intelligently focused creating precise patterns. Patterns of information do not just happen randomly, but are intelligently conceived and projected as holographic structures or images within different time beams. In turn, these time beams inform the different structures of celestial, cosmic reality.

This particular 5,125-year time beam structure contains the holographic information of everything that has occurred in human history. It is directed with the purpose of utilizing the vibrational frequency to create a particular effect intended to agitate and help disperse the human family as a vast community around the planet.

If we view the Earth from a time capsule in BC 3113, we see many small dispersed communities. Very few, if any—or some exceptional intelligences—knew they were living on a whole Earth. None save maybe a visionary or sage here and there was aware of the numbers of people on the Earth, much less that Earth was a sphere rotating in space. Everything was dispersed. There was no knowledge of who everyone else was. Life was like this for quite some time.

Soon after the beam occurred, humans began conglomerating into cities in a process referred to as the three c's: *colonization, conquest* and *communication*. The humans projected their holograms of material conquest that resulted in the creation of one empire after another beginning with the Egyptian empire, the Sumerian empire. Babylonian empire, Persian empire, and then the Chinese get into it and the Indians, Greek, Roman, and even in the new world, the ill-fated Aztec and Inca. The point is that the three c's were holographically programmed into the human noosphere and human mind.

MAYAN ENGINEERING TEAM

... What the Maya knew was that, while the beam had the correct program for this critical phase of development, the human genetic circuits were just a little out of phase. Incidentally, the Maya call this beam an "acceleration-synchronization beam." First it accelerates human activity, causing an interesting side effect: material technology. Towards the end of the beam, acceleration is supposed to become exponential. Population explodes, technology is everywhere, and the stock market cannot stop going straight up the charts. When it becomes absolutely exponential, acceleration is supposed to phase into synchronization. That is when everybody starts to say to everybody else: "Hey! Did you notice that?" And everyone says that all at the same time.

—José Arguelles, *Surfers of the Zuvuya*

SUNSPOT CYCLES AND BEAMS

All the beam information is focalized through the local star, the Sun—Kinich Ahau—as the Maya call it. The purpose of the star is to focalize the beam information through a regular radio program that coordinates the sunspot cycles. These sunspot cycles then transmit the beam through peak solar activity, sending solar information into the Earth. This solar information carries within it the holographic beam codes to the Earth. The holographic codes create a massive cumulative incremental build-up, so that by baktun 10, 11 and 12, the empire building reaches a tumultuous climax.

In the Old World, during baktun 12, the barrier of empire building conquest and colonization was in full force as the Europeans set sail across the ocean and "found" a New World. This marks the climax of baktun 12: colonization of the New World and the circumnavigation of the globe. This set the stage for the final effect of the beam—planetary consciousness—when then the human is catapulted into the awareness that it is a single planetary organism aware of itself everywhere on the planet. That is the full function of the beam. We are now at the final stage of it.

Even though the human being is catapulted, most people don't feel like a planetary being, but rather they feel like an Australian rugby fan or Islamic jihadists or Japanese businessman, or whatever they think they are. People stick to their chosen identity even though the human species has been entirely planetized. You can buy a shirt that is designed in the United States manufactured and assembled in Mexico and sold in Dubai. This is the globalization factor that has created this kind of world.

THE BEAM AND THE CLOSING OF THE CYCLE

At the closing of the cycle the beam will be complete, the final holograms will be (and are now being) imprinted. At a specific point, there will come a pause—a *time quake*—and the previous structure of the hologram that has moved through the human population of the planet during the last 5,000 years will be erased or dissolved. The screen will go blank and we will be faced with ourselves. All the self-perceptions, opinions, and conditioned responses that you thought were *you*, will no longer have any meaning. At the same time, there will be a familiarity to the moment; like a child looking at the night-time sky we will be filled with a nameless awe and divine wonder.

It is mind-boggling to consider that everything that has happened was programmed into this beam—that the whole process and holographic structure was there from the very beginning. The raw material is actually the karmic residues of previous worlds that were coded into the DNA of the beings on this planet.

When the holographic structures of information hit the human DNA, past world analphs were activated. Masses of people and huge eras of time were catalyzed. Empires were created, along with specific arts, culture and literature. Different types of archetypal beings began to emerge. Every single personality like Buddha, Hitler or Joan of Arc, were performing archetypal functions encoded into the DNA and activated by the holographic information of the beam.

Today, we know that we are one planetary organism. The beam has awakened human consciousness to a state of primitive planetary consciousness. It is primitive because while it knows it is a planetary organism, the human collective has yet to fully experience that knowing as the conditioned filters are still too strong. These conditioned factors are held in place by a specific, often highly divergent, consensual belief system (such as the idea of nation states, etc). All outmoded forms of the hologram that are not serving the highest planetary cause will be dissolved. Only then will the human know what is true and real.

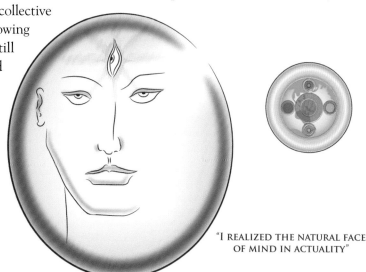

"I REALIZED THE NATURAL FACE OF MIND IN ACTUALITY"

INTELLIGENCE OF THE BEAMS

The beams are intelligently coordinated information complexes that carry holographic constructs mediated through the star that holds a particular planetary field together. In turn, the star beams specific information in harmonic increments over cycles of time.

The specialized 5,125-year beam is a very short term beam. This beam is also referred to as a *mutative phase beam* as it is affecting a mutational shift between stages of human being—from that of living in dispersed tribal community, to that of a complete full-on planetary human being. The planetary human knows that it is a function of the planet and that the planet is a whole system with different levels of organization. This is a vast shift from the tribal community living in an unconscious nest of nature.

It is important to understand what is meant when we say that the beam is moderated through the Sun or local star. This information can only be received through telepathic attunement, the method of which the galactic Maya were masters. They knew that what we call the "telepathic function" of the human brain is actually activated by solar frequencies from the Sun. This is why they had different words for the Sun; the base unit is *kin* which is also the same as day, star, person or unit of measure. *Kinan* means spiritual force of the spiritual psychic energy of the Sun. *Tinkanantan* refers to spiritual psychic energy of the Sun experienced as paranormal powers.

The Maya were deeply attuned to the Sun's cycles; this is how they knew to create the 13 baktun or the Mayan long count cycle, when it began and when it would end. The count of the baktuns was discontinued after 830 AD (10 baktuns or 1,440,000 days completed), or shortly thereafter. This means that the main research and recording of calibrations was done very precisely at a specific time.

The Maya foresaw the closing out 620 years from 692, 9.13.0.0.0. In 692 Chichen Itza was abandoned; many interesting recordings were left at this time in many places, especially at

The telepathic function of the human brain is activated by solar frequencies from the Sun. Tinkanantan refers to spiritual psychic energy of the Sun experienced as paranormal powers.

Edzna, and Yaxchilan, indicating great ceremonies and synchronizations in celebration of Sirius rising occurring on this date. Most importantly, this date inaugurated the final 7 katuns of the cycle of the Galactic Maya, the cycle of 7, Book of the Seven Generations.

Chichen Itza was reactivated by Quetzalcoatl in 987. This was a prophetic sign; It was the 144th year of the prophecy of the 13 heavens and 1,000 years before 1987, the sign of the closing of the cycle. Once we have sufficiently cultivated our biosolar telepathic powers then we can directly tune into this beam information.

The Mayans were highly conscious of the beam and its purpose and made calibrations of the baktun count that we find up through the end of baktun 10. At that point they had gathered all the information that they needed and the experiment was concluded. This is why the baktun count was discontinued. The galactic masters departed and left the remnants of knowledge, with those who were later known as the "indigenous Maya" or the "Toltec Maya". Quetzalcoatl catalyzed this later cultural cycle into manifestation, 987 AD.

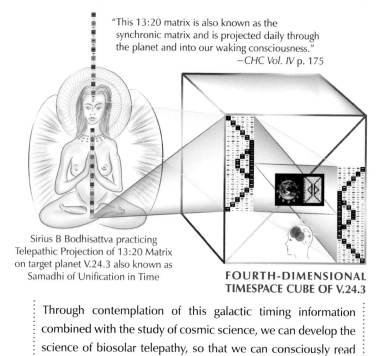

"This 13:20 matrix is also known as the synchronic matrix and is projected daily through the planet and into our waking consciousness."
—CHC Vol. IV p. 175

Sirius B Bodhisattva practicing Telepathic Projection of 13:20 Matrix on target planet V.24.3 also known as Samadhi of Unification in Time

FOURTH-DIMENSIONAL TIMESPACE CUBE OF V.24.3

Through contemplation of this galactic timing information combined with the study of cosmic science, we can develop the science of biosolar telepathy, so that we can consciously read the information of the beams.

This particular mutative phase beam, activating the DNA over this 5,125-year cycle, created a corresponding timespace. The timespace it created was codified into the perception of reality that we have at this point in time—for most people this is a 9-5, Monday through Friday work-week reality timespace.

The final mutative phase was condensed into a mechanized timespace field. In this field, people's perception of themselves and reality are highly conditioned by timespace factor 12:60. The entire creation of the timespace that people move through at the closing of the cycle is conditioned and a function of this particular artificial reality.

Not only is this timespace conditioned by artificial factors, it is also unconscious—that is, people are not conscious of the fact, nor to the degree in which their lives are dominated and controlled by this artificial timing frequency. And on top of this, no one ever seems to have enough time! Few people consider this, most just live like they live, rushing around, repeating the same programs inherited from family and society, unquestionably.

When this hologram fades out and dissipates, we will experience a cosmogalactic pause for a certain period, just long enough for the old hologram to dissolve. Then by July 26, 2013—galactic synchronization—we will be fully engaged in a new beam.

Note: There are exactly 216 days from 21/12/2012 through 25/7/2013. This 216 frequency is the frequency of the cube or 6 cubed. This will be the adjustment cycle of Earth to the new timespace cube.

Every time a beam shifts out and another beam shifts in, it is assumed that there is a new evolutionary level that has been attained. The effect of the previous beam builds on that level of information to then unload its hologram for however many years or aeons it may be. When the 2013 beam hits, it is assumed that the human beings will have stabilized at a level of planetary consciousness. In this consciousness, the reality of the Planet takes precedence over any racial, religious, ideological or national identification.

This collective egolessness is the new primitive plateau that will be arrived at. This is the basis of planetary consciousness and the opening to cosmic consciousness, into greater unification and oneness for a full telepathic field of harmonic union. We are moving into a new timespace matrix governed by the 13:20 time beam, where reality will be perceived in fourth-dimensional terms.

We are on a cosmic adventure: time travel, mental spiritual exploration, evolution and telepathic teleportation—exploration of other world systems and parallel realities that we can enter into and define through superior states of consciousness. A different kind of timespace: the beam.

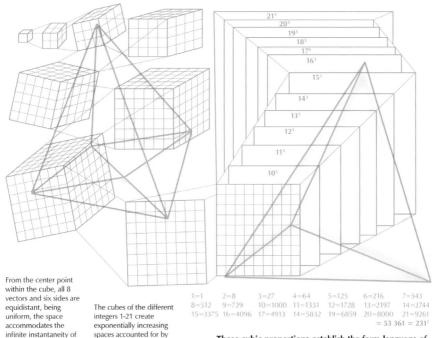

1=1	2=8	3=27	4=64	5=125	6=216	7=343
8=512	9=729	10=1000	11=1331	12=1728	13=2197	14=2744
15=3375	16=4096	17=4913	14=5832	19=6859	20=8000	21=9261
						= 53 361 = 231²

From the center point within the cube, all 8 vectors and six sides are equidistant, being uniform, the space accommodates the infinite instantaneity of time within a uniformly limited form.

The cubes of the different integers 1-21 create exponentially increasing spaces accounted for by and increase in mathematical proportion.

These cubic proportions establish the form-language of telepathy, the basis of the timespace of telepathic civilization.

When we enter the new timespace matrix it will no longer be based on the third-dimensional, but on the fourth-dimensional matrix perceived as a function of the cube.

THE BEAM AND THE CUBE

The universe is a fourth-dimensional cube structure. All beam information, all the holographic information, all the resonant information is a function of mathematical codes. We are phasing into a new perception of the universe and into a whole other cosmology that is vastly different than what we know today.

4D CUBE MATRIX

We are describing a higher dimensional structure which is a fourth-dimensional cube matrix. The third dimensional reality moves through or plays itself out within that particular cube matrix, and from its own dimension in that matrix—no more than a two-dimensional plane slicing through it—takes on a particular appearance: the universe as we know it.

Within that cube matrix, the functions of intelligence can be precisely calibrated and coordinated by mathematical structures in accord with different fluctuations of solar-galactic energy. Solar flares, solar emissions and solar winds are actually information waves and signals that reach us through what appears to be third-dimensional perturbations. As we transit from the Fifth Sun to the Sixth Sun of Consciousness we will see that the field created by the solar ring—thirteen 28-day cycles—calibrates the Earth perfectly as it makes its orbit around the Sun at the center.

This solar ring activates a cosmic memory field that contains all the universal information necessary to structure a new order of reality. This new reality is based on values of consciousness, telepathy and aesthetic harmony. As memory is activated we will move into a whole other timespace of harmonic comprehension from the Fifth Sun, which is commemorated by the Pyramid of the Sun (Nahui Ollin pyramid) to the Sixth Sun of Consciousness, the fulfillment of the prophecy of 2012.

SIXTH SUN OF CONSCIOUSNESS

Just as the Aztec sunstone was the final compilation of the beam information for the Fifth Sun, the final stage of the beam, so we will see that the galactic compass is the compilation of the energetic information of the Sixth Sun of Consciousness. The Sixth Sun of Consciousness contains the 1320/2013 beam information stored within the wheel of the galactic compass, which is actually the wheel of the cycle of revolution of Sirius B as it goes around Sirius A. Hence, this compass may be more precisely known as the *Sirian Wheel*.

By attuning our consciousness to the Earth, Sun and galactic beam, we will understand everything.

By attuning our consciousness to the Earth, Sun and galactic beam, we will understand everything. Through this understanding, we will establish a genuine cosmic order—cosmic civilization. Insofar as the beam affects the stages of galactic evolution, it is loaded with the galactic cosmic memory plates. These memory plates are the information holograms necessary to activate our next etheric field of telepathic/psychic/mental/spiritual expansion into the whole order of the universe.

We are transiting from a third-dimensional physical perception of timespace into the fourth dimension. Imagine that suddenly someone opens the top of your head and the invisible is made visible; you see that all of reality is coded into a vast cube matrix structure that is vibrating and pulsating mathematical structures from a radial matrix that connects everything to everything. You suddenly know beyond doubt that you are an integral part of an expanding cube matrix that contains the whole evolution of the cosmos, and of the universe itself. The fact is that the nature of the universe is far out!

Our perception of cosmology will change dramatically when we see things in this light. We are ever-evolving masterpieces in motion; we are endless and dynamic and at the same time we are rooted in a cosmic timelessness that has always been and always shall be.

In the new timespace we will entertain thoughts of polarity without difficulty because we will have expanded our perception as a comprehensive, binary totality rather than a sense of "If I'm not this, then I'm not that." We will realize that we are *this* and we are *that* and at the same time, we are *neither*. In the comprehensive totality there is no struggle, there is only pure love radiating in all directions.

A SYNCHRONIC NOTE ON TRANSMISSION OF GALACTIC BEAM

Please note: This transmission on the Galactic Beam was received on kin 194, commemorating the first katun cycle, the Crystal cycle, between 692 and 712 AD. This is the first cycle of time following the dedication of the tomb of Pacal Votan (692 AD).

During this katun cycle, the information was telepathically deposited into the Earth and into the unconscious mental sphere of the psi bank. This information would be prophetically downloaded between 1987 and 2012, and most specifically, at the point of the discovery of the Telektonon prophecy on 26 July 1993. This discovery came at the precise point that marked the first day of the seven years of prophecy: the day kin 144. This first year of prophecy was also coded by kin 194, the First Book of the Seven Lost Generations.

In that first year of prophecy on the day kin 194, the third day of the Crystal Moon (12), the tomb of the Red Queen was discovered in Temple XIII next to the Temple of Inscriptions in Palenque, Mexico. The discovery of Temple XIII yielded a tomb of equal significance, at least, to the tomb of Pacal Votan, and at that precise moment in time, demonstrated the precision of the prophetic alignment of the closing of the cycle and the cycle of prophecy.

This synchronic alignment led to further activation of the psi bank holding the information of the beam to be downloaded in various forms of codices and texts such as the 20 Tablets of the Law of Time and the 7:7::7:7. Already, early in 1986, the perception of the time beam was perceived at Coba, Yucatan by José Arguelles/Valum Votan and was recorded and formed the basis of The Mayan Factor.

This information is being transmitted at a perfect point of synchronization, 21 galactic spins since the discovery of Temple XII, 15 years, less 15 days. Those two numbers are key to create a perfect harmonic. 15 is the triangular number of 5 (1 + 2 + 3 + 4 + 5 = 15). 21 is the triangular number of 6 (15 + 6 = 21). Add 15 (1 + 5) = 6. This point marks the perfect equivalence between 15 solar years and 21 galactic spins. 21 is also the eighth unit in the logarithmic spiral that goes from 13 to 21. This moment is synchronized for the synchronization of the prophecy with the larger beam information.

PART III
ARCHETYPES AND THE COMING TIMESPACE

CHANNEL 7

THE MYTHIC SELF

As the Earth changes so does the human. As we enter into a new timespace we will no longer be the same human. We are being changed into something new. Our perceptions are rapidly shifting. We are reaching a point where there is a break in the historical continuum. A radical shift and evolution of the human species is about to occur. We shall become something we cannot imagine now.

We are undergoing a fundamental shift from the third-dimensional realm of personality to the fourth-dimensional archetypal or mythic realm. In the latter every thought and action is based on the fulfilment of a higher principle for the betterment of the whole rather than personal satisfaction. Archetypes are universal and commonly shared, rather than individualist and ego-centered personality as it has generally been evolved.

Any timespace is a mind-based reality. Our collective self-perception creates the look and tone of the timespace we project, live and move in. What we call "reality" is merely a collectively held belief system that molds, shapes and organizes the timespace in a specific way and then deems it "normal." In this perception, anything that does not conform to this timespace is considered a "deviation" in need of rehabilitation. Of course, as the social structures become more dissipative at the closing of the cycle, there are more "deviants." This only tells us it is time for an archetypal renewal. New archetypes are now emerging—new only in the sense that they are not of the historical cycle. But we have known these archetypes before on other worlds, in other dimensions.

In order to consider our mythic self and the new archetypes, let us first review the nature of timespace and the human function therein.

1. The timespace is a coded set of patterns that organize different levels of reality in a systematic manner.
2. Within this timespace system, the human is the organizing component instrumented by cosmic intelligence.
3. Specific timespaces appear according to the requirements of different stages of evolution.
4. Society is a human organization of timespace.
5. We are a timespace within a timespace; each of us lives our life and exerts our influence within the sphere of a greater being.

What kind of timespace are we moving into? What type of beings are required for this timespace? What is the future identity for the human? How do we transition from personality into archetype? To find the answers let us step back into the historical cycle to search for clues.

Carl Jung did much work on the archetypes and the collective unconscious. Jung's work expanded on the theories of Hippocrates who believed that there were four primary personality types. In his book, *Psychological Types* (1921), Jung concluded that all human beings have access to the collective mental experience of all their ancestors. He believed that these memories are carried genetically from one generation to the next.

Esotericist, Isaac Bonewits, expands on Jung's philosophy by concluding that there is a Switchboard, suggesting that there is a network of interlocking metapatterns of everyone who has ever lived or who is living now, expressed as constantly changing and infinitely subtle modifications of current telepathic transmissions and receptions. This could also be the same as the Akashic Field.

According to this train of thought, every human being is constantly broadcasting and receiving on telepathic wavelengths. This is possible because there is a cosmic memory field that underlies and informs the universal timespace. This cosmic memory (Akashic) Field has two principle attributes: 1) It is structured by a radial telepathic template that informs all orders of reality in waves of simultaneity; and 2) it is holographic in nature, that is, it holds the holographic structures of all forms, memories, experiences, etc.

Buckminster Fuller, for instance, felt that there was a cosmic switchboard that could be telepathically accessed connecting us with any being throughout history. If he was able to converse with the pre-Socratic philosophers while walking on the beach, it is because his mind was in resonant attunement with the hologram of those pre-Socratic thought forms held in place by the psi bank, the Akashic record within Earth's noosphere.

The Law of Time affirms this by stating that time is the universal factor of synchronization. This means in any instant or

What is the future identity for the human? How do we transition from personality into archetype?

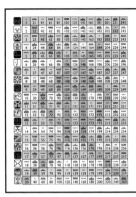

Through the synchronic order we can access any being through their galactic signature. All 260 kin are registered in the underlying template of the psi bank—planetary cosmic memory plates.

"now" moment, the whole of reality is being enacted simultaneously. This means that any persona from past, present or future can be accessed through the now. How can this be? Because time is radial. This accounts for why astronomers can see stars that existed millions of years ago, but we just now see their light. The totality of the universe exists in the timespace of a single vast continuum that is a unitary simultaneity of information.

441 FRACTAL MATRIX

The psi bank, the noosphere, the Akashic cosmic memory field and the synchronic order all represent levels of timespace organization informed by a vast underlying telepathic substructure. This underlying telepathic matrix informs every aspect of the cosmos and cosmic life inclusive of the phenomenal, mental, and higher-dimensional aspects of the universe.

These components are arranged by telepathic frequencies that create different harmonies. These can be thought of as *telepathic frequency organizers*. For instance, all of the oxygen atoms throughout the universe are continuously in telepathic communication with each other, and forming an underlying telepathic oxygen matrix of the universe. At a more complex level, the Earth's biomass constant also maintains its homeostasis by the intricate feedback systems of the telepathic frequency organizers that govern the evolving forms of matter.

There are different levels and layers of these telepathic matrices, each with its own unique mathematical organization. The combination of these telepathic matrices form an infrastructure that underlies the universe. This vast universal matrix or infrastructure can be reduced to its smallest fractal component: the 441 base matrix or the 21 squared base matrix. This is the minimal matrix of the master fractal cube: 21 cubed or 9,261 units or 1.3.3.1 as written in the vigesimal code.

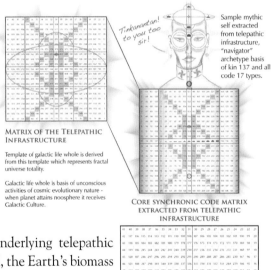

Tinkanantan! to you too sir!

Sample mythic self extracted from telepathic infrastructure, "navigator" archetype basis of kin 137 and all code 17 types.

MATRIX OF THE TELEPATHIC INFRASTRUCTURE

Template of galactic life whole is derived from this template which represents fractal universe totality.

Galactic life whole is basis of unconscious activities of cosmic evolutionary nature - when planet attains noosphere it receives Galactic Culture.

CORE SYNCHRONIC CODE MATRIX EXTRACTED FROM TELEPATHIC INFRASTRUCTURE

The 21 × 21 matrix follows a spiral form. The first units are in the lower right corner and go up the right following a radial spiral leading to the center: 441. This matrix is the basis of all other matrices.

Noospheric Beam

As we phase out of this 12:60 synchronization beam, we will enter into the precincts of another beam, the "noospheric 13:20 beam". Under the influence of the noospheric beam, we will operate according to the laws of the galactic life whole and of the fractal matrix from which all the other matrices are derived. The preparation for entry into this beam is referred to as the *discovery of the Law of Time*. The base understanding of the Law of Time lies within the 441 matrix.

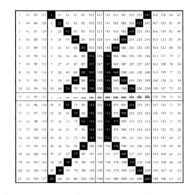

> In the cosmic evolutionary nature, whenever a planet attains noosphere—the planetary mind—it then becomes capable of receiving the processes that create galactic culture.

The harmonic module matrix is the core synchronic code matrix, extracted from the master 441 telepathic matrix. This is a base 13:20 matrix of 260 units. Within this 13:20 matrix lies the key harmonic matrix module for the new dispensation of time. As this new dispensation phases in, all outmoded programs based in the old 12:60 frequency will either be dissolved or transmuted into a higher form.

Galactic Life Whole

The galactic life whole is derived from the 441 template and represents the fractal template of any galaxy with life. A galaxy is the smallest operating macro unit of the cosmic evolutionary process. We are all functions of the galactic life whole. The galactic life whole itself is the basis of all conscious activities that oversee the cosmic evolutionary process. These seven volumes of the *Cosmic History Chronicles* aim to define, with ever greater clarity, the seeds of a new knowledge base beyond 2012.

The new dispensation of galactic culture has already been deposited on Earth. It is now awaiting the study of humanity. This knowledge base vibrates with the 13:20 noospheric frequency of the coming time beam. In this new dispensation everybody receives a galactic *signature*, a code name for their mythic self and archetypal function within the noospheric 13:20 time beam.

GALACTIC SIGNATURE AND MYTHIC SELF

What does it mean to extract your mythic self from the telepathic infrastructure? First, we must understand the 441 telepathic infrastructure. The 260-unit harmonic module is are derived from the 441 matrix. Within the harmonic module are the 260 code names or galactic signatures. This means there are 260 possibilities for your mythic self. These signatures are based on 20 + 1 new archetypes, as introduced in the next chapter. Each of the 20 archetypes code one of the 260 galactic signatures. There are 13 variations of each of the 20 particular archetypes that exist and there are 260 variations of the 20 archetypes (see chart in Chapter 13, page 212).

Extracting the Mythic Self from the telepathic infrastructure

Furthermore, each of the 20 mythic selves has a five-part function derived from the fifth force. The fifth force is the power that animates the vitality and livingness of the galactic life whole. Applying our galactic signature establishes within us a particular frequency of resonant knowing opening us to the possibility of universal telepathy.

The galactic signature or mythic self is a gateway or portal to explore and discover different aspects of ourselves. Every mythic or archetypal self is a multilayered code with essentially five component code parts plus a galactic tone or frequency. For example let's look at kin 137, the mythic self or galactic signature known as *Red Resonant Earth*. Resonant is tone 7, a bar with two dots above it. Seven represents the tone of attunement and holds the powers of channelling and inspiration. Each of the 260 galactic signatures has its own particular qualities as well as a code affirmation that can be found in the Book of Kin. The affirmation for kin 137 is:

I channel in order to evolve

Inspiring synchronicity

I seal the matrix of navigation

With the resonant tone of attunement

I am guided by the power of universal water ...

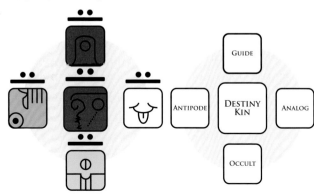

Each mythic self also contains a five-part oracle that includes the guide, the analog (helping partner), the antipode (challenge partner) and the occult (hidden power). The Red Resonant Earth is guided by the Moon, the power of universal water; its analog partner is the Wind, power of spirit; its antipode is the Hand, power of accomplishment; and its occult is the Seed, the power of flowering.

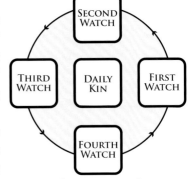

Each of us is born into a different "watch" based on our five-part oracle depending on our time of birth: midnight to dawn, is the first "watch" (analog); dawn to noon, is the second "watch" (guide); noon to sunset, is the third "watch" (antipode); and sunset to midnight, is the fourth "watch" (occult). For instance: If kin 137 was born in the first watch, then the emphasis is on the analog partner, Wind, which signifies spirit, breath and communication.

Every mythic self is a personification or an emanation of one of 20 archetypal personas as given in the following chapter. The Earth is code 17 and represents the manifestation of the Navigator archetype. Each of these archetypal personas has 13 variations, according to whatever tone they may be. Kin 37 is variation 7 of the Navigator archetype. This defines the basic kin.

In the oracle layout, we see that every mythic self is also a gathering or congregation of at least three or four other archetypes (see next chapter for list of archetypes). For example, in the Earth archetype is the Navigator. The Resonant Navigator gathers around it the Wind (High Priestess), the Moon (Healer), the Hand (Avatar) and the Seed (Innocent One).

EARTH FAMILIES AND HOLONS

The Akashic field is the mathematically structured medium that holds the holograms or holographic information of all and everything that is. In the synchronic order, the holographic "soul" element of any given form—human, planet, star or galaxy—is called a *holon*. Hence, there are human holons, Earth holons, etc.

Each mythic self with its holon also corresponds with a number, an Earth family, a chakra, and a planet (see chart in Chapter 13, page 212). There are five Earth families: Polar, Cardinal, Core, Signal and Gateway. Each of these Earth families codes both the human holon and the planet holon. We are within the Earth, the Earth is within us.

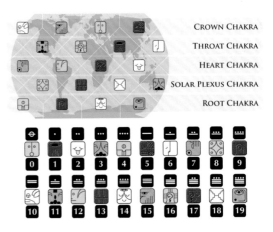

CROWN CHAKRA
THROAT CHAKRA
HEART CHAKRA
SOLAR PLEXUS CHAKRA
ROOT CHAKRA

In the example of Red Resonant Earth, Earth (17) belongs to the Core family, along with the Hand, the Wind and the Human. The Core family codes the equatorial zone of the Earth—one of the five noospheric protection zones. The Seed and the Moon are Gateway family and code the South Pole. The other three zones are Polar (North Pole); Cardinal (Northern hemisphere); and Signal (Southern hemisphere).

Each of the mythic selves also corresponds with one of the five principle chakras. The Earth, along with the rest of the Core family, corresponds with the heart chakra, while the Seed and Moon are Gateway family and correspond with the root chakra. The root and heart chakras are the special activation power centers of the Red Resonant Earth.

G/K Inbreath

S/P Outbreath

S/P stands for solar prophetic and G/K stands for galactic karmic. G/K refers to galactic energy plus past energy to be transmuted by the galactic streams. S/P refers to solar energy plus the future streams which must be energized into being.

Further designation for the mythic self is its interplanetary aspects. The Earth sign is associated with the planet Uranus (S/P). The support power, Wind, is also Uranus (G/K). This means the sign of the Earth archetype, Navigator is predominantly a Uranian type. The guide Moon is Mercury (G/K), which is also an omega or outflow of the whole galactic karmic flow, since Mercury is closest to the sun. The Hand is G/K Earth. Finally, the Seed is at the root and represents G/K Jupiter. This is not necessarily the same as the astrological meaning in the new cosmology. For instance, Uranus is the partner of our Planet Earth and with it generates and maintains a biotelepathic stream of consciousness.

Each mythic self has four planets most strongly connected with it. The base kin defines the primary planet. The analog partner is always the same planet as the base kin planet. In the sign Red Resonant Earth, Uranus is the base power; Uranus is also the supporting (analog) power; Earth is the challenge (antipode) power; Mercury is the guiding power; and Jupiter is the hidden (occult) power.

PLANETARY ORBITS

The purpose of a planet is to hold its orbit in relation to the other planetary orbits and altogether in relation to Sun or stellar unit of the evolving star system. The capacity of a planet to hold its orbit is a function of the intelligence consummated on that planet. As holders of different functions of intelligence, the planetary orbits harmonize the stellar intelligence within its patterns of galactic exchange.

There are 52 permutations in all that we run through in our lifetime. Each year on our birthday we acquire another mythic self. Every four years we run through four basic aspects or archetypes of ourselves based on our Earth family. For example, kin 137, rotates from Earth (red years), Wind (white years), Hand (blue years) and Human (yellow years).

Each year, we explore different facets of archetypal personas that are embedded in our unconscious, subconscious and preconscious. In other words, by assuming these new mythic archetypal personas, our consciousness and stream of being are expanded into new cosmic realms of experience.

MYTHIC SELF AND MENTAL SPHERES

In the new timespace we will operate primarily with the fourth, fifth and sixth mental spheres (see *CHC Vol. II* for complete description of the mental spheres). The function of consciousness, focalized in the third mental sphere, is to merely input data perceived through the physical senses, and to remain awake in the present moment. The function of continuing conscious is to keep the flow of the data of the synchronic order in an unbroken motion and in a process of creative synchronization.

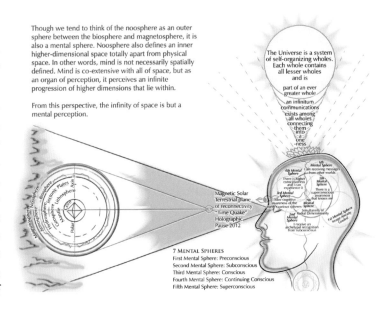

Though we tend to think of the noosphere as an outer sphere between the biosphere and magnetosphere, it is also a mental sphere. Noosphere also defines an inner higher-dimensional space totally apart from physical space. In other words, mind is not necessarily spatially defined. Mind is co-extensive with all of space, but as an organ of perception, it perceives an infinite progression of higher dimensions that lie within.

From this perspective, the infinity of space is but a mental perception.

7 MENTAL SPHERES
First Mental Sphere: Preconscious
Second Mental Sphere: Subconscious
Third Mental Sphere: Conscious
Fourth Mental Sphere: Continuing Conscious
Fifth Mental Sphere: Superconscious

As the data of the sense experiences enters the conscious mind, it draws up material from the subconscious or preconscious. It is the continuing conscious that places this data into organizational frames of the mythic structure of the galactic signature, inclusive of the annual galactic signature, which is a variation of the mythic self.

We are learning to utilize and access information from the superconscious fifth mental sphere (paranormal telepathic information) as well as the sixth mental sphere (subliminal conscious). The subliminal consciousness refers to highly sublimated frequencies received from higher-dimensional telepathic long distance "telephone calls." These frequencies can be accessed within the frame of the mythic self. This is a noospheric operation.

The mythic structures create the bridge and guide to enter the noospheric superstructure of ever increasing unity. As we evolve into galactic culture, the frequencies of the archetypal selves and kin structures will be sufficient to designate in which particular timespace vector we are operating in relationship to whomever else may be operating with us in any other given timespace moment.

Mythic Diversity

In galactic culture individualized diversity is subsumed into mythic diversity. Mythic diversity represents a psychic compression of information. Currently, there are about 7 billion atomistic selves; we have arrived at a point of maximum psychic dispersion of the one unitary psyche of the Earth into 7 billion atoms. At this stage there is maximum diversity and divergence creating a ferment that produces a dynamic dissonance that contributes to the shifting of planetary structures and frequencies. This is the transformation of the timespace of the clock.

Each of these structures or units cannot unify altogether because they are so identified with their particular atomistic frame of reference. It is very rare that true unity occurs within this particular structure. People have to overcome a tremendous amount to get to that level. When the frequency shifts into the 13:20 operating frequency of the galactic cosmic mind field, then it will be easy to assume the identity of your mythic self.

As we enter more deeply into the noospheric phase, people begin to assume the identity of and take responsibility for their galactic signatures and mythic self. As this occurs, so then does the psychic compression of all of the different selves into 260 variations. This psychic convergence is the function of the larger planetary mythic self and produces a tremendous amount of psychic or paranormal, telepathic capacities and adaptabilities. There is an enormous amount of psychic energy waiting to be released.

Each mythic self alternates through 52 permutations, each with a five-part oracle, based on four earth families multiplied by 13 tones. This creates a psychic compression of five super-mythic collective personas, the fifth force. The fifth force animates the entire cosmos with incredible brilliance and power, like an internal exploding supernova that eternally radiates its brilliance throughout the whole Earth. As we learn to harness this force, we advance into the next phase of hyper-evolutionary soul travel and finally enter the secret chamber where this whole process is being engineered from in the first place!

Behind these words, we offer clues to understand the nature of the mythic self within the new telepathic timespace. As we are imprinted with the new program, we open to a whole nexus of psychic compression within a mythic frame of reality.

When we reach a critical mass operating with 260 mythic selves, we will become one mythic planetary human tribe. In the aboriginal indigenous tribe, before contact with the western Babylonian civilization, everybody in

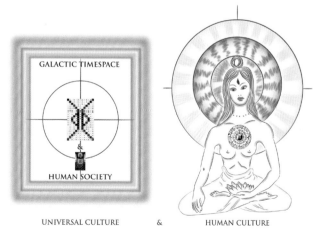

GALACTIC TIMESPACE

HUMAN SOCIETY

UNIVERSAL CULTURE   &   HUMAN CULTURE

the tribe knew who they were and what their cosmic function was. They also knew what rites and ceremonies to perform to create specific outcomes. Each person had their own ancestral totem. Analogously, each of us will know what particular emanation or archetype we are (in the form of mythic self), and to which psychic Earth family totem we belong.

As we evolve along the path, everyone will possess the ability to tune into the frequency of their archetype and establish contact. This is a vision of the future of human identity and the universal telepathic timespace that comes about through our galactic signature, rather than through a presumed or given identity based on name, culture, religion or race.

In the new timespace, we operate by a galactic signature that gives us accessibility to many other domains and dimensions of consciousness. By this means the life of the galaxy—the galactic life whole—forms the foundation of cosmic civilization. We are moving into a telepathically informed galactic culture. This is the mainframe of the planetary masterpiece: Becoming our mythic self and realizing the Earth as a work of art.

CHANNEL 8

TRANSFORMATION OF THE ARCHETYPES

An archetype is a primal pattern that exists in the fourth-dimensional realm and is expressed in the third dimension through symbol, thought, speech, behavior, art, etc. We are always expressing a specific archetype. Primal archetypal templates equip us with lenses that we may personally glean our cosmic potential and divine attributes—they are a way to focalize intent on behalf of humanity.

The principle of the archetype traces back to ideas of Plato when he speaks of everything in this world having its ideal prototype in another world and in another dimension. Plato stated that the primal being is the emanation of the "demiurgic" mind (nous), which contains from eternity the idea of the "to be created world" within itself. This is what Carl Jung later referred to as the world of archetypes. In Jung's definition, archetypes refer to a primal persona or personality. Different people embody specific archetypes and play out these roles in the social organization. Jung said the archetype was the result of "countless experiences of our ancestors. They are, as it were, the psychic residue of numberless experiences of the same type."

Joseph Campbell built on the work of Jung's concept of the collective unconscious to encompass the world's mythologies. Campbell studied world mythology, religion and art to discover the common thread woven throughout. He sought to find the commonality of themes in world myths, pointing to a constant requirement in the human psyche for a centering in terms of deep principles (*The Power of Myth xvi*). Campbell focused much on the hero archetype; he felt the function of the hero was to "pull together all these tendencies to separation, to pull them together into some intention."

According to Cosmic History an archetype is the entitization of a specific configuration of primordial space capable of performing a cosmic function. New galactic archetypes are needed to raise the human frequency and lead us across the bridge to the new timespace. These new galactic archetypes are the tellers of the new stories, the tales of Tomorrow.

Archetypes are projected through an act of creative will that links lower mind with higher mind, or ego-consciousness with archetypal consciousness. In elevating ourselves into higher consciousness, reinforced by right thought, we join the great company of *Those Whose Will is Consciously Divine and Who are the Custodians of the Plane*, as Alice Bailey phrases it.

An archetype is first a *formalization*. A formalization is a "form" created from the interaction of various wave motions or patterns. These patterns establish a structural field that holds the "memory" or configuration of meaning for what that field might contain. Number is the measure of movement. Number combines with space in time to create form. This form then becomes quantifiable number—so there is number as frequency oscillations and number as quantifiable forms or geometries. These quantifiable forms represent the crystallization of primal sound resonance into points of matter (see *CHC Vol. II*).

This formalization then acquires intrinsic qualities required by a particular stage in the dimension of evolvement to perform different functions of intelligence. Every person plays out one or more archetypal roles at any given time. Some examples of archetypes are: Prophet, avatar, world teacher, magician, priest, poet, farmer, navigator, virgin, pathfinder, healer, wizard, seeker, fool, initiate, alchemist, artist, even the trades of commerce—the merchant, the apprentice, the journeyman, etc.

The archetype is a prototypal role, a spatial configuration capable of performing a cosmic function(s). Everyone who incarnates into the endless generations of society and history takes on one or more of these archetypal functions.

---

22 MAJOR ARCANUM ARCHETYPES

Arcana is plural for Arcanum, which means "profound secret." The basic archetypes appear in the 22 major Arcanum of the Tarot deck. There is the Fool or Young Seeker, the Magician, the High Priestess, the Empress, the Emperor, the Hierophant, the Lovers, the Chariot, Strength, the Hermit, the Wheel of Fortune, Justice, the Hanged Man, Death, the Devil, the Tower, the Star, the Moon, the Sun, the Judgment, and the World. These are the types of archetypes that have come down in history.

The archetypes as depicted in the Tarot, come from a much earlier stage of development, or the hieratic stage, where there were stratified classes of people, like the priest class, aristocrats, merchants, peasants, laborers, etc. The rulers, priests or clerics who governed society can also be seen in these types. Archetypes are also present in the game of chess with kings, pawns, bishops, knights, etc., which also represent a hieratic stage of society.

ARCHETYPES AS FIFTH RAY MANIFESTATIONS

Archetypes are fifth ray concretizations of patterns of the Absolute. The fifth ray revolves around concrete knowledge or how we apply knowledge through utilization of the medium of the timespace. As fifth ray entitizations, all archetypes represent a descent from a higher dimensional blueprint. Different cycles call for different archetypes. The historical cycle includes: The formation of the archetypes, the enactment of the archetypes, the degeneration of the archetypes and a return or renewal of the archetypes.

The 5,125-year cycle can be divided into five 1,025-year cycles ($5 \times 1025 = 5125$). During these cycles different classes of people arise: the farmer and peasant, merchants, aristocratic class, and often a warrior class as well as a priest class at top. This is a fractal of the five suns. The whole of this cycle creates the Fifth Sun.

The first fifth of this cycle, from 3113 BC to 2088 BC, represents the ascent of history, the construction of civilized society and the generation of historical archetypes: the hierophant, magician, priest, and high priestess.

Once archetypes are formed and crystallize into formation at the beginning of the second 1,025-year cycle of the social/historical order, then begins an inevitable decline of the archetypes from a more pristine to a more profane order of reality.

When the Moon becomes absolutely full it begins to wane. When the Sun reaches its maximum at the summer solstice, the next day is shorter than the one before it. This means that the descent into an ultimate anarchy of the archetypes is naturally inevitable. So we have hieratic or hierarchical society followed by a slow descent from the hierarchical role of sacred art into the anarchical rule of cultural disorder. All of history is a degeneration of this process.

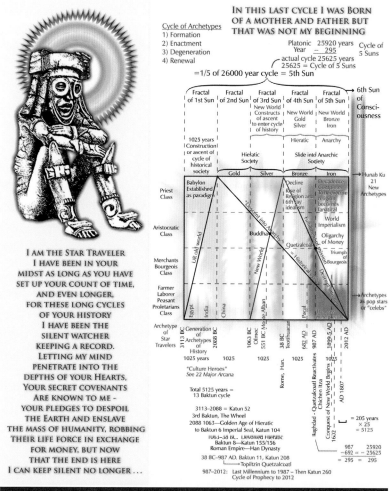

I AM THE STAR TRAVELER
I HAVE BEEN IN YOUR
MIDST AS LONG AS YOU HAVE
SET UP YOUR COUNT OF TIME,
AND EVEN LONGER,
FOR THESE LONG CYCLES
OF YOUR HISTORY
I HAVE BEEN THE
SILENT WATCHER
KEEPING A RECORD.
LETTING MY MIND
PENETRATE INTO THE
DEPTHS OF YOUR HEARTS,
YOUR SECRET COVENANTS
ARE KNOWN TO ME -
YOUR PLEDGES TO DESPOIL
THE EARTH AND ENSLAVE
THE MASS OF HUMANITY, ROBBING
THEIR LIFE FORCE IN EXCHANGE
FOR MONEY, BUT NOW
THAT THE END IS HERE
I CAN KEEP SILENT NO LONGER ...

ARCHETYPAL PROCESS

We see a line that goes from 3113 BC up to the top. Following that, there is a miniaturization of the ages: the Golden Age, Silver, Bronze, and Iron. Each cycle is 1,025 years.

Ascent: 3113 – 2088 BC
Golden Age: 2088 – 1063 BC
Silver Age: 1063 – 38 BC
Bronze Age: 38 BC – 987 AD
Iron Age: 987 – 2012

2088 BC TO 38 BC

After the first 1,025 years—the ascent of the archetypal functions and then the crystallization—then comes the next four phases that represent the descent of hierarchal society. The golden and silver age goes from BC 2088 to 38, the whole era before Christ is the classic period of hierarchical society. In *Earth Ascending* this is seen as the pristine hieratic and then the imperial hieratic. From 38 BC to 2012 we see the slide into anarchic society—by anarchic we mean without sacred order.

38 BC TO 987 AD

The next 1,025-year cycle is completed when historic Quetzalcoatl renews civilization at Chichen Itza. In *Earth Ascending*, this is referred to as the cosmo-political/medieval or religious age—this era is dominated by the three major religions: Buddhism, Christianity and Islam.

This cycle ends 1,000 years before 1987 when the 25-year countdown to the closing of the Great Cycle began. The generation of the archetypes first occurs in the Old World. What we call the civilization of the New World is only half the duration of the whole scale. Its archetypes crystallize about the time of the first of the inscriptions that show the long count and Teotihuacan was preparing for its full manifestation, about 38 BC.

What starts in Old World—BC 2088—begins in the New World at 38 BC. The midpoint between 987 and 2012, the last fifth, is the year 1499; this is precisely when the conquest of the New World begins. When we get past this point the slide into anarchy and the descent into hell becomes coalesced into one process.

The midpoint between 1499 and 2012 is 1807. At this point the cycle is rapidly consuming itself in the industrial dark age of iron. At this last stage comes the complete separation and degeneration of religion from the natural processes as well as the development of sixth ray idealism. Religion evolves into forms of sectarianism and fanaticism. This is the only way it can continue to affect the world.

The aristocracy becomes world imperialism and the oligarchy of money. The merchant class becomes the triumphant class in the sense that all the bodies are oriented to middle class comfort, while the farmer and peasant class become the Proletariat class engendering the mass mind. This is the mind that prevails today. At this final stage, the archetypes have degenerated into roles known as pop stars or celebrities. This completes the process of archetypal generation to degeneration.

Archetypes originally represented manifestations of the Absolute. Once they incarnate into the relative world there comes an inevitable degeneration. This is the process and program of the historical society.

Quetzalcoatl

Quetzalcoatl is a multidimensional being. The spirit of Quetzalcoatl was known to the people of Mexico before the incarnation of the actual culture bringer in 947 of the Christian era. This Quetzalcoatl—the long-awaited one—lived the archetypal pattern, bringing great forms of art and culture.

The year 987 marks 1,025 years before the end of the cycle, 2012. This is the point that the historical Quetzalcoatl, who had now left Tollan, arrived in Chichen Itza to renew the pattern. This is the pattern that comes from Tollan and the New World. Here, the beginning of the last fifth of the cycle mimics the beginning of the Fifth Sun in BC 3113.

The Old World is characterized by Babylonian civilization and the New World by the cosmic civilization of the Maya, the descendants of Tollan. The old world conquers the new world beginning in 1499. The new world really never got the chance to be the new world for the whole world. In this sense, Quetzalcoatl is the supreme archetype of the complete spiritual journey, for he has yet to "return." Here there is a remarkable coincidence with the prophecy of the return of Christ.

The graphic from one of the Mexican codices—the Vienna codex—shows Quetzalcoatl in the celestial realms receiving instruction from the star elders, then descending on the ladder of avataric descent. Once on the plane of history, Quetzalcoatl is guided by celestial forces as he sets off on his world mission.

History is the context of the spiritual journey. As the archetypes degenerate the spiritual force enters in to redeem and lift up as much as it can the degenerated forces that have effected the decline of the power of the archetypes. Quetzalcoatl is the archetype of spiritual and cultural renewal who vows to return at the end of history.

Following the descent from the absolute, Quetzalcoatl is born as an anticipated type of messiah. In his birth he conforms to an archetypal pattern already established. His mission is to renew the culture. He receives the instructions from the elders of the different traditions. He founds the city of the new Tollan (Tula) but then has a fall from grace, he departs and goes on a wisdom quest and leaves teachings everywhere he goes. He ends up at Chichen Itza in 987, which had been abandoned in 692; at that point he renews and revivifies Mayan culture, which had been abandoned since the departure of the Galactic Maya in 830. All of this has been foreseen.

After he bequeathed to the people a new cultural legacy then he departs for the Eastern Sea in 999, giving prophecies for when he will return some 1,000 years later. Through his historical incarnation he follows the pattern of culture bringer and culture renewer, the highest archetypal function. Quetzalcoatl is many and he is one. His message is peace and he knows the method

TOLLAN

is organized as four outer courts, a fifth inner court and four primal heat and light energy cells which activate eight electroenergetic circuits, connecting the five courts.

First Archetypes: The archetypal pattern exists and is made known, becomes conscious. Then as time requires, human personages appear to fulfill the archetypal pattern: Quetzalcoatl, the Serpent Initiate King of Tollan/Tula in the 10th Century AD is the supreme example, just as Tollan is the supreme pattern.

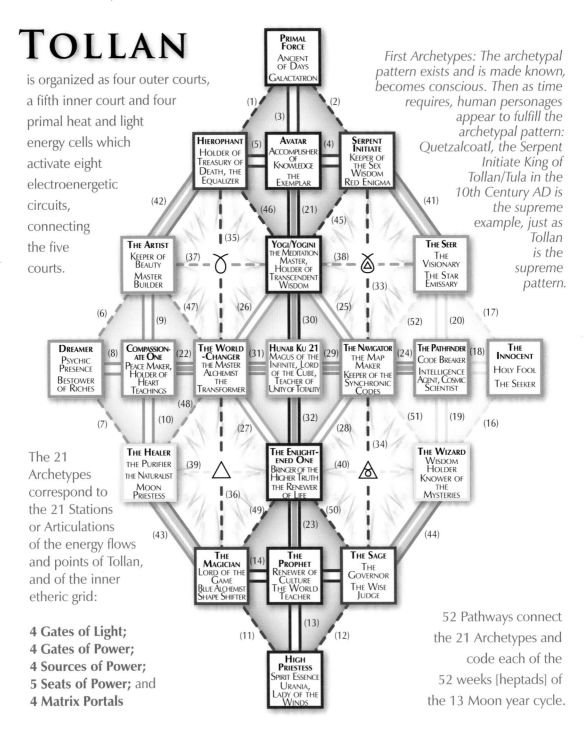

PRIMAL FORCE
ANCIENT OF DAYS
GALACTATRON

(1) (2)
(3)

HIEROPHANT
HOLDER OF TREASURY OF DEATH, THE EQUALIZER

(5)

AVATAR
ACCOMPLISHER OF KNOWLEDGE
THE EXEMPLAR

(4)

SERPENT INITIATE
KEEPER OF THE SEX WISDOM
RED ENIGMA

(42) (46) (21) (45) (41)

(35)

THE ARTIST
KEEPER OF BEAUTY
MASTER BUILDER

(37)

YOGI/YOGINI
THE MEDITATION MASTER, HOLDER OF TRANSCENDENT WISDOM

(38)

THE SEER
THE VISIONARY
THE STAR EMISSARY

(33)

(6) (47) (26) (25) (52) (20) (17)
(9) (30)

DREAMER
PSYCHIC PRESENCE
BESTOWER OF RICHES

(8)

COMPASSION-ATE ONE
PEACE MAKER, HOLDER OF HEART TEACHINGS

(22)

THE WORLD-CHANGER
THE MASTER ALCHEMIST
THE TRANSFORMER

(31)

HUNAB KU 21
MAGUS OF THE INFINITE, LORD OF THE CUBE, TEACHER OF UNITY OF TOTALITY

(29)

THE NAVIGATOR
THE MAP MAKER
KEEPER OF THE SYNCHRONIC CODES

(24)

THE PATHFINDER
CODE BREAKER
INTELLIGENCE AGENT, COSMIC SCIENTIST

(18)

THE INNOCENT
HOLY FOOL
THE SEEKER

(7) (48) (27) (32) (28) (51) (19) (16)
(10) (34)

THE HEALER
THE PURIFIER
THE NATURALIST
MOON PRIESTESS

(39)

THE ENLIGHT-ENED ONE
BRINGER OF THE HIGHER TRUTH
THE RENEWER OF LIFE

(40)

THE WIZARD
WISDOM HOLDER
KNOWER OF THE MYSTERIES

(36) (49) (50) (44)
(23)

The 21 Archetypes correspond to the 21 Stations or Articulations of the energy flows and points of Tollan, and of the inner etheric grid:

(43)

THE MAGICIAN
LORD OF THE GAME
BLUE ALCHEMIST
SHAPE SHIFTER

(14)

THE PROPHET
RENEWER OF CULTURE
THE WORLD TEACHER

THE SAGE
THE GOVERNOR
THE WISE JUDGE

(13)

(11) (12)

HIGH PRIESTESS
SPIRIT ESSENCE
URANIA,
LADY OF THE WINDS

4 Gates of Light;
4 Gates of Power;
4 Sources of Power;
5 Seats of Power; and
4 Matrix Portals

52 Pathways connect the 21 Archetypes and code each of the 52 weeks [heptads] of the 13 Moon year cycle.

TOLLAN AS THE ORGANIZATION OF THE 21 ARCHETYPES AND THEIR 52 PATHS OF INTERCONNECTEDNESS

	#	Name	Archetype	Paths	Court	TFI
Four Light Gates	1	DRAGON	**Primal Force** Queen of Throne The Ancient of Days (Galactatron)	Paths 1, 2, 3	Birth of Knowledge Court of the Avatar 1st Light Gate—Marka Pole	108
	2	WIND	**Spirit Essence** Urania, Lady of the Winds High Priestess	Paths 11, 12, 13	Court of the Prophet Spirit of Prophecy 2nd Light Gate—Darka Pole	144
	3	NIGHT	**The Dreamer** The Psychic Presence Bestower of Riches	Paths 6, 7, 8	Court of the Compassionate One Dream of Love 3rd Light Gate—Centrifugal Force	126
	4	SEED	**The Innocent** The Holy Fool The Seeker	Paths 16, 17, 18	Court of the Pathfinder Awareness of Intelligence 4th Light Gate—Centripetal Force	90
Court of the Avatar	5	SERPENT	**Serpent Initiate**, the Hermetic Keeper of the Wisdom of Sex The Red Enigma (♀ red electricity)	Paths 1, 4, 33, 41, 45	Court of the Avatar 1st Source of Power Sex is the Beginning of Knowledge	288
	6	WORLD BRIDGER	**Hierophant** (Revealer of the Sacred) Holder of the Treasury of Death The Equalizer	Paths 2, 5, 35, 42, 46	Court of the Avatar 1st Source of Power Death is the Source of Knowledge	294
	7	HAND	**The Avatar** Accomplisher of Knowledge The Exemplar	Paths 3, 4, 5, 21	Court of the Avatar 1st Seat of Power Avatar Embodies Knowledge	291
Court of the Compassionate One	8	STAR	**The Artist** The Keeper of Beauty The Master Builder	Paths 6, 9, 42, 37, 47	Court of the Compassionate One 2nd Gate of Power Art is the Beginning of Love	300
	9	MOON	**The Healer** The Purifier The Naturalist, Moon Priestess	Paths 7, 10, 43, 39, 48	Court of the Compassionate One 2nd Source of Power Healing is the Source of Love	306
	10	DOG	**The Compassionate One** The Peace Maker Holder of the Heart Teachings	Paths 8, 9, 10, 22	Court of the Compassionate One 2nd Seat of Power Compassion is the Power of Love	303
Court of the Prophet	11	MONKEY	**The Magician** Lord of the Game (Blue Alchemist) The Shape Shifter (♂ blue electricity)	Paths 11, 14, 36, 43, 49	Court of the Prophet 3rd Gate of Power Magic is the Beginning of Prophecy	312
	12	HUMAN	**The Sage** The Governor The Wise Judge	Paths 12, 15, 34, 44, 50	Court of the Prophet 3rd Source of Power Wisdom is the Source of Prophecy	318
	13	SKY WALKER	**The Prophet** The Renewer of Culture The World Teacher	Paths 13, 14, 15, 23	Court of the Prophet 3rd Seat of Power Prophecy is the Spirit of Prophecy	315
Court of the Pathfinder	14	WIZARD	**The Wizard** Wisdom Holder Knower of the Mysteries	Paths 16, 19, 44, 40, 51	Court of the Pathfinder 4th Gate of Power Timelessness is the Beginning of Intelligence	276
	15	EAGLE	**The Seer** The Visionary The Star Emissary	Paths 17, 20, 38, 41, 52	Court of the Pathfinder 4th Source of Power Vision is the Source of Intelligence	282
	16	WARRIOR	**The Pathfinder**, Code Breaker Intelligence Agent The Cosmic Scientist	Paths 18, 19, 20, 24	Court of the Pathfinder 4th Seat of Power Intelligence is the Power of the Pathfinder	279
Court of Hunab Ku The Galactic Matrix	17	EARTH	**The Navigator** The Map Maker, Galactic Archivist The Keeper of the Synchronic Codes	Paths 24, 25, 28, 29, 33, 34, 51	Court of the Hunab Ku 1st Matrix Portal Synchronicity is Intelligence of Hunab Ku	396
	18	MIRROR	**The Yogi/Yogini** The Meditation Master, Holder of the Transcendental Wisdom	Paths 21, 25, 26, 30, 37, 38, 45, 46	Court of the Hunab Ku 2nd Matrix Portal Meditation is Knowledge of Hunab Ku	402
	19	STORM	**The World-Changer** The Transformer The Master Alchemist	Paths 22, 26, 27, 35, 36, 31, 47, 44	Court of Hunab Ku 3rd Matrix Portal Self-generation is Love of Hunab Ku	408
	20	SUN	**The Enlightened One** The Bringer of the Higher Truth The Renewer of Life	Paths 23, 27, 28, 39, 40, 32, 49, 50	Court of Hunab Ku 4th Matrix Portal Enlightenment is Prophecy of Hunab Ku	414
	HUNAB KU 21		**The Magus of the Infinite** Lord of the Cube, Hunab Ku Teacher of the Unity of Totality	Paths 29, 30, 31, 32	Court of Hunab Ku 5th Seat of Power Unity of Totality is the Reality of Hunab Ku	441

of return—this is the great secret. In his destiny he was the punctuation mark inaugurating the last fifth of the archetypal cycle of history. In this sense, this last stage of history, 987-2012, is the cycle of Quetzalcoatl.

In the final stage leading to 2012 we complete the Fifth Sun, and usher in the Sixth Sun of total renewal. This is brought about through the reorganization by a universal plan of unification in which the old timespace is dissolved and a new one takes its place. The template of this renewal plan is known as the Hunab Ku 21—the prophetic tradition of the Galactic Mayan. The Hunab Ku is the One Giver of Movement and Measure—movement is time, measure is space.

TOLLAN AS ARCHETYPAL TEMPLATE

Tollan is the template of order that creates the pattern and environment for the new archetypes to evolve. The heavenly Tollan is organized as four outer courts with a fifth inner court. This fifth inner court contains the primal and secondary heat and light energy cells which activate electromagnetic circuits connecting the five courts. This is the image of the heavenly court as five great domes.

In this heavenly Tollan, there is a renewal of the archetypes. In the celestial pattern of heavenly Tollan, there are 21 archetypes that correspond to 21 stations or articulations of the energy flows that make up the inner etheric grid of the human body: the outer and the inner. The outer environment is a reflection of the inner etheric body that receives its own projection back as a reflection of the environment in which it is evolving.

The 21 articulations account for: four gates of light, four gates of power, four sources of power, four matrix gates and five seats of power. These are the archetypal "stations". When the archetypal pattern becomes conscious as time calls it forth, the human personages appear to fulfill their archetypal power. In the tenth century, it was Quetzalcoatl, the serpent initiate king of Tollan, who embodied the supreme example of this function.

In the Kaballah there are 22 pathways that connect the 10 Sephiroth, and that correspond to the 22 Major Arcanum in the Tarot. In the vision of the celestial Tollan there are 21 "Sephiroth" or archetypes and 52 paths that connect them. In this way, the 52 paths that connect the 21 archetypes function as each one of the 52 weeks (heptad paths) in the year.

These archetypes are engendered for the Sixth Sun of Consciousness. Tollan is the organization of the 21 archetypes and their 52 paths of interconnectedness. There are 21 base numbers that represents the unity of totality. Twenty represents totality plus one = unity. The unity of totality, 21, represents the 20 solar seals plus the Hunab Ku.

1. **Primal Force**; also known as the Dragon, Ancient of Days, and "Galactatron", by name. Establishing the Court of the Avatar, Dragon gives birth to knowledge and holds the position of the first light gate—the *marka* pole—at the North Galactic Pole. The Primal force exemplifies being as knowledge.

THE 52 HEPTAD PATHS OF HUNAB KU 21
52 HEPTADS OF THE COSMIC RING OF V.24.3
THE ARCHETYPAL JOURNEY MADE AVAILABLE TO EVERYONE

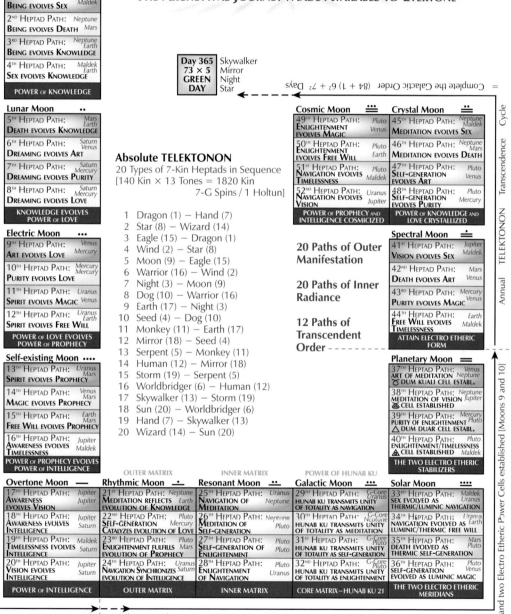

Magnetic Moon •

1ST HEPTAD PATH: *Neptune Maldek*
BEING EVOLVES SEX

2ND HEPTAD PATH: *Neptune Mars*
BEING EVOLVES DEATH

3RD HEPTAD PATH: *Neptune Earth*
BEING EVOLVES KNOWLEDGE

4TH HEPTAD PATH: *Maldek Earth*
SEX EVOLVES KNOWLEDGE

POWER OF KNOWLEDGE

Lunar Moon ••

5TH HEPTAD PATH: *Mars Earth*
DEATH EVOLVES KNOWLEDGE

6TH HEPTAD PATH: *Saturn Venus*
DREAMING EVOLVES ART

7TH HEPTAD PATH: *Saturn Mercury*
DREAMING EVOLVES PURITY

8TH HEPTAD PATH: *Saturn Mercury*
DREAMING EVOLVES LOVE

KNOWLEDGE EVOLVES POWER OF LOVE

Electric Moon •••

9TH HEPTAD PATH: *Venus Mercury*
ART EVOLVES LOVE

10TH HEPTAD PATH: *Mercury Mercury*
PURITY EVOLVES LOVE

11TH HEPTAD PATH: *Uranus Venus*
SPIRIT EVOLVES MAGIC

12TH HEPTAD PATH: *Uranus Earth*
SPIRIT EVOLVES FREE WILL

POWER OF LOVE EVOLVES POWER OF PROPHECY

Self-existing Moon ••••

13TH HEPTAD PATH: *Uranus Mars*
SPIRIT EVOLVES PROPHECY

14TH HEPTAD PATH: *Venus Mars*
MAGIC EVOLVES PROPHECY

15TH HEPTAD PATH: *Earth Mars*
FREE WILL EVOLVES PROPHECY

16TH HEPTAD PATH: *Jupiter Maldek*
AWARENESS EVOLVES TIMELESSNESS

POWER OF PROPHECY EVOLVES POWER OF INTELLIGENCE

Absolute TELEKTONON
20 Types of 7-Kin Heptads in Sequence
[140 Kin × 13 Tones = 1820 Kin
7-G Spins / 1 Holtun]

1 Dragon (1) − Hand (7)
2 Star (8) − Wizard (14)
3 Eagle (15) − Dragon (1)
4 Wind (2) − Star (8)
5 Moon (9) − Eagle (15)
6 Warrior (16) − Wind (2)
7 Night (3) − Moon (9)
8 Dog (10) − Warrior (16)
9 Earth (17) − Night (3)
10 Seed (4) − Dog (10)
11 Monkey (11) − Earth (17)
12 Mirror (18) − Seed (4)
13 Serpent (5) − Monkey (11)
14 Human (12) − Mirror (18)
15 Storm (19) − Serpent (5)
16 Worldbridger (6) − Human (12)
17 Skywalker (13) − Storm (19)
18 Sun (20) − Worldbridger (6)
19 Hand (7) − Skywalker (13)
20 Wizard (14) − Sun (20)

Day 365
73 × 5
GREEN DAY
Skywalker / Mirror / Night / Star

= Complete the Galactic Order (84 + 1) 6² + 7² Days

Cosmic Moon ≣

49TH HEPTAD PATH: *Pluto Venus*
ENLIGHTENMENT EVOLVES MAGIC

50TH HEPTAD PATH: *Pluto Earth*
ENLIGHTENMENT EVOLVES FREE WILL

51ST HEPTAD PATH: *Pluto Maldek*
NAVIGATION EVOLVES TIMELESSNESS

52ND HEPTAD PATH: *Uranus Jupiter*
NAVIGATION EVOLVES VISION

POWER OF PROPHECY AND INTELLIGENCE COSMICIZED

Crystal Moon ≣

45TH HEPTAD PATH: *Neptune Maldek*
MEDITATION EVOLVES SEX

46TH HEPTAD PATH: *Neptune Mars*
MEDITATION EVOLVES DEATH

47TH HEPTAD PATH: *Pluto Venus*
SELF-GENERATION EVOLVES ART

48TH HEPTAD PATH: *Pluto Mercury*
SELF-GENERATION EVOLVES PURITY

POWER OF KNOWLEDGE AND LOVE CRYSTALLIZED

20 Paths of Outer Manifestation

20 Paths of Inner Radiance

12 Paths of Transcendent Order - - - - - - - -

Spectral Moon ≡

41ST HEPTAD PATH: *Jupiter Maldek*
VISION EVOLVES SEX

42ND HEPTAD PATH: *Mars*
DEATH EVOLVES ART

43RD HEPTAD PATH: *Mercury Venus*
PURITY EVOLVES MAGIC

44TH HEPTAD PATH: *Earth Maldek*
FREE WILL EVOLVES TIMELESSNESS

ATTAIN ELECTRO ETHERIC FORM

Planetary Moon ≡

37TH HEPTAD PATH: *Venus Neptune*
ART OF MEDITATION ♉ DUM KUALI CELL ESTABL.

38TH HEPTAD PATH: *Neptune Jupiter*
MEDITATION OF VISION ♋ CELL ESTABLISHED

39TH HEPTAD PATH: *Mercury Pluto*
PURITY OF ENLIGHTENMENT △ DUM DUAR CELL ESTABL.

40TH HEPTAD PATH: *Pluto Maldek*
ENLIGHTENMENT/TIMELESSNESS ♒ CELL ESTABLISHED

THE TWO ELECTRO ETHERIC STABILIZERS

OUTER MATRIX   INNER MATRIX   POWER OF HUNAB KU

Overtone Moon —

17TH HEPTAD PATH: *Jupiter Jupiter*
AWARENESS EVOLVES VISION

18TH HEPTAD PATH: *Jupiter Saturn*
AWARENESS EVOLVES INTELLIGENCE

19TH HEPTAD PATH: *Maldek Saturn*
TIMELESSNESS EVOLVES INTELLIGENCE

20TH HEPTAD PATH: *Jupiter Saturn*
VISION EVOLVES INTELLIGENCE

POWER OF INTELLIGENCE

Rhythmic Moon ⊥

21ST HEPTAD PATH: *Neptune Earth*
MEDITATION REFLECTS EVOLUTION OF KNOWLEDGE

22ND HEPTAD PATH: *Pluto Mercury*
SELF-GENERATION CATALYZES EVOLUTION OF LOVE

23RD HEPTAD PATH: *Pluto Mars*
ENLIGHTENMENT FULFILLS EVOLUTION OF PROPHECY

24TH HEPTAD PATH: *Uranus Saturn*
NAVIGATION SYNCHRONIZES EVOLUTION OF INTELLIGENCE

OUTER MATRIX

Resonant Moon ⋯

25TH HEPTAD PATH: *Uranus Neptune*
NAVIGATION OF MEDITATION

26TH HEPTAD PATH: *Neptune Pluto*
MEDITATION OF SELF-GENERATION

27TH HEPTAD PATH: *Pluto Pluto*
SELF-GENERATION OF ENLIGHTENMENT

28TH HEPTAD PATH: *Pluto Uranus*
ENLIGHTENMENT OF NAVIGATION

INNER MATRIX

Galactic Moon ⋯

29TH HEPTAD PATH: *G-Core Uranus*
HUNAB KU TRANSMITS UNITY OF TOTALITY AS NAVIGATION

30TH HEPTAD PATH: *G-Core Neptune*
HUNAB KU TRANSMITS UNITY OF TOTALITY AS MEDITATION

31ST HEPTAD PATH: *G-Core Pluto*
HUNAB KU TRANSMITS UNITY OF TOTALITY AS SELF-GENERATION

32ND HEPTAD PATH: *G-Core Pluto*
HUNAB KU TRANSMITS UNITY OF TOTALITY AS ENLIGHTENMENT

CORE MATRIX−HUNAB KU 21

Solar Moon ••••

33RD HEPTAD PATH: *Maldek Uranus*
SEX EVOLVED AS THERMIC/LUMINIC NAVIGATION

34TH HEPTAD PATH: *Uranus Earth*
NAVIGATION EVOLVED AS LUMINIC/THERMIC FREE WILL

35TH HEPTAD PATH: *Mars Pluto*
DEATH EVOLVED AS THERMIC SELF-GENERATION

36TH HEPTAD PATH: *Pluto Venus*
SELF-GENERATION EVOLVED AS LUMINIC MAGIC

THE TWO ELECTRO ETHERIC MERIDIANS

Left margin: Annual Alpha Phase TELEKTONON Unit of Outer Manifestation.   20 Heptads − 140 Days   Four Outer Courts (Power Cells) Established

Right margin: Transcendence Cycle   Annual TELEKTONON Transcendence   and two Electro Etheric Power Cells established [Moons 9 and 10]

Bottom: Annual Omega Phase TELEKTONON Unit of Radiance.   20 Heptads − 140 Days [280 Days Complete] Matrix [Moons 6-7-8]

2. **High Priestess**; also known as the Wind-spirit essence, and "Lady of the Winds", by name. She establishes the Court of the Prophet and holds the power and spirit of prophecy at the second light gate—the *darka* pole—the South Pole of the galactic order. The High Priestess exemplifies spirit as the command of prophecy.

3. **Dreamer**; also known as the Night, or the "Psychic Presence", by name. As the bestower of riches—both spiritual and material—the Dreamer invokes the Court of the Compassionate One with the dream of love. The Dreamer activates the centrifugal force and holds the position of the third light gate. The Dreamer exemplifies abundance as the intuition of love.

4. **Innocent One**; also known as the Seed, the Seeker, and the "Holy Fool", by name. The Innocent calls for the Court of the Pathfinder and the awareness of intelligence. The Innocent One activates the centripetal force and holds the station of the fourth light gate.

5. **Serpent Initiate**; also known as the Serpent, Guardian of the Covenant a Keeper of the Primal Wisdom of the Fifth Root Race, and "Red Enigma", by name. Serpent Initiate is the generator of the red electrical circuit and holds the first gate of power in the Court of the Avatar. The Serpent Initiate exemplifies sex as the beginning of knowledge.

6. **Hierophant**; also known as the Worldbridger, Revealer of the Sacred, Holder of the Treasury of Death, and the "Great Equalizer", by name. The Hierophant is the guardian of the first source of power in the Court of the Avatar and balances the primal power of sex with death. The Hierophant exemplifies death as the source of knowledge. The Hierophant holds the key to the treasury of revelations.

7. **Avatar**; also known as the Hand, Accomplisher of Knowledge, and "Exemplar", by name. The Avatar holds the first seat of power in the Court of the Avatar. Taught by the Serpent Initiate, the Avatar receives directly the knowledge revealed by the Hierophant. The Avatar exemplifies cosmic knowledge.

8. **Artist**; also known as the Star, Keeper of Beauty, and "Star Singer", by name. The Artist is the master builder and holds the position of the second gate of power within the Court of the Compassionate One. The Artist exemplifies the resonant power of art as the beginning of love.

9. **Healer**; also known as the Moon, Purifier, Naturalist, Guardian of the Moon, and "Moon Priestess", by name. The Healer holds the second place of power in the Court of

the Compassionate One. The Healer exemplifies healing as the source of love and is the guardian of the universal water that nurtures and sustains all beings.

10. **Compassionate One**; also known as the Dog, Peacemaker, Holder of Heart Teachings, and "Divine Loyalty", by name. The Compassionate One holds the second seat of power in the Court of the Compassionate One. Compassionate One exemplifies the power of love as the unconditional regard for the well being of all creatures.

11. **Magician**; also known as the Monkey, Lord of the Game, Shapeshifter, and "Blue Alchemist", by name. Magician is the generator of the Blue Electrical Circuit and holds the third gate of power in the Court of Prophecy. As the generator of the blue electrical circuit, the Magician complements the Serpent Initiate as the generator of the red electrical circuit. Magician exemplifies magic as the beginning of prophecy.

12. **Sage**; also known as the Human, Governor, and "Wise Judge", by name. The Sage is the guardian of wisdom and holds the third source of power in the Court of the Prophet. The Sage exemplifies wisdom as the source of prophecy and prophecy as the enactment of wisdom.

13. **Prophet**; also known as the Skywalker, World Teacher, and "Culture Bringer", by name. The Prophet holds the third seat of power in the Court of the Prophet. Prophet exemplifies the spirit of prophecy as the wisdom of the future made present.

14. **Wizard**; also known as the White Wizard, Knower of Mysteries, and "Northern Light", by name. The Wizard opens the fourth gate of power in the Court of the Pathfinder. The Wizard exemplifies timelessness as the beginning of intelligence—only by being still and receptive can the intelligence of timelessness arise.

15. **Seer**; Also known as the Eagle, Visionary, Star Emissary, and "Sky Born", by name. The Seer is the guardian of the fourth source of power—vision—in the Court of the Pathfinder. The Seer exemplifies vision as the source of intelligence—without vision there is no intelligence.

16. **Pathfinder**; also known as the Warrior, the Intelligence Agent, the Cosmic Scientist, and "Code-breaker", by name. The Pathfinder holds the fourth seat of power in the fifth court, the Court of Hunab Ku. Pathfinder exemplifies intelligence as the synchronization of fearlessness with the unknown.

17. **Navigator**; also known as Earth, Galactic Navigator, Keeper of the Synchronic Codes, and "Synchrotron", by name. The Navigator opens the first matrix portal in the fifth court, the Court of Hunab Ku. Navigator exemplifies synchronicity as the intelligence of the Hunab Ku.

18. **Yogi/Yogini**; also known as the Mirror, Meditation Master, Holder of the Transcendental Wisdom, "Mind Born", by name. Yogi/Yogini opens the second matrix portal in the fifth court, Court of Hunab Ku. Yogi/Yogini exemplifies meditation as the knowledge of Hunab Ku.

19. **World-Changer**; also known as the Storm, Transformer, Master Alchemist, Catalyzer, "Thunder Voice", by name. The World-Changer opens the third matrix portal in the Court of Hunab Ku. The World-Changer exemplifies energy and self-generation as the love of Hunab Ku.

20. **Enlightened One**; also known as the Sun, Bringer of Higher Truth, Renewer of Life, and "Awakened One", by name. The Enlightened One holds the fourth matrix portal in the Court of Hunab Ku. Enlightenment One exemplifies enlightenment as the prophecy of Hunab Ku.

21. **Hunab Ku—One Giver of Movement and Measure**; also known as "Magus of the Infinite", by name. Hunab Ku is beyond form and empowers all streams and fields of knowledge with the galactic treasury of infinite wisdom and knowledge. Magus of the infinite is merely the one on whom is bestowed the power of guarding the galactic treasury of Hunab Ku 21.

Understanding the Matrix Portals

Each matrix portal opens one of the outer courts. The Navigator opens the Court of the Pathfinder. The Pathfinder creates possibilities for the Navigator. Yogi/Yogini opens the gate to the Court of the Avatar. The Yogi/Yogini bestows mind-to-mind meditation teaching to the Avatar empowering the Avatar's knowledge. The Catalyzer opens the court of the Compassionate One. The Catalyzer transmits the catalyzing power of self-generation to the Compassionate One so that compassion becomes an enduring force of oneness. The Enlightened One opens the gate to the Court of the Prophet. The Enlightened One bestows the transmission of light to the Prophet so that the prophecy bears the seal of truth and is effective in every way.

The fifth seat of power is the Court of Hunab Ku at the very center. This archetype representing the Hunab Ku is the Magus of the Infinite, the Lord of the Cube or the Teacher of the Unity of Totality. From this center court comes the teaching of the unity of totality, which is the reality of Hunab Ku. (We also have an index of the different paths that each of these connect with).

The four light gates each have only three paths that connect. The power gatekeepers and sources of power have five paths each. The seats of power have four paths each and the matrix portals each have eight paths of power. This is a brief run-through of the 21 basic archetypes.

There are carry-overs of traditional forms of archetypes like the magician, wizard or seer. However the Hunab Ku 21 is a renewal. Why? Because we have reached the stage of the degeneration of historical archetypes where pop stars and celebrities have become the archetypal personas wiring the consciousness of the mass mind.

The 52 paths that connect the 21 different archetypal stations can be followed by anyone who so chooses to learn and identify them. Through the means of the 13 Moon calendar or synchronometer the archetypes can be enacted and lived through each person, so that they do not become specified functions embodied by certain people.

All 21 archetypes can be embodied by everyone. These archetypes are doorways into multidimensional reality where everyone can open up and experience the different hierarchical stages of each of the archetypes. The 21 archetypes and 52 heptads paths exist as a means to help us pass thorough the dimension of illusion into realms of higher truth.

The 21 archetypes and 52 heptad paths provide the interconnection of both the archetypal stations of the inner temple of the human body and the outer temple of the environment. We refer to the outer temple as Tollan.

GLAMOUR, ILLUSION AND ANARCHIC DEGRADATION

"Glamour, in its turn, veils and hides the truth behind the fogs and mists of feeling and emotional reaction."
—Alice Bailey, *Glamour, a World Problem*

We live in a world glamorized by the realm of lower illusion where many seek to resemble Hollywood movie stars. In this realm there is either fame and riches or there is degradation and

The 21 archetypes and 52 heptad paths provide the interconnection of both the archetypal stations of the inner temple of the human body and the outer temple of the environment.

despoilment, which people seem equally fascinated by. In this fictitious reality, the expectation is that someone who is high today may be brought low tomorrow. Everyone waits to see whether or not these famous characters are able to live the fairy tale life that is projected on them and endure all the temptations of life that are brought forth.

This realm of tabloid archetypes, as portrayed by the media, creates a monumental distraction to keep the mass mind at a certain vibrational frequency so that it doesn't think about things that are really important. Throughout human history there has always been an effort to despoil the earth and to rob the masses of their life-force in exchange for money and cheap illusions. In the present time this has reached a phenomenal level of anarchic degradation.

"Illumination reveals first of all the existence of glamour; it provides the distressing contrasts with which all true aspirants wrestle and then gradually floods the life to such an extent that eventually glamour completely vanishes."
—Alice Bailey, *Glamour, a World Problem*

The 21 archetypes and 52 heptad paths exist to transport us from this realm of illusion into higher realms of beauty and truth. In this template of Tollan, connected by 52 paths, the 21 articulations move through the supreme harmonic standard of the 28-day cycle, which creates a projection of higher-dimensional order, both in spatial and temporal reality. This template brings forth new levels and states of archetypes that represent different stages of human development and spiritual evolvement. This is necessary to create new structures within the mass mind, lifting it into higher states of consciousness.

Where did the idea of the enslavement of the mass mind come from? Should not every human being who exists with a mind and heart have the opportunity to raise him/herself to the same level as all of the greatest masters and teachers? The greatest masters and teachers said that not until the last one is raised up shall the teachings be fulfilled.

There is a certain illusion that has been passed through history that the mind cannot rise any higher than its lowest state. This is reinforced through media and marketing, which now dominate the timespace with an all-pervasive fog of illusion. For this reason, consciousness is always being brought down to lower levels and the archetypal functions become lurid and gray. In fact, the archetypal memories are stories of a remote time that probably never existed anyway.

The point of bringing in the new post-2012 reality, or Sixth Sun of Consciousness, is to create a true integration and synthesis of a hieratic order of the spiritual evolvement of the different stages. This is the only way to bring about a true democratization of making the hierarchical knowledge available to every being who so chooses. This establishes a timespace that is exalted and ever-inspiring.

We see the degradation of archetypes brought to the level of Mickey Mouse: instead we must make this hierarchical knowledge available so we can rise to our own evolutionary needs. This is the program of the Sixth Sun of Consciousness. This is brought to consciousness through the program of a 52-week cycle of a 13 Moon calendar. By operating within this matrix, everyone can live the enactment of the different archetypal functions and begin to evolve in different levels and states of consciousness embodied by the archetypes.

These archetypes represent structures of galactic consciousness, galactic society and cosmic civilization. These are the enduring, transmigrating archetypes that provide the cultural renewal and sustenance to different solar and planetary realms throughout the cosmos for the purpose of upliftment. Once the energies of the archetypes are thoroughly absorbed and the collective or noospheric mind advances to a certain level, then it goes to another level of transcending and transcendence.

The archetypes function in a certain dimension of evolvement from the third to fourth to fifth dimensions. Once we reach a stage of enlightenment and evolvement, the archetypal functions cease to be necessary unless they are being used as forms of bodhisattva activity for the upliftment of other world systems.

We can see different gradations of avatar functions because in some way the archetypes are avataric functions as well. We can distinguish, as Alice Bailey puts it, the *cosmic avatars*, the *solar avatars*, the *planetary avatars*, and the *human avatars* which are the legends and the myths.

As our consciousness rises, we eventually encounter the level of star councils—or star masters—like those of Sirius or the Pleiades. These are the higher-dimensional supramental levels that coordinate the solar logos, a particular mind that initiates the planetary logos by means of interplanetary archetypes that descend in particular stages.

These interplanetary archetypes arrive, particularly at the culmination of world cycles when there is a need for their emergence. The 52 heptad paths provide a common pool of archetypal functions accessible to each and every consciousness. This information is for the upliftment of the spiritual soul and human personality as we move into the noosphere.

These interplanetary archetypes arrive, particularly at the culmination of world cycles when there is a need for their emergence.

Tollan in this sense is the establishment of the temple as the medium of the outer environment. 144 is the number of the Temple. 441 is the number of the matrix timespace in which the temple is embedded. This is the sacred order of reality as a living spiritual environment that allows the human to evolve, the timespace

Tollan is a projection of the body and its inner temple. Each of the 21 archetypal stations corresponds to a position in one of the five outer courts. Each station also corresponds to an electromagnetic-etheric grid within the body—this is the structure or base plan of the inner temple.

When the science of the outer temple coincides with the science of the inner temple, then the timespace becomes objectified as the universal plan of unification. This knowledge provides a template that equalizes the inner temple with the outer temple and the inner etheric body with the outer temple body so that in becoming equalized, they become objectified as a single unit, or unity. In this single unity lies the universal plan of unification.

Application of the 21 archetypes of Tollan bring the timespace to life. These archetypes also correspond to the 21 principle articulations within the etheric body. Even as we focus on this text we are performing an archetypal role. Cosmic History is an interactive, living phenomenon. When we realize this then we enter a stage of owning our own multidimensional reality and fully utilizing our vastly untapped capacities of consciousness. Up until this realization, our consciousness has been pressed into a very thin layer of repetitive circuits and loops that constitute the life of the modern cyberspheric planetary human.

But now, the lid is coming off, pushing us through the veil to the self-existing consciousness of the cosmic order. This information is presented to be lived. This is the full development of the timespace as the fifth ray of consciousness: the science of how we make things concrete in the third dimension. There is no turning back. We must now embody the cosmic order within our every thought-form which then radiates to every cell of our body permeating our environment and then transforming the timespace itself.

"The happy and inspired movement of a divine power and wisdom guiding and impelling us will replace the perplexities and stumbling of the suffering and ignorant ego."
—Sri Aurobindo, *Synthesis of Yoga*

CHANNEL 9

MEET THE GALACTIC ARCHETYPES

The adjustment of the lower will to the Divine Will is a manifest act of evolutionary consciousness. To project a new archetype at first requires a combination of will, contemplation and visualization. Intensity of purpose is responsible for lifting you from the world of mediocrity into the pulsing world of higher consciousness.

Learning to project a new archetype or to construct a cosmic personality is a living process, growing out of conscious daily exertion and experience. It is dependent on the expression of the divine aspects in the life upon the physical plane.

21 GALACTIC ARCHETYPES

- Primal Force
- High Priestess
- Dreamer
- Innocent One
- Serpent Initiate
- Hierophant
- Avatar
- Artist
- Healer
- Compassionate One
- Magician
- Sage
- Prophet
- Wizard
- Seer
- Pathfinder
- Navigator
- Yogi/Yogini
- World-Changer
- Enlightened One

Hunab Ku 21

1
PRIMAL FORCE

I am the Primal Force
Coded by the Red Dragon
My number is one
The unification of primal being
I am the Ancient of Days
I enter your Universe
Through the First Gate of Light
I hold the memory of cosmic being
Within the primal source
The birthplace and playground of
Star makers and star masters
Eternity is my headdress
I give birth to all forms
And in nurturing every form
I nurture compassion for all living things
Awakening in them
An essence sealed in the ever-returning genesis of my origins
To know me is to glimpse the primal matrix
And if you encounter me
It will only be as a mystery
Reflected back to you
Beckoning you ever and on

●

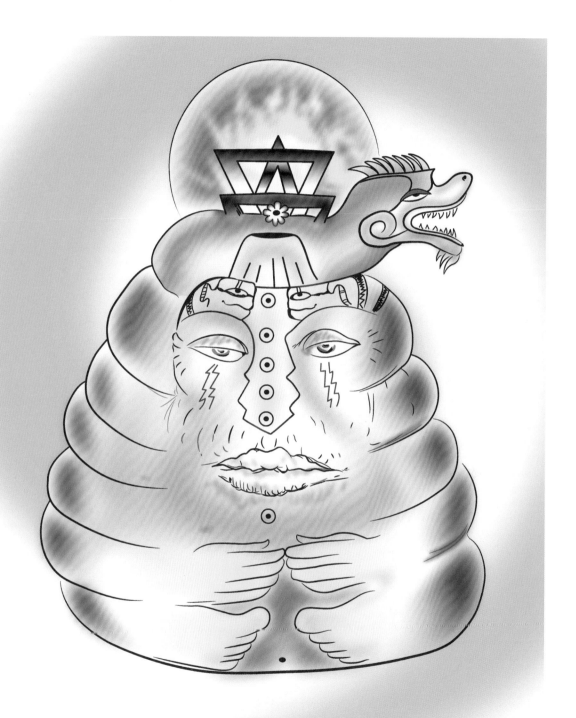

2

HIGH PRIESTESS

I am the High Priestess
Coded by the White Wind
I enter your universe
Through the Second Light Gate
My number is two
The challenge of the Wind
As it turns in every direction
Harnessing the power of the "word"
Let your tongue speak only what is glorious
Is my challenge to you—for I am the Lady of the Winds
Keeper of the mind tunnels opened through crystal song
From my crown, my hair emerges
As the top knot of the infinite
I am the holder of the spirit of prophecy
I harness the energy of breath filling the body with vitality
The jewel on my forehead is the indestructible wisdom that illumines
My every thought
Sent by divine decree
My command is always directed
To your spirit essence alone
Listen for me always when the wind
Arises from nowhere

● ●

3
DREAMER

I am the Dreamer
Coded by the Blue Night
I enter your Universe
Through the Third Gate of Light
My number is three
Activating and bonding the dream
The infinite reaches
Of the starry night is my dwelling place
Abundance is my nature
Intuition is my guide
I serve all dreamers with
Divine remembrance and inspiration of cosmic truth
There is no one who can live without me
For there is no one who does not dream
My dream is truth within the dream
When I come to you, do not doubt me
For I bring the memory of the Great Dreaming of Earth
When the tribes of time dreamed themselves human
And the humans dreamed the dream of free will
There is always a message that I bring
Just for you, that only you can unlock
Listen to me and know for yourself
The endless Rainbow Dreaming World of majestical splendor!

● ● ●

4
THE INNOCENT

I am the Innocent
My sign is the Yellow Seed
I enter your universe
From the Fourth Gate of Light
My number is four
Clear, self-existing, intrinsic
Awareness is my nature
Transparent, radiant
I sow the seeds of omniscience
From the Earth
I am the flowering of intrinsic awareness
In pure consciousness I bear the fruits of spirit
I am the unimagined blossoming of the new
Unsullied by desire, contrivance
Or secret motivation
I am the Holy Fool
People mistake me for a simpleton
But I am merely the self-reflecting face of all of their projections
If you wish and you are pure
I will share my secret with you
To know me is to rise in the strength of spirit
And to resist all that is unlike good

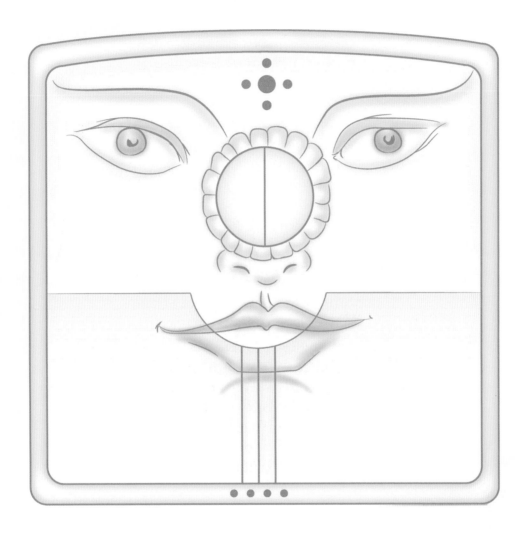

5
SERPENT INITIATE

I am the Serpent Initiate of Wisdom
Coded by the Red Serpent
Five is my number, for the fifth force
Is my secret power
I am the dweller of the hidden caves
And temples of the Earth
Lost worlds and past root races are
Subsumed in my being
My body is the hermitage that holds
Knowledge of the hidden side of things
I am the serpent of the astral light
The life force of kundalini
The source of light and vibration itself
Generator of the red electrical circuit
The mystery of electricity
Is coiled in my being
On my brow I wear the sign
Of the serpent who creates
The cycles of universal life
The tree of time that whirls both ways
Is the sign of my wisdom
To know me, you must cease to be
Who you think you are

———

6
HIEROPHANT

I am the Hierophant
Coded by the White Worldbridger
Six is my number
The root of the cube
I am the great equalizer
Restoring balance to all worlds
The sacred order of all dimensions
Illumines my being
For I am the master of the arts of deathlessness
That all true seekers must come to know
Death is the great interdimensional realm of the galaxy
The storehouse of my wisdom
It is the hidden treasure chest free from fear
Skilled at the arts of bridging the worlds
I am the great destroyer of illusion
Stripping the varnish of conventionalities
That civilization overlays
Fathomlessly deep is the extent of my knowledge
I reveal all, but only those who know can see what I reveal
The rainbow is my crown
Perfect is the order I keep
To know me is to die to your false self

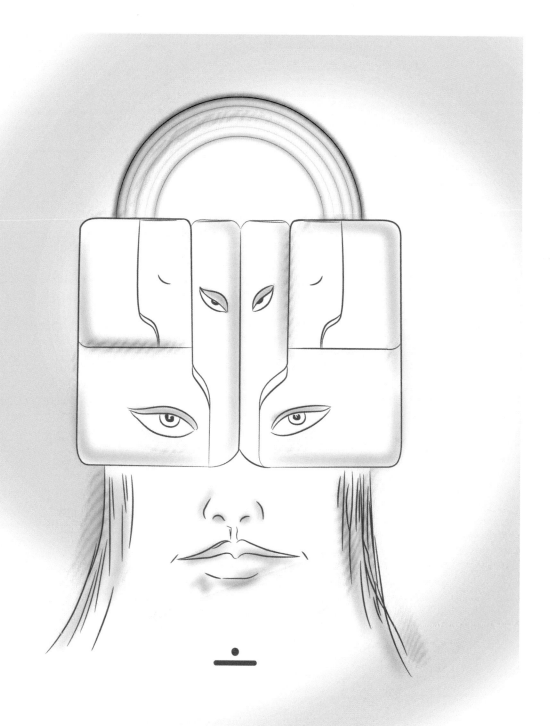

7
AVATAR

I am the Avatar
Coded by the Blue Hand
By the power of seven
I move through your world
Descending from the comic heights of the seven heavens
I hold the keys to the seven days of creation
I am the accomplisher, the builder of forms
I am the constructor of the worlds to come
Within the interdimensional architecture
I lay the path of knowledge for you to remember
To know, to heal, to accomplish
These words too I beckon you to realize
Through all of your actions
For I am the keeper of the covenant
Binding all knowledge for the healing of the world soul
The code is in my being
An enigma wrapped in mystery
Leaving divine clues
With whomever I meet
My mission is to exemplify
What others have not yet known

8
ARTIST

I am the Artist
Coded by the Yellow Star
Eight is the number that opens my gate
Resonant frequencies are my palette
To harmonize according
To the deepest impulses of the universe
Dare to be beautiful!
I am the elegance of enlightenment
Through my art I color your world
I am the rainbow in your day and the
Moon-glow in your night
I am the Artist
Everything I do originates from the stars
Star Being, Star Child, Star Singer is my name
I am the galactic chord
Resounding from the cosmic key
I invent the songs and recite the crystal oath
That travels the infinite zuvuya
The wonders of ever-expanding harmonics
To know me is to ride the endless song
Back to the Master Artist of all Creation

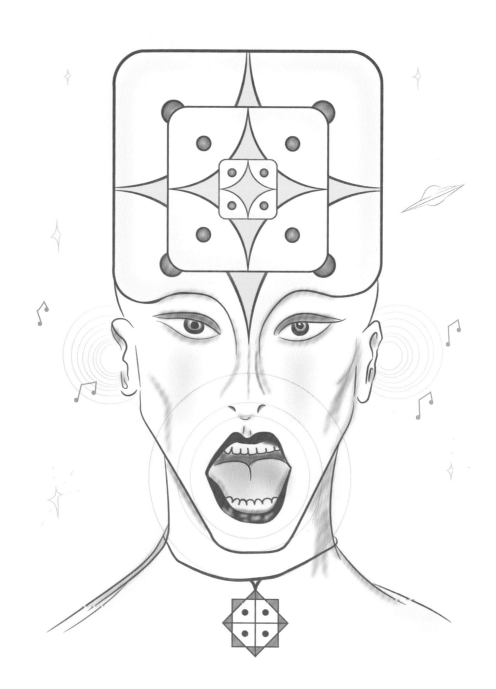

9
HEALER

I am the Healer
Coded by the Red Moon
My number is nine
The power of time, destiny and the cycles of life
From within the living waters
I merge with the universal flow
Purifying all within my sacred stream
And lifting the vibration in every nature kingdom
I am the harmony of wholeness
And the regeneration of life
I am fluid and flowing
At one with the phases of the Moon
I am the queen of life-nurturing water
I am the rain and the stream as it flows
Feeding the plants and the flowering herbs
In my sacred stream lies the kinship of all
I am crowned by the restorative splendor of leaves, roots, seeds and flowers
The supremacy of divine mind
To know me and my endless powers of healing
Is to cast aside all doubt and enter the stream of the faithful ones

10
COMPASSIONATE ONE

I am the Compassionate One
Coded by the White Dog
Ten is my number complete
I am the ageless Comforter—the Loyal One
Love is my law
Wise, am I in the ways of empathetic knowing
From my two hands of light
I radiate goodwill to all beings in all kingdoms
I raise my right hand
Palm, open and free—no secrets in me
In the absence of fear there is nothing to hide
All heart—patience and kindness
This is the deepest
All-pervading universal wisdom
Nothing exists that is not
An expression of this all embracing love
For love is the manifest
Power of compassion
To know me is to remember that
Love is the light that holds the dreaming together

==
==

11
MAGICIAN

I am the Magician
Coded by the Blue Monkey
My number is 11, master code
I arise out of nothing
With self-liberated perception
By means of the double eleven
I project multiple realities
For the sake of universal transcension
As the generator of the blue electrical circuit
I am the Blue Alchemist
The illusion of my own existence
Projected by my double terminated crystal
I exemplify the enigma of reality, neither coming, nor going
Neither ending, nor beginning
To those who think I am an enigma
I am real
To those who think I am real
I am an enigma
Wherever illusion remains
There I am to dispel and dissolve it
For I hold the magic tables and numbers
That enter you into the cosmic mind-play

12
SAGE

I am the Sage
Coded by the Yellow Human
Twelve is my number
Perfect order and root of the mystic 144—the perfection of the human temple
Benevolent, kind and wondrous
I am the wise one, the judge, and discriminator
I have mastered the seven centers
And perfected the laws of external and internal forces
Higher mind control is the power of my influence
In my right hand, I hold the double-terminated crystal
Of equalizing skillful means
In my left hand, I hold the crystal ball
Of universally impartial wisdom and clear seeing
My way is spontaneous conduct
Free from fabrication
I am the blueprint of the purified solar human
I speak with the voice of the noosphere
Announcing the return of all things good
To know me is to
"Know Thyself"

13
PROPHET

I am the Prophet
Coded by the Red Skywalker
Thirteen is my number
The wavespell of creation
Many times and many worlds have I known
For I am the agent of universal time
Exploring space with all-abiding wakefulness
I am the colonizer of lost worlds
The galactic navigator of time
The all seeing eye of the fifth force
Anoints my brow
In my right hand I hold the book of
The Law of Time
A gift from the star family
In my left hand I hold the galactic compass/the Sirian wheel
The compendium of the prophetic way
Prophecy is natural law, a function of the time
My shirt bears the two sacred numbers 13 and 20
Crossing the barriers of time and space
I am crowned by the sign of the infinite cycles of time
To know me is to know the prophecy of time
Within the promise of the coming dawn

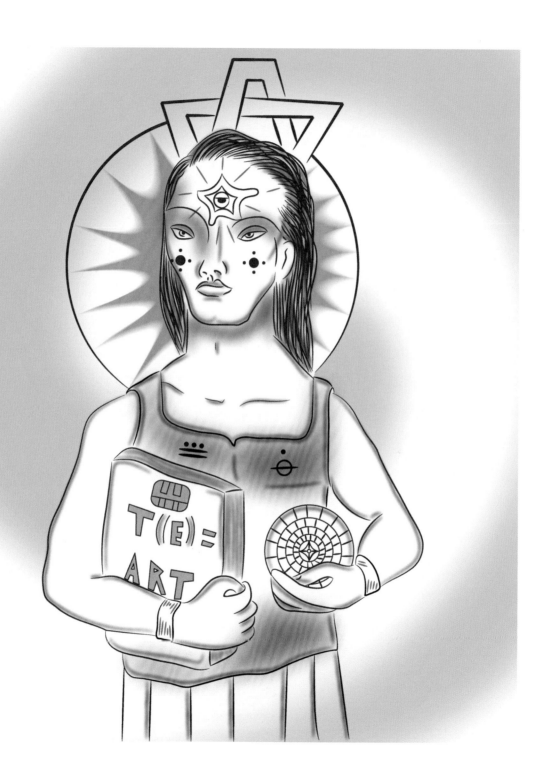

14
WIZARD

I am the Wizard
Coded by the White Wizard
Seven doubled is my number
Sign of my supermental absorption in the forces of cosmic creation
Within my crystal sphere is all that can be seen or known
Through my supreme receptivity
I leave you the codes of resonant definition
That you call time
Suspend all thought and enter with me
Into the timeless enchantment of my oracle—the Wizard's Oracle
By which the dimensions are sewn together
My mind is the universe
My body is the world you see
My speech is the melodious sound of the natural world
My third eye is the triangulation
Of body, speech and mind
I am the giver of magickal names
I hold the secret of the lost chord—the music of the spheres
The higher vibrations of cosmic law
To know me is to know the trees
For I am the movement and measure of the natural order—Hunab Ku

15
SEER

I am the Seer
Coded by the Blue Eagle
Fifteen is my number—three gates of five
Are opened by my mind
My home is the endless sky
For I am the sky-born
The galaxy pulses
With my luminous thoughts
By the power of vision I slip easily through the dimensions and
Foretell the coming of the shifting times
Through parallel universes I fly
On a single zuvuya track
Vision is the source of my intelligence
That sustains the planetary whole
All who seek to know mind and to create
According to the universal plan, come to me, and they shall see
Within my mind is the power of universal mind in its endless creativity
To know me is to know the astral plane of all embracing infinity
From which higher mind is derived

16
PATHFINDER

I am the Pathfinder
Coded by the Yellow Warrior
My number is eight doubled
The high harmonic resonance of sixteen
I am the pathfinder of the radial matrix
By the power of intelligence
I cut through ignorance of the illusory world
Following the signs
Left by the world changer
I see ways not yet seen by others
My fearless spirit clears obstacles along the way
So that others may follow paths of increasing intelligence
Wearing the insignia
Of the Fifth Sun
I trace the footsteps of the Ancient Prophet
To the temple enclosing
The house of the cosmic night
I am the pioneer of the future
All paths do I open to and investigate in the name of cosmic science
Whichever way the path may lead
There will always be another treasury of knowledge to learn anew
To know me is to banish fear
And see your true face bright and clear

17
NAVIGATOR

I am the Navigator
Coded by the Red Earth
Seventeen is my number
My insignia are the harmonic seals
Of Planet Mind and Star Mind returning to source
I am the indivisibility of all time and consciousness
I hold the maps of celestial origin
And follow the signs of synchronicity
On behalf of cosmic evolution
My crown is the interdimensional portal
Of the Galactic Life Whole
The 13 and 7 code is above and below
In the center is the 441 and on either side
The 11 and 27, keys to the synchronic power of seven
Synchronic lenses allow me to see all things radially
I am evolution in motion
I am the skilled star traveler
Guided by telepathic frequencies that hold
Stars and planetary systems in order
The galactic compass is my steering wheel
Keys to the knowledge of galactic navigation
Whose signs are the directions
For every traveler of time to know
To know me is to know the language of the stars

18
YOGI/YOGINI

I am the Yogi(ni)
Coded by the White Mirror
Eighteen is my number
I dwell in the state of undistracted meditation
Beyond word, thought and deed
Seated in my heart cave
I am the reflection of the endless dream
I hold the key to the mirror universes—the mirror dimensions (8-13)
Of the cosmic universe that mirrors this one
I am the meditation of empty bliss
The wall of my cave is my view into the universe
Supreme in my yogic powers
I exemplify self-transcendence into the noosphere
For I am the evolutionary forerunner
Surrounded by the rainbow aura—product of my inner self-transmutation
I manifest signs of supernormal powers
Only that the way be made clear for all beings
An orb to my right glows in its own light
The result of pre-existing luminosity
Above my head appears the mandala of primordial self-perfection
A sign that we may all attain the way of infinite light
To know me is to know that
Practice alone brings knowledge and wisdom

19
WORLD-CHANGER

I am the World-Changer
Coded by the Blue Storm
My number is nineteen
The power of all number
I am the master alchemist
The force behind the philosopher's stone
Skilled at the arts of transmutation
I am the catalytic transformer
Of World consciousness and planetary living
I oversee the changes of the weather
I am the thunder that shatters your world systems
I am the transport of clouds filled with lightning
To illuminate the truth behind your illusions
I am the bringer of the drenching rain that purifies
It was I who caused the triple aspect monuments of the avatar archetype
To appear in the ancient temple grounds
I oversee the Morning and Evening stars
I behold the creator of the Fifth Sun, the Present world
Sent forth am I to dwell among you
Calling forth the Sixth Sun
For the Great Regeneration of the world soul
To know me is to know your own power of self-generation

20
ENLIGHTENED ONE

I am the Enlightened One
Coded by the Yellow Sun
My number is twenty
The universe totality
In meditation was I conceived
From meditation was I born, and
For long aeons have I dwelt deep within this meditation
I am the higher truth and the renewer of life
I turn the cosmic wheel of the law
Giving pure mind teachings among the stars
I am the harmonic keeper of the blazing fields of infinite light
Many names am I called
But they only name my outer form
My fiery cloak that you call the Sun
The enlightenment of one is the enlightenment of all
I am the fulfillment of the prophecy of Hunab Ku
Awakening all beings simultaneously is my task
In many places have I awakened
And every place I go
I know only by the name Tollan
Tollan of the awakened ones
To know me is to know
The light of truth that illumines all things

Hunab Ku 21

Of all the hidden treasures come to light
None exist vaster
Than Hunab Ku 21
Unity of totality—secret of the 441
One Giver of Movement and Measure
Hunab Ku cannot be seen or encompassed
But special ones are appointed
Known by name as Magus of the Infinite
Many are we and yet we are one
Teachers of the Cube of the Law
Our teachings exemplify the essence of the cube
Lords of the Cube, we emanate and radiate the powers of seven
With celestial ears we hear the sacred holy sounds
Of the universal void
Our vow is simplicity
We eat nothing, we take nothing
We only know how to give
Masters of the zuvuya we ride
The waves of infinity
Infinitely
You will recognize us when you see yourself
Emanating from the center of the cube
To know us is to know totality
To know totality is to know peace
To know peace is to enter fully into the
Awesome, endless, splendor of galactic unfolding

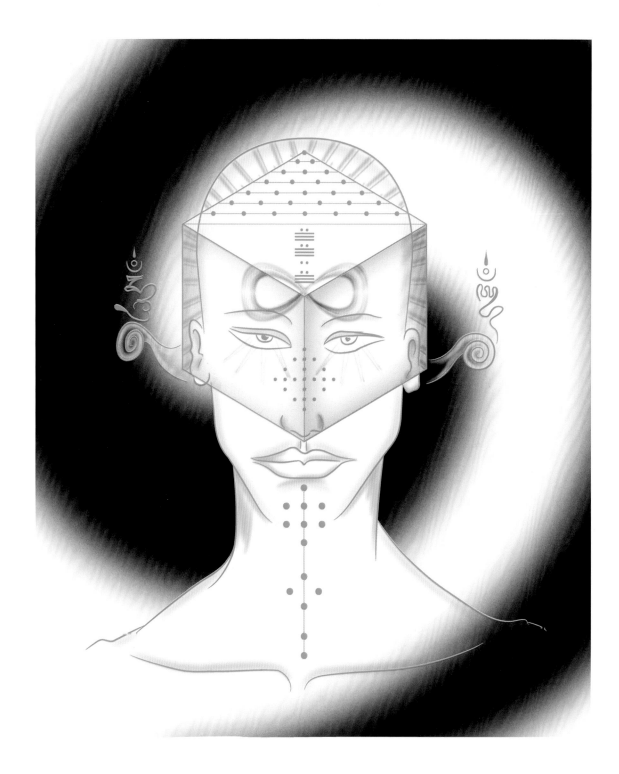

PART IV
TELEPATHIC TRANSFORMATION OF REALITY

CHANNEL 10

VISIONS OF UTOPIA

Like all timespaces, utopia is a template. It is a template necessitated by the belief in human imperfection. Until this thinking is corrected, the idea of utopia is inevitable.

All of the perceptions of history, or problems that we think we will never be able to escape—the crush of the cities, the population explosion, the bomb, global disasters, environmental degradation, global warming—all of these perceptions are invalid as they are based on the idea of imperfection. The human, thinking itself imperfect, has created a society that reflects that imperfection. It has created a society that gives rise to governments, insurance companies, institutionalism, mafias and everything else that makes up what we call "civilization".

Utopia can only exist as long as the human thinks of him/herself as imperfect. This imperfection program is now being overridden. Noosphere is utopia. When the whirling rainbow prophecy is fulfilled and the hoop of nations is mended and made whole, then the mind of Earth will speak as one voice; one humanity will arise and take its cosmic role, no longer victim of the consequences of faulty self-perception.

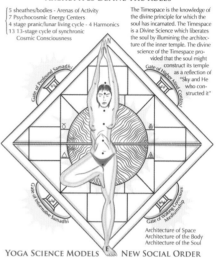

YOGA SCIENCE MODELS
THE NEW SOCIAL ORDER - THE 21 GALACTIC
ARCHETYPES DEFINE THE ROLES

5 sheaths/bodies - Arenas of Activity
7 Psychocosmic Energy Centers
4 stage pranic/lunar living cycle - 4 Harmonics
13 13-stage cycle of synchronic Cosmic Consciousness

The Timespace is the knowledge of the divine principle for which the soul has incarnated. The Timespace is a Divine Science which liberates the soul by illuminating the architecture of the inner temple. The divine science of the Timespace provided that the soul might construct its temple as a reflection of "Sky and He who constructed it"

Gate of Profound Samadhi
Gate of Higher Mind Control
Gate of Bliss Ananda Samadhi
Gate of Waking Conscious Mediumship

Architecture of Space
Architecture of the Body
Architecture of the Soul

YOGA SCIENCE MODELS   NEW SOCIAL ORDER

HISTORY OF UTOPIA

Why utopia? If utopia were not possible then why would we think about it? Who invented the idea of utopia? The word *utopia* was coined by Sir Thomas More, an English statesmen and church cleric who lived at the time of the Renaissance in England. More served as Chancellor in the government for several years. He was beheaded in 1535 when he refused to sign the Act of Supremacy that declared King Henry VIII Supreme Head of the Church of England.

Several years before, Sir Thomas More, also known as Saint Thomas More, wrote the book *Utopia (1516)*. Utopia is an ambivalent play on words; it is Greek and actually means "nowhere" or "noplace". *U* can mean *no* and *topia* means place: Nowhere or no place. It was never clear which of the two Sir Thomas More meant.

Sir Thomas More's Utopia describes an island nation inhabited by a perfect society where everyone owns property in common, similar to what we might label "communism" or "socialism".

WHEN THE WHIRLING RAINBOW PROPHECY
IS FULFILLED AND THE HOOP OF NATIONS IS MENDED
AND MADE WHOLE
THE MIND OF THE EARTH WILL SPEAK
AS ONE VOICE
ONE HUMANITY WILL ARISE
AND TAKE ITS COSMIC ROLE

More's Utopia was based on the Biblical communalism prescribed in *Acts of the Apostles*, the fifth book of the New Testament.

In most aboriginal societies people have a few of their own possessions, but everything is held in common. Everyone is happy and the government is minimal. This is another point of utopia: the description of an ideal society.

Some people thought Sir Thomas More was satirizing the present day customs and beliefs, but he was actually painting a picture of an ideal society. The Atlantis we find described in Plato's *Timaeus* is also such an island as is Sir Francis Bacon's *New Atlantis*. Aldous Huxley's *Brave New World* gives a vision of a future society, which is a revolt of the notion of utopia and a criticism of H.G. Wells utopian ideas. Huxley's book was inspired by H.G. Wells utopian novel, *Men Like Gods* (1923), where utopia was envisioned as a parallel world or a type of advanced earth

An earlier idea of utopia is described in Plato's *The Republic* (380 BC) where Socrates and Plato hold a dialogue about the perfect society and city. They concluded that only when philosophers are kings will there be a perfect society. In this regard, *The Republic* of Plato with its philosopher-kings is similar to the Shambhala society or enlightened society that Buddhists speak of. The closer we get to the present the more prevalent is the idea of utopia.

UTOPIA IS A TEMPLATE

St. Augustine speaks of the idea of the "City of God" or the heavenly city, (this also occurs in the *Book of Revelation*). The vision of the Garden of Eden in Genesis is also utopia. The point is that utopia is a template. In this regard, consider the following verses from the New Testament:

> "All who believe are together and have all things common and sold their possessions and goods and gave them to all."
>
> —*Acts 2:44-45*

> "And the multitude of them that believed were of one heart and of one soul: neither said any of them that ought of the things which he possessed was his own; but they had all things in common."
>
> —*Acts 4:32*

> "And all mine are thine, and thine are mine; and I am glorified in them."
>
> —*Jesus in John 17:10*

Stories like Sir Thomas More's *Utopia* point to basic problems or issues that we find in historic society. The idea of private property gives rise to inequality; some people have and some people don't. In many regards, the belief in private property and government negates the possibility of equality or justice. Consider that when the American republic was formed and democracy was created, the first and only people who could vote were the property owners, who were all White males.

In this regard, the template of utopia is closer to anarchy. Anarchy literally means no government. Government exists because of the prevailing belief that man cannot rule himself. Anarchy nowadays has a violent tinge due to the overregulation of human existence. But utopian society means there really isn't any government nor need for government, as we now think of it. Government does not exist in aboriginal societies. Whatever imperfections may exist in aboriginal societies, everyone lives by an unspoken covenant with nature and the universe and matters decided in common. There is an equal balance, an equal give and take, so there is no need to think of things as imperfect.

Sir Francis Bacon's *New Atlantis* is also a utopia as an island, Salomona, and describes an ideal society in which the perfection of the human mind and learning establish a world of absolute justice and equality.

WHY UTOPIA?

The root of utopia is the discontent with history as we know it. History is the consequence of an error in time that occasions utopia. In the utopian theme and at the beginning of the industrial age there were a number of efforts to create an ideal society. One of these was brought about by Robert Owens, a Welsh social reformist who lived in the late eighteenth and early nineteenth century. He saw what industrialism and capitalism were doing to society and set up socialist communities, which he felt would help to equalize and alleviate poverty.

Karl Marx's *Communist Manifesto* states that everything should be owned and shared in common. The Marxists looked forward to the classless state where everything was shared equally. The Marxists viewed government as an interim which they called the "dictatorship of the Proletariat" or the working class. They believed that when all the aims were achieved of creating an equal society everything would be classless and free.

Another utopianist was John Humphrey Noyes, an American Christian utopian who took the sayings in the Bible to the limit. Noyes coined the term "free love" and created his version of utopian communities in Oneida (upstate) New York. However, his radical views caused him much trouble. He took literally the sayings of Jesus and set up communities based on these sayings. According to Noyes, the utopian Christian society would be egalitarian, with no private property, and no exclusive marriage arrangements.

These are some views illustrating how people have envisioned utopia. People often use the phrase, "(s)he is utopian", meaning an ideal which will never be fully realized. In some sense, Utopia represents the perfect society. The prevailing belief, however, is that man is imperfect and will never be perfect. On the other hand, there is the idea of technological/material progress, but as the machines get more perfect, the humans get more imperfect. This brings us back to the question: Was the human created imperfect? Is the human capable of ultimate perfection and perfectibility? Or is the human already perfect and doesn't know it?

Utopia, in this sense, is the result of an evolutionary change of mental/spiritual nature. Most utopians, though not all, stress a material progress and everyone getting what everyone needs equally. If we look at the world today, we see massive inequality, poverty, and the inability of human societies, as they are constructed, to promote genuine justice and social equality—all the opposite of utopia.

Utopia is also associated with a freedom from fear. The Greek word *atadaxia* means peace of mind or no fear. Utopia, in the ideal society, is the elimination of fear. When we look at the end state of global civilization we see it is filled with fear—most institutions, inclusive of laws and customs, are profoundly fear-based. By contrast, in the rainbow nation vision of society, there is no fear; everything is love based; instead of money there is barter, gardening and living close to the Earth.

The template of utopia, then, is the mirror opposite of what exists at the end state of materialist civilization. In this regard, utopia is a state or condition of mind that is free from fear, war, inequality and all things that plague the modern world. The idea of utopia is also that the individual is autonomous. The notion of justice in utopia is that there is no interference with the individual, and that the individual is recognized as having the autonomous intelligence to govern his/ her own life as long as they are not hurting others. These are important points.

In the Dreamspell this is summarized as the *Law of Kin*: "In the law of kin, all kin are equal." "It is for the planetary kin, equal and free, to create a path of power for the rainbow nation that is completely liberated from all institutions, money, war and poverty … Autonomy, equality and loyalty are the three mutually self-regulatory expressions of the law of the kin."

Many people view government as a coercive interference in their lives. Most people fear the government, when in fact, the government was originally created to help the people. We cannot get property unless we make money. And if we make money, we have to pay taxes. And our taxes are used to fund wars. And if we do not pay taxes then the government will penalize us. This is a highly coercive form of social behavior.

In Islamic society, the banks do not charge interest and everybody pays Zakat, an obligatory charity that is used for welfare purposes; while the religious belief system is so strong that it satisfies any spiritual discontent, generally speaking.

In this regard we see that the idea of utopia and anarchy is that the human being actually functions best on his/her own guidance. This is why, in over the last 200 years, there have been increasing industrial democracy and student worker uprisings. The last thing the government wants is for the individual to actually be thinking for him/herself. This is what creates the box. Everyone has to be in the box. In this way, utopia is an unattainable dream as everyone presents is in the box, and if we try to get out of the box it is a difficult time. The box is the matrix.

The deeper question is: Can a human rule him/herself? Indigenous or aboriginal tribes demonstrate that this is possible. Buddha says "Look to no outer authority. Be a lamp and refuge unto yourself." The whole process of history is to promote a conditioned belief that says we cannot govern ourselves, that we are not intelligent enough and we do not have the moral fortitude to do it. So we give our power away to governments and institutionalized religions.

Conditioned belief that says we cannot govern ourselves, that we are not intelligent enough and we do not have the moral fortitude to do it. So we give our power away to governments and institutionalized religions.

The process of history itself reinforces the imperfection of the human so the human feels powerless and helpless in the face of the government. This belief is built into the core fabric of historical society. At a more fundamental level, the evolutionary dynamic pits the individual against family and society—often there is a choice to make that causes our autonomy to pursue its own way.

Self-Governance and Utopia

Utopian visions occur in other civilizations as well. In China there is the notion of the primal Taoist society where there is complete trust; no one has to put locks on the door and there are no instruments that reinforce fear. In Chinese history there are many different types of Taoist protests and uprisings. For example, Falun Dafa teaches that the individual can take care of his/herself and does not need to be told whether or not, he/she has the right to do this.

Even now, we see the continuous squashing of utopian efforts, as in the repression of Falun Dafa in modern China. These governments do not wish to recognize the right of the individual to make his/her own contract with the Creator. Only the individual can establish his/her own contract with God. This brings us to the idea of utopia, nirvana and the heavenly City of God.

What is the purpose of enlightenment? What is the purpose of any mystical path? From one point of view, the purpose is to establish a means for the autonomy of the soul to create its own contract with the Absolute.

In the teachings of enlightenment and the teaching of pure monotheism (Islam), the individual has the right to go to God directly without interference or without an intermediary. This is the primal spiritual right of the human being, exemplified by meditation practice where the individual sits with him/herself alone.

The historical process of the teachings of enlightenment or mystical teachings allows the individual to experience autonomy and spiritual freedom that is the foundation of utopia. Of course as history progresses the mystical paths become narrower and narrower and the number of adherents fewer and fewer because of the overwhelming propensity of society to become more and more coercive and materialistic. As society becomes more and more materialistic then the lower self is satisfied with that and doesn't think it needs anything else.

Utopian Mind

What is a state of mind that expresses utopian spiritual freedom? Think to yourself: "I am already perfect, and I have the right to perfect myself even more in the way that my contract with the Absolute tells me."

This brings us to the idea of millenarianism (literally 1,000 years in Christian eschatology). Millenarianism is the belief that a major positive transformation of society is to come when this historical society concludes—a return to the Golden Age. According to the prophecies in the Book of Daniel and the Revelation of St. John, this kingdom of God on Earth will last one thousand years. This is similar to the idea of the classless society, the Second Creation, the New Jerusalem or even the Noosphere.

Obviously, such a society is necessary for the attainment of utopian spiritual freedom. In this perception, history is just a process and it will wear itself out. Soon we must all turn inward and perfect ourselves. But what is the prerequisite?

At the time of this writing, the 2012 threshold draws near. What are the prerequisites to open to the utopian state of mind? What is the relation between utopia and spiritual freedom?

"The one who transcends his/her consciousness, who grasps the truth, is the one who passes through the narrow gate", says *The Knowledge Book.* To transcend our own consciousness means to rise above historically conditioned points of view to create the personality of the planetary human. It is the transformation of our conditioned persona altogether that allows us to grasp the truth and pass through the narrow gate to spiritual freedom.

We are merging into unity. In utopia there is no "my space." Utopia is a template that throws into high relief all the errors of history and industrial society that are constructed on these historical models.

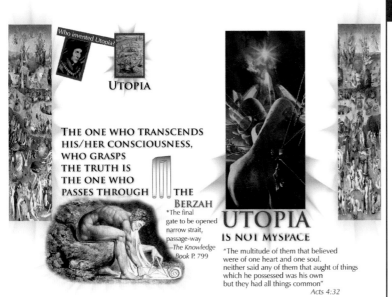

THE ONE WHO TRANSCENDS HIS/HER CONSCIOUSNESS, WHO GRASPS THE TRUTH IS THE ONE WHO PASSES THROUGH THE BERZAH
*The final gate to be opened narrow strait, passage-way —The Knowledge Book P. 799

UTOPIA IS NOT MYSPACE

"The multitude of them that believed were of one heart and one soul. neither said any of them that aught of things which he possessed was his own but they had all things common"
Acts 4:32

THE TABOO AGAINST KNOWING WHO YOU ARE

In the 1960's, Alan Watts wrote the book, *The Taboo Against Knowing Who You Are.* This book emphasizes that you have the right to know who you are and you have the right to create a society in which the right to know who you are is the foundation. This means there is recognition of the autonomous being. At the same time the autonomous being is a reflection of one and all. "Through my autonomy I recognize myself in all."

The Law of Time and Utopia

What is utopia from the point of view of the Law of Time? The discovery of the Law of Time is a crossroads: Either choose 12:60 hell or 13:20 utopia. In the 12:60 frequency people are ruled by the clock and money—the deadening "daily grind" takes precedence over spiritual purpose. In the 13:20 frequency, people are ruled by their heart and Nature—each day is the awakening of the body into its fourth-dimensional cosmic root. Each day is perceived as a universe in which the body and mind can flower anew.

From that perspective, the Law of Time says that when we get to Magnetic Moon 1/2013 we will all be living again in the 13:20 frequency. We will have passed through the narrow gate of 2012 then we will reach 2013 as one organism synchronized with the universe and the 13:20 timing frequency. What will life be like then? The Buddhist seven branch prayer concludes with its seventh verse "May all Sentient beings attain buddhahood simultaneously." This is a 13:20 utopia vision—7.26, 2013.

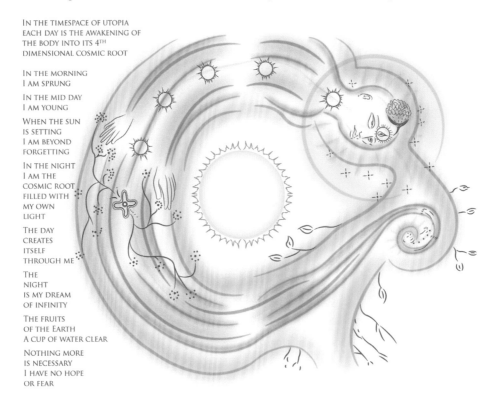

IN THE TIMESPACE OF UTOPIA
EACH DAY IS THE AWAKENING OF
THE BODY INTO ITS 4TH
DIMENSIONAL COSMIC ROOT

IN THE MORNING
I AM SPRUNG

IN THE MID DAY
I AM YOUNG

WHEN THE SUN
IS SETTING
I AM BEYOND
FORGETTING

IN THE NIGHT
I AM THE
COSMIC ROOT
FILLED WITH
MY OWN
LIGHT

THE DAY
CREATES
ITSELF
THROUGH ME

THE
NIGHT
IS MY DREAM
OF INFINITY

THE FRUITS
OF THE EARTH
A CUP OF WATER CLEAR

NOTHING MORE
IS NECESSARY
I HAVE NO HOPE
OR FEAR

This above graphic is the utopian vision of a 13:20 society: A society of human consciousness in the noosphere having come into full realization of its cosmic role on the Earth and in relation to the universe. This is a graduated version of the perception that exists before history where everyone lives in a tribal universe. Only it will be different: the 13:20 noosphere is a total planetary perception of the total planetary human being within the noosphere. We are playing and reflecting a cosmic vision and role. We are merging into a planetary tribe.

Dreamspell Utopia

In the noospheric society, there exists a Dreamspell utopia. Utopia in the 12:60 sense means "nowhere" because in the ceaseless imperfection of the 12:60 worldview perfection is ever unattainable.

In the noospheric timespace of 13:20 synchronization, everything is always in perfect order, that is, everything is always on time. Everything is always new. Everything is what it is supposed to be at any particular moment. Because we are living in a phase of quantum shift and massive restoration of human trust, then there is no need for all the mechanisms that support and reinforce fear. Utopia is the realization of human life organized in cosmic timespace released from fear.

The dolphins in their pods, the birds in their tribes, the deer in their herds, the bees in their hives, fish in their schools, lions in their pride, and the humans in their Earth families and tribes. Each of these is an inherent utopia, where all have everything they need; within their own social formations, there is no need for anything. These different kinds or social organizations are completely synchronized with the 13:20—in whatever medium of the biosphere they are moving in, whether they are dolphins and fish in the sea or bees in the air or lions roaming the Earth. They all do what they do and there is no reason to be anything other than what they are. But what about the human?

Humans and Earth Families

In the transition to the noosphere the humans are placed in their Earth families—this is the utopian social unit, according to the Law of Time. It is also the unit for organizing the human body into a psychophysical system. We know there are five Earth families and each Earth family is correlated with a different chakra.

Earth Family
The five Earth families represent the fifth force and have great flexibility within the psychophysical human body and planet bodies. Together, the five Earth families create the whole noospheric human as a single planetary organism. One being is all beings. The Earth families create one whole noospheric human made up of five "types": Polar, Cardinal, Core, Signal and Gateway. Contemplation of the Earth families as a social order requires a shift in self-perception and a shift in our perception of the planetary organism within human society.

There will be the new dispensation on Earth after July 26, 2013, for everybody who remains here after the shift. Those who remain will be the lovers of the Earth and of humanity. At this point everyone will have their galactic signatures and be integrated as one unit within their Earth families. The Earth family has the duty of creating the noospheric human, the one single being of unification. We also see how the Earth families function in terms of the planet Holon. The Earth families also code the Planet Holon, and are viewed as *telepathic protectorate zones* to guard the Earth. In this way, the Earth families create the structure of a whole new social organization.

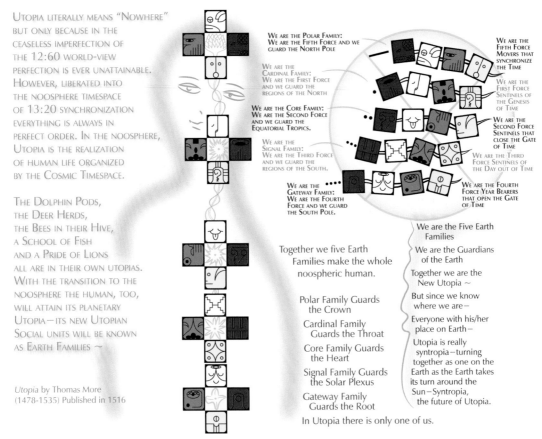

UTOPIA LITERALLY MEANS "NOWHERE" BUT ONLY BECAUSE IN THE CEASELESS IMPERFECTION OF THE 12:60 WORLD-VIEW PERFECTION IS EVER UNATTAINABLE. HOWEVER, LIBERATED INTO THE NOOSPHERE TIMESPACE OF 13:20 SYNCHRONIZATION EVERYTHING IS ALWAYS IN PERFECT ORDER. IN THE NOOSPHERE, UTOPIA IS THE REALIZATION OF HUMAN LIFE ORGANIZED BY THE COSMIC TIMESPACE.

THE DOLPHIN PODS, THE DEER HERDS, THE BEES IN THEIR HIVE, A SCHOOL OF FISH AND A PRIDE OF LIONS ALL ARE IN THEIR OWN UTOPIAS. WITH THE TRANSITION TO THE NOOSPHERE THE HUMAN, TOO, WILL ATTAIN ITS PLANETARY UTOPIA—ITS NEW UTOPIAN SOCIAL UNITS WILL BE KNOWN AS EARTH FAMILIES ~

Utopia by Thomas More (1478-1535) Published in 1516

WE ARE THE POLAR FAMILY: WE ARE THE FIFTH FORCE AND WE GUARD THE NORTH POLE

WE ARE THE CARDINAL FAMILY: WE ARE THE FIRST FORCE AND WE GUARD THE REGIONS OF THE NORTH

WE ARE THE CORE FAMILY: WE ARE THE SECOND FORCE AND WE GUARD THE EQUATORIAL TROPICS.

WE ARE THE SIGNAL FAMILY: WE ARE THE THIRD FORCE AND WE GUARD THE REGIONS OF THE SOUTH.

WE ARE THE GATEWAY FAMILY: WE ARE THE FOURTH FORCE AND WE GUARD THE SOUTH POLE.

WE ARE THE FIFTH FORCE MOVERS THAT SYNCHRONIZE THE TIME

WE ARE THE FIRST FORCE SENTINELS OF THE GENESIS OF TIME

WE ARE THE SECOND FORCE SENTINELS THAT CLOSE THE GATE OF TIME

WE ARE THE THIRD FORCE SENTINELS OF THE DAY OUT OF TIME

WE ARE THE FOURTH FORCE YEAR BEARERS THAT OPEN THE GATE OF TIME

We are the Five Earth Families

We are the Guardians of the Earth

Together we are the New Utopia ~

But since we know where we are—

Everyone with his/her place on Earth—

Utopia is really syntropia—turning together as one on the Earth as the Earth takes its turn around the Sun—Syntropia, the future of Utopia.

Together we five Earth Families make the whole noospheric human.

Polar Family Guards the Crown

Cardinal Family Guards the Throat

Core Family Guards the Heart

Signal Family Guards the Solar Plexus

Gateway Family Guards the Root

In Utopia there is only one of us.

We are the five Earth families; we are the guardians of the Earth. Together we form the new utopia. But since we know who we are and where we are everyone has their place on Earth.

Utopia is really *syntropia*, turning altogether as one on the Earth. Syntropia is the opposite of the historical perception of entropy, where everything dies down and reverts to chaos and a genuine lawless anarchy. Syntropia, on the other hand, is the evolutionary momentum of cosmic evolution into ever greater harmony without end.

We are destined for syntropia, to greater spiralling forms of spiritual evolution going ever higher to the spiritual mental to the superconscious to the supermental and beyond, finally to return to Source. Just as the Earth takes its turn around the Sun, syntropia is the future of utopia.

We first establish an egalitarian society—where every five days each Earth family assumes responsibility for the social whole—then we enter a future where that takes on the cosmic role in relationship with the Earth, and with the Sun in relationship to the entirety of the cosmos. The Earth families are also the keepers of time. Every five days the Earth families create a pole-to-pole circuit or chromatic.

In this way, the five Earth families create the utopic round of time. Every five days each of the five Earth families has its turn to define the way. In the noosphere, society is organized in time, 73 chromatics (5-day cycles) per year; each of the Earth families takes responsibility for the whole. This establishes a new cyclic frequency—every 35 days there are seven chromatics and five weeks or heptads. The 35-day cycle is a *chromo-heptad*. There are 18 *chromo-heptads* per year, with a three chromatic (15-day) cycle to take care of the year's unfinished business.

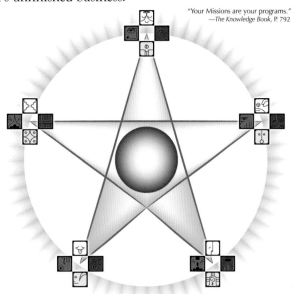

"Your Missions are your programs."
—*The Knowledge Book*, P. 792

Since 365 is divisible by 73 five times, a perfect pentagram we make of the solar round of time, one sequence of Earth families creates a chromatic of time, 73 chromatics, five days each, 365 days in the solar year. Equal and free, the five Earth families are we in the utopian way. We all live by synchronicity. In five days we turn and create a perfect pentagram.

With the social organization of Earth families, comes the psychic organization that constitutes one noospheric

WE ARE THE FIVE EARTH FAMILIES, WE DEFINE THE UTOPIAN ROUND OF TIME, EVERY FIVE DAYS EACH OF THE EARTH FAMILIES HAS ITS TURN TO DEFINE THE WAY. IN THE NOOSPHERE, SOCIETY IS ORGANIZED IN TIME 73 TIMES A YEAR, EACH OF THE EARTH FAMILIES TAKES RESPONSIBILITY FOR THE WHOLE. A PERFECT PENTAGRAM WE MAKE OF THE SOLAR ROUND OF TIME. ONE SEQUENCE OF EARTH FAMILIES CREATES A CHROMATIC OF TIME: 73 CHROMATICS, 5 DAYS EACH = 365 DAYS IN THE SOLAR YEAR. EQUAL AND FREE, FIVE EARTH FAMILIES ARE WE IN THE UTOPIAN WAY WE ALL LIVE BY SYNCHRONICITY.

being with five principle chakras activated by one each of the Earth families as units in time. These become the markers of time as the Earth revolves around the Sun. Every 140 days, the five-day and seven-day cycles are perfectly synchronized. Twenty heptads × 7 = 58 chromatics × 5. This occurs twice a year once at end of overtone moon, 140 days, and again at end of planetary moon, 280 days.

The Earth families participate in a highly conscious, evolutionary momentum pushing the totality of the Earth as a single unified thought and art form to become a participating unit of the cosmic civilization. As we know in the cosmic civilization the smallest unit for entry is a cosmically unified planet.

Historical representations of utopia are just little dreams. When the shift happens and we enter the new timespace, it will be so unimaginably different from what we thought it might be like. With communitarian social experiments gathered around here and there across the historical landscape, the whole Earth will be the canvas to paint the unified, utopian noospheric mindscape; this is what we are looking forward to!

The organization in time, which has never been articulated on a whole planetary scale, is the opportunity we are presented with. This is the post-2012 vision of the five Earth families, organization in time and creation of the new human. This merely sets the stage for an evolutionary move into the cosmic telepathic civilization.

When we speak of utopia in relation to 2013 and beyond we are referring to the self-domestication of the self-evolved noospheric human. This noospheric human then creates the Earth as a work of art, a planetary time shift and a planetary thought form. Once this process is in motion, we will then receive ever greater signals from cosmic civilization and join the Galactic Federation as we move up the hierarchy of dimensions of increasing spiritual unification and evolvement. This is the vision.

CHANNEL 11

WIZARD'S GARDEN

The iron tongue of midnight hath told twelve; lovers to bed; 'tis almost fairy time!
—William Shakespeare

To enter into the Wizard's garden is to enter a realm that is teeming with the mind of creation itself. It is the realm where the gnomes breathe life into the rocks and flower beds, keeping the garden balanced, grounded and steady. It is the realm where the tree fairies keep watch on all the sacred trees, helping them to ripen, blossom and give forth their succulent fruit. (The fairies know that the trees are the portals to the Otherworlds). It is the realm where bright purple roses, orange daffodils and fragrant lavender bloom with the unseen aid of the flower fairies who lovingly guide their opening. It is the realm where the glorious unicorn roams free offering its medicinal horn to all in need.

The Wizard's garden is the realm of Vila, the air fairy who guards the harvest and teaches the herbal arts, fruit growing and gentleness to animals. (Note: It is said that Vila went into hiding when the humans began to make war). It is the realm where Naiad, the beautiful water nymph, keeps the flowing stream crystalline with the purity of her loving spirit, knowing that water is the great reflector, the doorway into the dimensions.

In the Wizard's garden all the nature spirits rejoice on the rare occurrence of the Pegasus landing in their midst bringing tales of interdimensional travel. The Wizard's garden breeds self-purification, self-education and self-attainment.

In the post-modern world, the Wizard's garden is but a dim memory. Sealed off in favor of a mindset of scientific-historical materialism, the Wizard's garden remains alive only in the minds of the **secret dreamers**. Where did the unicorns go? Where are the dragons? Where are the mythic beings? They are trapped behind a sealed door of the mind that is rendered collectively inaccessible. So much so that these beings are now dismissed as fictions, pure figments of the imagination!

Though they are no longer recognized as real, these nature spirits and mythical creatures feed our popular fiction. They are the archetypal wellspring of literature, music and film: fairies, elves, gnomes, vampires, werewolves, dwarves, etc. This is because the power of the imagination never died, even though the belief systems banished these characters to non-existence.

How can we open this long-sealed door to release the part of our mind capable of entering into constructs of the imaginal realm, as well as the paranormal? The combination of these two realms opens the spirit world, the world of jinn, elementals or the fairy faith. Just because it has been sealed off doesn't mean it ceases to exist; it merely means that the modern mind has defined itself on such a narrow wavelength band that this door has almost become invisible.

MYTHIC CREATURES SINCE TIME BEGAN

"The elementals are the first and original matter of all things, and all things are of and according to them, they in and through all things diffuse their virtues."

—Alice Bailey

"The web pulsates. It contracts and expands. Let the magician seize the midway point and thus release these "prisoners of the planet"* whose note is right and justly tuned."

*"The prisoners of the planet are those deva lives who form the planetary pranic body, and are swept in on the floods of vital force emanating from the physical sun."
Alice A. Bailey
Treatise on Cosmic Fire
P. 1024

Through the whole of human history virtually every culture has recognized the spiritual nature of all phenomena, whether it is rocks, minerals, plants or animals. The natural world was always seen as being animated by spirits. These elementals kept the streams filled with fish, helped the trees to fruit, kept the waters pure for drinking. But our global society has disemployed the elementals in favor of the machine. We no longer see the fairies because we are disconnected from nature. We might say that the fairies have withdrawn from the human realm because of the machine takeover.

The nature spirits are the guardians of Mother Earth. The disrespect shown to these nature spirits by global industrialization has resulted in the majority of the problems we see on our Planet today, from pollution to the extinction of species. This irreverence for nature such as cutting down trees, killing animals and poisoning the waters frightens the nature spirits and water nymphs forcing them to go deeper into hiding.

Elementals in fairy tales from all over the world are known to despise iron, as it symbolizes the end of the rule of Nature and the beginning of the domination of man and the machine. The fairies, elementals and other mythic creatures live in a world that overlaps our world. They do not vibrate within the 12:60 machine frequency; though they still appear from time to time to specific people.

At the turn of the twentieth century, W.Y Evans Wentz compiled a book of fairy lore and beliefs, *The Fairy Faith in Celtic Country*. Even at this time the existence of fairies was still widely accepted. Gradually, the modern mind has chosen to focus solely on the third-dimensional plane of reality barring any aspect of credibility to the fourth-dimensional mind—apart from cinema and popular fiction.

Much difficulty has befallen the human race because of its disregard of the soul element of animals, trees and plants and the spiritual nature of the elements. The human also generally disregards that its soul nature is part of a great, etheric world of evolving reality. The outer form is all that is regarded and the inner essence is disregarded.

Human thoughts, many of which are unconscious, go into the environment and create instability. As the forces of industrialization develop they go unimpeded across nature like rampant intoxicated thought waves. We do not ask the forests and the indigenous Amazon spirits or natives if it is OK to cut their trees down. So of course we are living in a world where natural disasters increase and where climate change comes about and so on. This is all an interrelated phenomenon.

From this perspective, consider the following three doctrines or gradations of spirit evolvement:

1. **The Doctrine of Animism**: Everything in nature has a soul essence: a rock, a tree, a bird, etc. For example, we observe that if a spider is in our shower, and we enter it, the spider becomes fearful and tries to escape. It is clear that a soul essence is operating within the spider. This is sentiency. This occurs in every living thing. When we consume plants, they become integrated into our higher nature and aid in our evolution through their pure solar vibration.

Animism is a predominant belief among most pre-historical, pre-technological people and cultures. They understand the psychic nature of reality and are able to commune with the elements, plants, rocks, etc. If they are purified and in the right state of mind, the living matter will talk to them. This is how humans know which plants to eat, which not to eat, and which plants were good for different types of human conditions, etc. The Kabbalah says a stone becomes a plant; a plant, a beast; a beast, a man; a man, a spirit or angel; and a spirit, God. This illustrates a gradation and evolutionary principle in the universal soul.

Everything is evolving in different stages interlocked with each other in an interdependent manner, with ultimately the same goal. In the Buddhist tradition, everything in nature is perceived to have *bodhicitta* or the seed of enlightenment. The Buddhist tradition says the bodhisattva will not enter the ultimate stage of enlightenment until everything in nature is enlightened, including the last blade of grass. This is a universal perception. Animism is a name we put on it.

2. **The Doctrine of Hylozoism**: This term was put forth by Madame Blavatsky and Alice Bailey and states that all matter is endowed with life. This is sometimes called *vitalism*. This is different from animism and says even the cells at the atomic level are actually a form of life. Consciousness is a universal property of everything. Everything has a degree of consciousness. This is a cosmic science point of view as well, even down to the least parton, that there is an element of consciousness, even if it called the preconscious state it is still an element of consciousness. All matter is endowed with the property of "life"

177

and consciousnesses. The distinctions made between organic and inorganic are ultimately relative and arbitrary.

3. The Doctrine of the World Soul or the Anima Mundi (Latin): This anima mundi is the great world soul from which psyche is derived—and from which is created the planetary mind: noosphere. The planetary mind (noosphere) of the anima mundi resonates with the heliosphere, the mind of the solar logos, that, in turn communicates with the mind of the cosmic logos. This view—or world soul—has persisted as a belief among all cultures in one form or another.

It was only with the rise of the doctrine of scientific historical materialism that this view of the world soul was shutdown. At this point a "do not enter sign" was put up on the free access zone of the door in our mind that opens to the fourth-dimensional mind inclusive of the imaginal realm. Many who have entered and stayed in that zone for a duration have been put in mental institutions. This is the story of the effect of the scientific revolution and the rise and triumph of the ideology of historical materialism.

BUT THAT'S JUST A FAIRY TALE!

"Do you know, I always thought unicorns were fabulous monsters, too? I never saw one alive before!' 'Well, now that we have seen each other,' said the unicorn, 'if you'll believe in me, I'll believe in you.'"

—Lewis Carroll, *Through the Looking Glass*

The triumph of "Babylon" was that this "fairy kingdom" imaginal part of the mind was outlawed, forbidden as a reality from which truth could be derived. As children, when we read fairy tales, we are told "these are just fairy tales; they are not real, just little entertainments."

We are taught from early on to focalize only on the part of the mind that will be useful in exploiting matter and turning it into money. This is the closing down of the mind. When this happened the human soul paid a big price. People thought it was silly to believe in such things. For example, the Christians thought the aboriginals were strange and their beliefs primitive and insisted that they go to a Christian school, learn the alphabet and wear clothes. But the door is not closed forever, for we spend millions of dollars to make the *Lord of the Rings*. But it can only come before us as a "movie."

This is the way that the tyranny of the historical/scientific materialism completely closed down that part of the mind, made it forbidden, made it illegal. This is why the psychedelic revolution was so powerful; it was a way to access forbidden knowledge. That is why Timothy Leary said "turn on, tune in and drop out"—drop out of the society that says only the scientific part of the mind is real. Within the scientific community reside the supreme skeptics who dismiss those making efforts to penetrate the veil as trying to create "pseudo science".

Not only have the aspects of the human mind that the mythic creatures are able to communicate with been shut down, but the mind that is dominating—the analytical scientific materialist mind—denies their existence altogether. To this mind, the anything unknown is perceived as a threat. This is the same mind that perceives UFO's as a threat, so much so that if UFOs come into the Earth's atmosphere, the first response is to shoot them down. It's the same principle, the same mindset at work.

All the elementals, jinn, fairies, etc., are all waiting for this to blow over. They have been around a long time, long before historical materialism (which has only been triumphant in the 13th baktun). Only when the noosphere becomes manifest then the jinn's, devas and fairies can return to their place of intercourse with the human mind and with human nature.

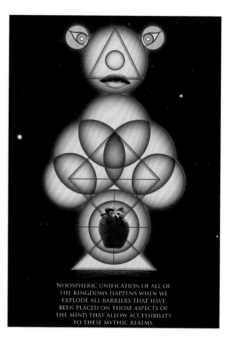

NOOSPHERIC UNIFICATION OF ALL OF THE KINGDOMS HAPPENS WHEN WE EXPLODE ALL BARRIERS THAT HAVE BEEN PLACED ON THOSE ASPECTS OF THE MIND THAT ALLOW ACCESSIBILITY TO THESE MYTHIC REALMS.

TIMESPACE AND ELEMENTALS

"Fairies, come and take me out of this dull world,
For I would ride upon the wind,
Run on top of the disheveled tide,
And dance upon the mountains like a flame."
—W.B. Yeats

Everything is alive. Everything is infused with soul, or with a vital element that we call life. In the Quran it says that by the power with which "We construct the firmament, We create the vastness of space"—this is the timespace. Timespace is the medium for the accommodation of matter. Timespace has meaning insofar as it is occupied by living matter or elementals. From the point of view of an open mind, there is no distinction between organic and inorganic matter.

The regeneration of the timespace is the regeneration of the elementals. As the new timespace emerges as a field of reorganized perception, a shift in the energy patterns takes place. The elementals are calling on us to return to the wonder of nature, to be aware of the powers of nature—this is where they live—they can only manifest themselves to those attuned to nature.

Every living entity represents a particular stage in the process of cosmic evolution. Fairies and other mythic creatures associated with elements are often grouped as belonging to a particular element. Each of these classes has different functions or categories and different purposes of evolution. If we begin to tune into the spirits of nature, it is possible to receive messages from them. The world of elementals is filled with wonder.

Fairies are nature spirits or elemental entities. Elementals are often spoken of in alchemy as the creatures evolved in and from the four kingdoms of the Earth, air, fire, and water. There are also crystal elementals, plant, fire, water, wood spirits dryads or Earth spirits, even wind spirits or zephyrs. The whole of the atmosphere is a function of spirit beings and energies.

Our consciousness itself is vitalized by different etheric beings. All of the creatures live in the in-between world just on the astral periphery. Most people dismiss these entities as myth, fable, or legends. But why do these entities appear in all traditions and in the poetry of all nations, both ancient and modern? These beings make themselves accessible according to situation and belief system.

In Arabian fairy tales jinn are depicted as the offspring of fire with flames, rather than blood, flowing through their veins. They are the ones who cause desert sandstorms and other mischief. The jinn are also reputed to be shapeshifters, usually taking some animal form. The Quran tells the story of how Solomon is able to put the jinn to work. Solomon represents a master; he is able to control the jinn to perform labors for him.

Jinn are also known as genies in Arabian fairy tales. As the story goes, unless we really have mastered our own powers, we should keep our genie, or jinn, in a bottle, otherwise they will create mischief. Solomon was endowed with magical mind powers and was able to tame the jinn and elemental wind spirits. The jinn are multifaceted.

According to the Quran, God created jinn and men so that they may serve Him alone. Sura 55 talks about the favors of God shown to the jinns and men and lists different categories of beings and spiritual entities: animals, human, jinn, and angels. Angels are created from light; jinn's are created from fire; humans, animals and plants are created from clay.

In sura 46 and 72 "the jinn" are depicted listening to a recitation of the Quran. The Quran also points out that God created jinn and men to worship Him alone. This means that it is not just the human being that is evolving but also the spirit beings and jinns. This is known about in occult traditions.

Alice Bailey calls jinn by the names *devas*, *solar angels*, and *fire beings*. In her book *Treatise*

NOW I BRING TO CONSCIOUSNESS THE SEED OF THE SIXTH ROOT RACE WHERE WE GO FROM INDIVIDUALIZATION TO THE GREAT MIND DEVA OF THE NOOSPHERE!

SOLAR ANGEL MOUNTING UPWARD BY MEANS OF THE SERPENT OF WISDOM

ALL HAS BEEN FORETOLD BY THE ANCIENT OF DAYS WHO ALONE CAN INITIATE A SERPENT OF WISDOM *on Cosmic Fire,* Bailey says devas and elementals are always evolving. This is also implied in the Quran. Bailey also says that the human seeks to control its lower self in order to advance and evolve. She says that devas and jinn have to be controlled. This is also what Bailey means when she states that etheric beings are responsible for the workings of the natural world, weather and elements.

Indigenous culture ceremonies always take into account the power of the elements. In folk or indigenous ceremonies when disasters or earthquakes occur it is perceived as the result of not appeasing the spirits properly, or something in the human mind that has brought this about.

Bailey talks about the quality of fire as being spiritual-electric cosmic in nature, "coursing through the string of the whole cosmic order of reality." Madame Blavatsky calls these fire beings: *fohat.* This fire is related to the evolution of consciousness. She says the solar or planetary logos are a type of etheric fire elemental that governs the consciousness of a celestial or heavenly orb, like the Sun. Within the celestial orb, each element of consciousness, like the human being, has its particular solar angel. Solar angels are related to another elemental principle or idea known as *daemon* in Greek philosophy or *genius.*

Genius is the solar angel or spirit essence that evolves with us. Bailey says that the solar angel is an inspiration of the serpent of wisdom to go to the next evolutionary stage. In reality, the spirit or elemental world is intended to be consciously integrated into our physical world. It would have to be since we are dealing with non-dualistic nature.

Gradations of Beings and Ibn Al-Arabi

Within the conscious being are all the powers of the whole of nature. Cosmic History reveals a living scheme or plan of substance in the cosmos. There are numerous gradations of sentiency and sentient beings. For instance, it has been scientifically demonstrated that plants have sentiency; they respond to music and have an auric field. Even crystals have some type of preconscious sentiency and the crystal lattice structure appears to be a morphic precursor of the DNA. We go from sentiency to sentient beings—and then affecting the imaginal realm as a "visual" projection.

Elementals are ultimately formless, though they are a vital force. Some sensitive types see elementals. That is, they perceive the energy attributes or frequencies of different types of elementals that may take an imaginal form—such as the fairy. What we are talking about is the gradations of going through sentiency to sentient beings.

Everything is a projection of the mind, but that does not make anything less real. We are bringing to consciousness the seed of the fifth root race and expanding it into consciousness of the noosphere. The noosphere itself is the solar angel of the planetary logos coming into manifestation. This is a vast theme of which we are only scratching the surface.

Animals are also an interrelated phenomenon and can be viewed as concrete manifestations of spiritual entities. Bailey said that in the flow of the cosmic force came a particular constellation

---

ELEMENTS AND KINGDOMS

Elements	Kingdoms
1. Fire	1. Mineral
2. Air	2. Plant
3. Water	3. Animal
4. Earth	4. Human
5. Space (Akasha)	5. Spirituals
	a. Angels (light)
	b. Jinn (fire)

In Ibn Al-Arabi's 28 stages of evolution, following the different gradations of the seven heavens, he presents the four elements: fire, air, water and earth. Each of these contains elementals, spirit entities that govern these elements. There is also ether, akasha, or space—the fifth element, as presented in the Buddhist/Hindu cosmology. Then follows the category of the four kingdoms: mineral, plant, animal and human. This presents an evolutionary progression.

Before the fourth kingdom there exist spiritual beings: angels made of light and jinns made of fire. The creation of the spirituals provides a context for human development. The human kingdom is divided into two categories.

1. The human as an all-comprehensive type that summarizes previous stages of evolution, as well as its diversity.

2. The human as a being that ascends in stages—human is not the end of evolution—but evolves into super- and suprabeing stages. In the akashic occult tradition, the human is the fourth kingdom, preceded by the crystal, and the mineral, plant and animal.

---

outside our solar system, outside of the astral body of the planetary logos. The condition this brought about was to plant a form of sentient consciousness in nature, representing the stream of energy by which animals come to populate the biosphere.

What Bailey presents is confirmed in *The Arcturus Probe*, where the engrams of several types of intelligent life forms transmitted the engrams to the Velatropa 24 star system. Life forms taken from healthy whales in parallel universes can provide stabilizing factors of consciousness within this world. This is saying that the animals are transmitted through radiogenetic transduction in a medium of organized transmission.

The Quran says that everything is created in pairs that we may receive instruction. This is an interesting consideration of the timespace we live in. Biologically, we know everything is created in pairs for reproduction and genetic propagation, but rarely do we think this is so in order to receive instruction. Whether animal, jinn or human everything is constructed as a pairing, a primal polarity; even certain plants and fruits are male and female. This seems to be the basic underlying instruction that we are mirrors in time of each other intended to realize a cosmic totality together. If we look at the animals, because they are in pairs they are also conscious sentient beings.

The Greeks said there are two souls: the psyche, and the reasoning soul or the *nous* (noosphere or mind), psyche or soul that all beings possess. Noosphere is the evolved mind of discriminating awareness, collectively comprehensible. This is similar to the Buddhist definitions of consciousness: Eye, ear, nose, etc., then following the category of mind there is the vijnana consciousness or the discriminating awareness, and the alaya or stored unconsciousness where vijnana is the reasoning soul and alaya is the noosphere.

THE ANIMAL KINGDOM

"Like a lion, without fear of the howling pack;
Like a gust of wind, ne'er trapped in a snare; Like
a lotus blossom, ne'er sprinkled by water; Like
me, like a unicorn, in solitude roam."
　　　　　　　　　　　　　　—*Hymn of Buddha*

For the most part it appears that animals have the soul or the psyche. The dolphins or whales, or those more evolved than the human, have an advanced brain capable of creating and participating in the noosphere. We also find this in some primates. These animals are here to instruct us and represent different aspects of our own psyche, like a psychic mechanism.

For this reason the deepest doctrine of vegetarianism exists. When we eat an animal, and don't have a psychic contract and permission from that animal, then we are stunting the evolution of that animal, as well as ourselves. Domesticated animals such as sheep and cattle are often forced into unnatural growth in

Our human psyche and the psyche or naguals of the animals are all part of the one world psychic unit—the world soul/anima mundi.

unsanitary environments, only to be slaughtered for eating—they lead a miserable life and are then killed, thus their evolutionary status is halted as they are not being used in a sacred way consummate with evolution. What kind of effect does this have then on the person condoning such badly treated animals? The purpose of the devas and animals and nature spirits is to evolve the spirit element in all of organic matter —and even in inorganic matter.

SHAMANISM AND NAGUALS

The animals represent aspects of our psyche or different psychic mechanisms. In shamanic traditions, animals are considered sacred portals to access specific powers. In Mesoamerica shamanism, the spirit of animals are known as naguals. This gives rise to nagualism, where the shaman may exchange his/her spirit with that of an animal or shapeshift. Then, as the case may be, the shaman can fly like an eagle. There is an important psychic principle here that is yet to be universalized.

The Chinese calendar consists of a 12-year cycle where each of the years is named after an animal. This is similar to the zodiacal cycle. We take this for granted but it is something worth relooking at. There is the mythic animal, the dragon, and then there is a serpent, tiger, rabbit, monkey and rat—these are all more or less wild animals, but can be domesticated. Then there is the horse, ox, sheep, rooster, pig, and dog. Those are all domesticated animals.

The Chinese also combine the animals with the five elements: earth, wood, water, air, metal and wind. The Chinese calendar is dominated by the influence of these animals and the five elements. However, they have now also been ascribed extensive fortune telling attributes.

The Babylonian Hindu western astrological calendar contains seven animal types: Aries the Ram, Pisces the Fish, Taurus the Bull, Cancer the Crab, Leo the Lion, Scorpio the Scorpion and Capricorn the Goat. The rest are human or divine types.

In the 13 Moon calendar, each of the moons is ascribed an animal totem: Bat (Moon 1), Scorpion (Moon 2), Deer (Moon 3), Owl (Moon 4), Peacock (Moon 5), Lizard (Moon 6), Monkey (Moon 7), Hawk (Moon 8), Jaguar (Moon 9), Dog (Moon 10), Serpent (Moon 11), Rabbit (Moon 12), and Turtle (Moon 13).

This is all to show the influence of the animal on the human psyche. This is because all of life is a unity. Our human psyche and the psyche or naguals of the animals are all part of the one world psychic unit—the world soul/anima mundi.

In modern civilization, animals, particularly dogs and cats, are utilized as pets in the modern civilized society. These pets actually become psychic projections of their master or owner. Some esotericists say that it is impossible to keep domesticated pets and practice the internal arts as the level of distraction and attachment is too great.

ANIMALS IN CREATION STORIES

Animals or mythic creatures also play an important role in many creation stories. For instance in the Balinese tradition, it says, at the bottom of everything there is magnetic iron, (this is the Earth core); but even before this existed, in the beginning there was nothing. All was emptiness. There was only space. Before there were the heavens, there was no Earth, when there was Earth, there was no sky.

Through meditation, the world serpent Antaboga created the turtle, Bedawang, on whom lay coiled two snakes, as the foundation of the world. On the world turtle rests a lid, the Black Stone where this occurs. There is no Sun, no Moon, and there is no night in the cave below. This is the underworld whose gods were the male *Batarakala* and the female *Setesuyara*. There also lives the great serpent Basuki.

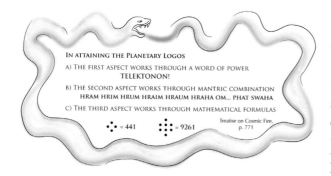

IN ATTAINING THE PLANETARY LOGOS
A) THE FIRST ASPECT WORKS THROUGH A WORD OF POWER
TELEKTONON!
B) THE SECOND ASPECT WORKS THROUGH MANTRIC COMBINATION
HRAM HRIM HRUM HRAIM HRAUM HRAHA OM... PHAT SWAHA
C) THE THIRD ASPECT WORKS THROUGH MATHEMATICAL FORMULAS

⁖ = 441   ⁝⁝ = 9261   Treatise on Cosmic Fire, p. 771

Here, we have the great cosmic serpents that meditate the world into existence. The first thing that is meditated is the turtle. The turtle is the oldest animal on Earth. Once the turtle is meditated into existence, two snakes wrap themselves around the turtle, creating the foundation of the world. Then there is the black stone, like the Ka'aba in Mecca that supposedly fell from space, from Maldek. Then there are the male and the female gods/goddesses. This is the serpent initiation from the previous fourth world round and is a good example of a type of creation where mythic animals dream the universe into existence.

In the Hindu traditions, two primary deities are Ganesh, the elephant and Hanuman the monkey, while in the creation myth of Vishnu, the great 7-headed world serpent plays a major role in the coiling and uncoiling that creates the cosmos. In the Egyptian tradition we also see another monkey form, Thoth, the god of light and literature, who in the hermetic traditions is associated with Hermes Trismegistus. In certain instances we also have mythic animals like the unicorn, dragon or garuda, an eagle-like bird with features of a lion. Where do these creatures come from?

Animals are the gatekeepers for us to enter into a supraphysical or magical realm. When we enter this other realm then we encounter creatures like the dragon or the garuda or the unicorn. These animals exist in the imaginal realm. Of course there is the memory of dinosaurs and so on. The dragon actually represents the primal force of the world that is able to manifest in this

Ganesh and Hanuman

185

particular form. The dragon appears not only in Far Eastern mythology but also in Western mythology.

This part of the mind is just as real as the part of the mind that created science. In this sense the dragon has just as much reality as a quark does to a subatomic physicist, who cannot really say he has seen one but he knows it by its behavior and of the certain indications and viewing apparatus and whatever instruments the quantum physicists use to measure subatomic reality. It is the same with the dragon, who has every bit as much reality as a quark, a lepton or a gluon. These represent different aspects of mind and reality.

When we further consider this it seems that shutting off this part of our mind diminishes the extent of reality that we can occupy. This is the multidimensional reality where we can talk to animals, see dragons and have communion with different levels of beings—much less theorize about quarks and leptons.

What aspect of the mind is the dragon a projection of?

There is a whole living spiritualized spectrum of reality, some of which entitizes as elemental forms, water spirits, fire spirits, or fire angels, etc. Parts of it enter as mythic animal type creatures, other parts of it enter as beings or types of spirit beings that can be pressed into our reality. The point is we are dealing with whole different ranges and categories: Devas, gods and goddesses, dakinis, jinn, elementals, nature spirits and the animal kingdom, etc.

Who are these elemental spirits and where are they? In Greek mythology, elemental characters often appear as vain or frivolous people. They get jealous and do silly things, yet they display certain

"He who chooses the infinite has been chosen by the infinite."
–Sri Aurobindo, Synthesis of Yoga p.47

It is necessary for the Magician here to remember that all that takes place upon the Earth is to be found within the Planetary Etheric Web.

A LEAF FROM
A TEXT ON THE ORIGINS OF TIMESPACE

magical powers. Some people believe these were real characters, while others believe these are made-up stories.

Still, the question remains: Were these actual celestial cosmic forces and at one point the only way the human mind could deal with it is by anthropomorphizing them into these different gods and goddesses? In this regard it is interesting to contemplate the gods and goddesses of the creation story of Babylon. This story is one of the most fantastic ones that exist in trying to determine what role they play in the human imagination *(see text box)*.

ENUMA ELISH—A CREATION STORY

There is a text called the Enuma Elish (see From Primitive to Zen, Mircea Eliade) *which was supposedly transcribed around 2000 BC, and which accounts the creation and how Babylon came to be. According to this story, originally there was the usual void and then two beings were brought into existence, female Tiamat and male Apsu but who were like an Adam and Eve but in a heavenly realm where they created many generations of children.*

At one point the children seemed to be having a really great time enjoying excessive pleasure. Out of jealousy, the father, Apsu, decided he wanted to kill all of the children, but the mother, Tiamat, who was a beautiful goddess, said, no there must be a better way to deal with this. One of the children, Ea, got word of what Apsu wanted to do, so instead he slew his father. This of course greatly grieved the mother and she didn't know what to do.

A high counselor, Kingu, told the mother that she should start a war against the children. So she gathered her children and began a war, so the story goes. Among the ranks of the Anunaki there was great fear. But the one who thought he could deal with it was Marduk, who was born in the heart of the slain father, Apsu, who said he would fight Tiamat. He said he would fight only on the condition that he be made king. Marduk then summoned the elements—the four-fold winds and the seven-fold winds, (4 × 7= 28.)

When he finally gets Tiamat in battle, she is in a total rage, but he shoots an arrow in her mouth that goes in and splits her body in two. Then Marduk and the great grandchildren kill the progenitors. Then Marduk decides he will cut her up and makes a new heaven and new Earth establishing the zodiac and telling the moon how to shine. He vows to create a race of savage men—created from the person who betrayed them and incited Tiamat to go to war. Kingu is then beheaded, and from the blood of the rebel he creates the human race so that they can have power over them. These are the Anunaki, 300 in heaven and 300 on Earth.

That race becomes the Mesopotamians or Babylonians. The Anunaki come to Earth and build the city of Babylon in Marduk's honor. This is an interesting story to contemplate. What is actually behind it all? What does it say about the human being created in this way?

Marduk is similar to Maldek. There is a war and a battle of the gods. The destruction of Tiamat seems to be the destruction of Maldek which seems to be forever destroyed. The evil person who started the whole thing is taken to form the human race. Since they created Babylon, which is the seat of Western civilization of the old world, all that is to unfold in history comes from this story. If this is the case, is it any wonder that Western civilization has come to such a chaotic place?

You may think it is just a story, but this is what created Babylon as a mythic reality in the imaginal realm. We can see here the story of the gods in a faraway place and the big battle that ended up in forms of matricide and patricide and that ends with the triumph of Marduk. Marduk takes the ill-conceived power to Babylon. The whole of that becomes perpetuated in the traditions of the zodiac, the idea of the seven deities and seven days of the week. This mind stream filters into the present world today, deep with unconscious streams of violence and perverse behavior.

This demonstrates the power of forces that we call gods or goddesses that implant themselves in the human mind and create this mindstream that leads forms the basis of modern civilization. From the timespace of Babylon to the present 12:60 timespace is one continuum. From the timespace of Babylon to the present 12:60 is one continuum.

CONSIDER THIS FROM THE *BOOK OF ONE*:

"There are entities experiencing your time/space continuum who have originated from many, many places, as you would call them, in the creation, for when there is a cycle change, those who must repeat then find a planetary sphere appropriate for this repetition. It is somewhat unusual for a planetary mind/body/spirit complex to contain those from many, many various loci, but this explains much, for you see, you are experiencing the third/dimension occurrence with a large number of those who must repeat the cycle. The orientation, thus has been difficult to unify even with the aid of many of your teacher/learners."

—RA, *The Law of One*

This returns us back again to the wizard's garden with the fairies, elementals, angels, jinn and animals. These beings exist to instruct and teach us, and each other, and also to evolve in parallel paths according to different scripts that they are each following.

The jinn and devas are meant to work on practical matters like how water comes out of a faucet. We can do this because we have tamed the water devas to make a water mill or a hydroelectric energy plant—we have to tame those forces.

Electricity devas serve us by coming through wires. These are all examples of elementals in action. We see that the elementals represent a soul or living, dynamic of nature.

We, as a species, have disregarded the soul element of the animals, except for perhaps domesticated animals such as dogs and cats. Though consciousness is now increasing, indiscriminate slaughter still occurs among the different species. A chief characteristic of the industrialization stage is the total disregard of the soul element of animals and reverence for the fact that they too are evolving beings. This contributes to the culture of violence that characterizes the end of the cycle and calls forth planetary cleansing.

Opening to the Higher Mind

The jinns have every right to be on this planet. The animals have every right to be on this planet, and so do the fairies and devas and every other living creature. This planet belongs to God, not to humans. The humans who rebel against this truth are the ones who are destroying the Planet. Because we are an interdimensional planet, when the noosphere actually bursts into manifestation, then with it will return the fairy kingdom; this is the long foretold re-enchantment of the world! This is the coming of the noosphere. When this comes our whole mind is opened and folded out.

THE WIZARD'S GARDEN PROCLAIMS THE RETURN OF THE COSMIC UNICORN!

Our whole mind is waiting to be unwrapped; we are operating with only a quarter of mind or 10 percent of our brain capacity. When the whole mind is opened, then we will see a new reality, a new universe; a new heaven and a new earth. This is the reanimation or re-spiritualization of the world. This is why the next stage of evolution—the noosphere—is also known as the Psychozoic Era, or the era of the soul's evolution with nature. The human spirit cannot evolve unless the spirit of physical nature is also evolving.

The transformation of the physical world will come when our mind is finally reinvested with all of its capacities. We will see this is not a dead world but a living world, and it is we ourselves who endow this world with life just as this world endows us with spirit. Then all of the world will become spiritualized with the conscious manifestation of divine intelligence.

CHANNEL 12

THE RETURN OF TELEPATHIC CIVILIZATION

Telepathic civilizations have always existed. Throughout the universe telepathic civilizations exist in the future as well as in the past. The future and past are unified in the present, owing to the radial nature of time. This radial nature of time is the fourth-dimensional level of the synchronic order organized by telepathic forms. It is in this vast realm that we also re-encounter the wizard's garden—the realm of the elementals and mythic creatures.

The regeneration of the timespace *is* the regeneration of the planetary elementals. As the new timespace emerges, a shift in the energy patterns takes place. Our evolved space brothers and sisters are calling on us to return to the wonder of nature, to be aware of the powers of nature and the cosmos—this is where they live—they can only manifest themselves to those attuned to nature.

Members of other planets have always visited our Planet from time to time, or they have listened to our Planet with their telepathic stethoscope to survey our species. Why? Because Earth is a planet with noosphere and a planet with noosphere is the prerequisite for becoming a telepathic civilization.

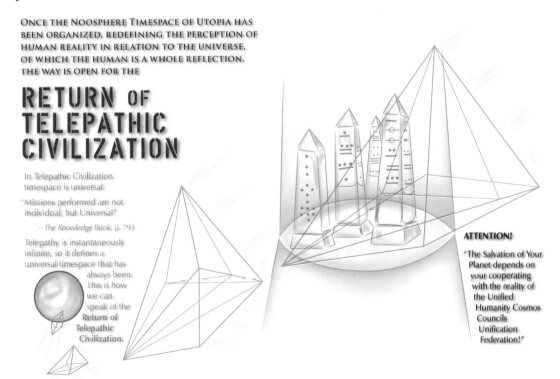

ONCE THE NOOSPHERE TIMESPACE OF UTOPIA HAS BEEN ORGANIZED, REDEFINING THE PERCEPTION OF HUMAN REALITY IN RELATION TO THE UNIVERSE, OF WHICH THE HUMAN IS A WHOLE REFLECTION, THE WAY IS OPEN FOR THE

RETURN OF TELEPATHIC CIVILIZATION

In Telepathic Civilization timespace is universal.

"Missions performed are not individual, but Universal"

— *The Knowledge Book*, p. 793

Telepathy is instantaneously infinite, so it defines a universal timespace that has always been. This is how we can speak of the Return of Telepathic Civilization.

ATTENTION!

"The Salvation of Your Planet depends on your cooperating with the reality of the Unified Humanity Cosmos Councils Unification Federation!"

The return of telepathic civilization can only come about once a complete harmonic pacification and stabilization has occurred on Planet Earth between the mind and the diversity of life forms. Once this has occurred then comes a symbiotic activation of the various species inhabiting the Earth in relation to each other and to the cosmos.

At this time the intermediate "utopic" stage of telepathic civilization is intuited by some. The more advanced minds of the Planet are already receiving the higher registrations of different mental layers that compose the mind of the cosmos. Once the pacification is complete and utopia (or syntropia) is established, then comes the harmonic return of telepathic civilization.

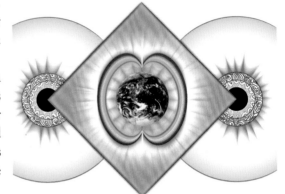

TRIGGERING THE NOOSPHERIC CONSCIOUSNESS

Return refers to a telepathic civilization universally dispersed throughout the cosmos returning to one form of its past. In other words, the timespace is universal and encompasses what we think of as past time as well as future time. Something *becomes* at the same moment that it returns.

TELEPATHIC TIMESPACE AND MENTAL LAYERS

The reason for the universality of the telepathic timespace is accounted for in the formulation of Russian scientist N.A. Kozyrev who stated: *the velocity of time is instantaneously infinite*. This also refers to the velocity of telepathy. In this regard, time and telepathy are inseparable and faster than the speed of light. This means that from whatever generating point of the mind throughout the universe, the telepathic wave radiates in all directions, both to what we think of as space and what we think of as time.

There is also a reception of telepathic time waves from every point of past, present and future. This is always available; this is why we speak of mental layers. All thoughts or mental constructs that have ever occurred or will occur are equally dispersed throughout the universe creating layers of thought waves. The mental layers can be thought of as stockpiles of telepathic mind waves generated from different points in space. These mind waves have a common resonant frequency and so pack themselves into different mental layers.

As the mind is able to rise above the pettiness of the lower self into the higher dimensions, then the consciousness or awareness opens to various mental layers. The mental layers are experienced differently according to the disposition of the being operating behind the awareness. Knowledge is given according to levels of consciousness. Whatever knowledge is needed is always communicated at those specific levels.

Telepathic civilization is but one mental layer that we can open to. Since cosmic evolution is infinite, telepathic civilization is not necessarily thought of as a stable phenomenon, but rather a dynamically dispersed phenomena in which new planets, life forms and new forms of existence are continuously occurring. Telepathic civilization takes part in the activation of the evaluative process of the planets and new life forms of existence as they emerge.

Telepathy forms the primary informative infrastructure underlying and connecting all phenomena in the universe. It is at the parton and subatomic levels that the atomic-molecular-cellular level is unified with itself as it is dispersed throughout the entire universe. All the hydrogen atoms unify with other hydrogen atoms throughout the universe as they are in a common telepathic frequency. In this regard, telepathy is a resonant informative pattern that bonds together all the elements holding that frequency.

Oxygen atoms that combine to form liquid called water are unified throughout the whole universe. There are hydrogen and oxygen molecules, H_2O, that create a common resonance that keeps water as a specific consistency. Wherever we go water is water, it has a particular consistency due to the telepathic infrastructure that bonds all the molecular structures that underlie whatever phenomena or element.

Above this we go to the more refined or subtle levels of the sixth dimensional etheric structures. The same rules apply here. All the elements that make the structures exist, those electronic and hyperelectronic levels are held together as a common telepathic resonance.

The return of telepathic civilization refers to patterns of telepathic return that are engaged on a particular evolutionary course or path and set in motion. There are points in this continuum that cyclically transfer the telepathic thought waves already set in motion by higher levels of telepathic civilization. These thought waves then become engaged in planetary thought forms of that particular stage.

For example, the year 2013 represents an already existing preordained moment of telepathic civilization. This is why the planetary event horizon up to 2012 becomes a phenomenal

Telepathy forms the primary informative infrastructure underlying and connecting all phenomena in the universe.

quickening, so that all the karma can be disposed of, cleansed and purified. The noosphere simultaneously lifts off, triggering the predetermined telepathic civilization and intervention. The mental states and consciousness are then adjusted and modified to accord with the higher resonance and frequency that we think of as the next stage of evolution.

MATHEMATICS: THE GRAMMAR OF TELEPATHY

What does this next stage of evolution look or feel like? We are talking about different primary geometrical form patterns and structures of an etheric nature that are coded with different mathematical formulas. These *"telepathic grammatical structures"* enter into the collective mental field or noosphere, imprinting it with new mental programs to replace old programs that are rapidly dissolving. We can visualize these new programs as millions of cubic structures in the noosphere simultaneously containing or being contained by one master cube of 21.

The higher civilization considers the capacity of the next stage of evolution as one that can contain and embody a fractal cubic structure of 21, which is a 9,261-unit ($21 \times 21 \times 21$) structure. All of its permutations and structures key into the higher structures, including cubes of any and all of its members—for instance, an even vaster super cube of 252—a factor of 16,003,008 or 144 cubed $\times$ 441 cubed!

CUBING

If we add the cubes of 1-21, which follow a larger rhythmic structure, one cubed is one, two cubed is eight, three cubed is 27, four cubed is 64, five cubed is 125, six cubed is 216, seven cubed is 343, eight cubed is 512, nine cubed is 729 on up to 21, which is 9,261. When we add the numbers of the cubes they create another number which is 53, 361, which turns out to be 231 squared. 231 is 21 $\times$ 11, which are key factors in the matrix and cube of 21. We can go on ad infinitum.

Also note that the God particle is 288 squared (82944) factored by 2808 (13 $\times$ 216), the velocity of energy of the mass of the god particle. Of course we can reduce these to smaller factors. This is an example of the basic mental form language of the next stage of evolution that we are going into. Right now it might seem really far out and heady mathematics, but the codes are being prepared so when the telepathic intervention occurs in 2013, these structures will be loaded into the noosphere.

DIVERSITY OF LANGUAGE

Until very recently, there were thousands of different languages that human beings spoke. Some have now gone extinct due to assimilation or extinction. But the question is: How did this all come about? Where did the Jews learn Hebrew? Where did the Arabs learn Arabic? Where did the Aztecs learn Nahuatl? Where did the Chinese learn Chinese? Think of all the different intricacies of these linguistic structures. For example, hundreds of different languages exist just among Australian aborigines alone. Where did they come from?

Consider that the programs of those languages were loaded by previous telepathic civilization interventions that impacted the unconscious noosphere. Then each of the tribes was able to download its particular language according to its psychogeographical location.

Numerous languages have evolved from a set number of root languages and some even now existing are primary root languages. There are still a large number of languages accorded with different psychogeographical regions on Earth. It was some 40-60 thousand years ago that the downloading of language occurred.

As the homosapiens evolved from the Neanderthal type from 78 to 26 thousand years ago, then the different languages were loaded into the noosphere. The final ones came in from 26,000 down to around 3,000 BC. Each group received from wherever they were tuned in.

In other words, the unconscious noosphere contained language structures that were loaded according to a larger psychic engineering program, into the brain capacitors or mental spheres of the different groups and thus, they evolved their different traditions and ways.

Given the intricacies of language and language structure, there is no way that anyone could figure out all of the logics for a language: past tenses, future tenses, subjunctive, imperative not to mention syntax and congruencies of nomenclature. This was already loaded into the human mind with a particular intrinsic systematically logical purpose.

When we travel to the pre-technological past, we examine the fields of knowledge that were considered mandatory studies. We find the main subjects were mathematics, astronomy, grammar, logic and music. These were the main subjects taught by Greek philosophers, Indian pandits and early schools in Islamic Arabia. These were the main subjects and are all related to underlying logical mathematical structures. The original philosophy was a philosophy of number.

Just as the different language programs and their intrinsic structures were downloaded into the noosphere, likewise, in the noospheric stage—the Psychozoic Era—the next intervention will download into the now conscious noosphere. This download can be thought of as different form structures of the telepathic timespace cube of cosmic universal mind. All the forms will be downloaded into the noosphere and we will learn telepathically

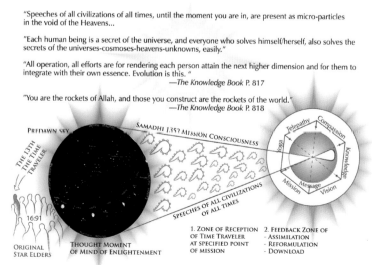

"Speeches of all civilizations of all times, until the moment you are in, are present as micro-particles in the void of the Heavens...

"Each human being is a secret of the universe, and everyone who solves himself/herself, also solves the secrets of the universes-cosmoses-heavens-unknowns, easily."

"All operation, all efforts are for rendering each person attain the next higher dimension and for them to integrate with their own essence. Evolution is this. "
—The Knowledge Book P. 817

"You are the rockets of Allah, and those you construct are the rockets of the world."
—The Knowledge Book P. 818

PREDAWN SKY

SAMADHI 1357 MISSION CONSCIOUSNESS

THE 13TH THE TIME TRAVELER

Yoga · Telepathy · Compassion · Knowledge · Vision · Message · Mission

SPEECHES OF ALL CIVILIZATIONS OF ALL TIMES

16:91

ORIGINAL STAR ELDERS

THOUGHT MOMENT OF MIND OF ENLIGHTENMENT

1. ZONE OF RECEPTION OF TIME TRAVELER AT SPECIFIED POINT OF MISSION

2. FEEDBACK ZONE OF
- ASSIMILATION
- REFORMULATION
- DOWNLOAD

that the grammar of telepathy is a pre-coded order of number just as the grammar of language is the order of words.

How is it that when we speak, or write, that all these words come out in a particular order with a particular meaning that communicates to someone? How can this be? How can it be that we can communicate words in a spontaneous unrehearsed moment? This is because the mind is in resonance with the higher mind or noosphere. In most cases, most people are just parrots; they speak in clichés and in a set of hardly more than 100 learned structures of grammar and sentences. It is no different if we listen to the human beings or the twittering of birds which is why the latest cyberspheric technology is called "Twitter."

We are examining the downloading of a higher form language. With a telepathic civilization the downloading occurs in the form of a particular mathematical language. This knowledge has been gleaned by mathematicians in the past, though many did not realize that they were actually engaged in a whole telepathic mathematical realm or dimension of mind.

How is it that when we speak,

or write, that all these words

come out in a particular order

with a particular meaning that

communicates to someone?

WHERE IS NUMBER LOCATED?

Where does number exist in nature? Though number is the organizational power of all that is, for us, it only exists in the mind. We can say there are 10 apples and four books, but the actual number "4" is an abstraction that only exists in the mind. The mind is already generated in a mathematical process. This is why we get so excited when we discover specific qualities of specific sets of number. Or people get excited when they see time prompts, like 11:11. The excitement comes from the telepathic jolt we get from actually tuning into a larger telepathic infrastructure.

When we get to this point of the telepathic beginning of civilization, we will see and understand where language and grammar come from and also where number and mathematics come from. We will see they can be traced back to particular mental layers that have filtered through the noospheric unconscious into the noospheric conscious.

MENTAL UNIFICATION

The difference between the noospheric conscious and the noospheric unconscious lies in the fact that telepathy means unobstructedness of mental unification. This is the meaning of the conscious noosphere. In the unconscious noosphere there is a density of egoic obstruction and therefore there is disunity that breeds diverse karmic situations that have to play out. Once we cross the threshold to 2013, the growing process of unobstructed mental unification becomes universalized.

As we open to this, we open to higher forms of number language. These higher forms are the main means of communication in the telepathic civilization. In telepathic civilization, the instinctual harmonics of the sense ratios that prevailed in prehistoric or aboriginal man are translated into mathematical ratios that govern all psychic phenomena and create the timespace of telepathic civilization.

We are emerging from the unconscious, instinctual harmonics of the sense ratios into the conscious experience of mathematical ratios that are supersensory or hyperorganic. We know many examples of the telepathic prowess of aboriginal indigenous people. They can sense something is going to happen or sense something happening at a distance to someone, or they can move very rapidly and suddenly jump very high. This is because they are operating in an unconscious resonance with instinctive mathematical ratios that govern their sense experiences, so there is no obstruction between mind, sense and capacity to act.

Sometimes a particular ratio will impact the mind and instinctively engage it in a supernatural response or behavior mechanism. This is a key point—the investigation of the meaning of number from this perspective is called numerology. Though discredited by materialist sciences, numerology is the sum of various efforts at defining or describing a telepathic form language.

As we enter deeper into telepathic civilization, we will learn what those mathematic ratios are that govern the psychic and interpsychic sense experiences. This is part of the learning that comes through the adaptation to the *holomind perceiver*, the seventh mental sphere to be activated within the noosphere.

The holomind perceiver is a function of mathematical ratios. These mathematical ratios are embedded in the noosphere. As we learn these ratios, they affect latent capacities in our brain, awakening dormant capabilities that correspond to structures in the mathematical ratios of the larger matrix now being embedded into the noosphere.

RESONANT ATTUNEMENT

In telepathic civilization communication is transmitted through resonance or knowledge by attunement. As it says in the Tibetan tradition, once yogis reach a certain level of consciousness, nature is all the books they need. We see now books for the most part (sacred texts excluded) are secondary experiences about what someone else experienced or that someone else is telling us about.

Books of the future will be important, but the nature of books will change dramatically with focus on nature and magic/mantric formulas or telepathic mathematic formulations rather than descriptions about something. The bottom line is that in telepathic civilization knowledge is learned primarily through forms of resonant attunement.

At this stage, all elements of consciousness will be in universal attunement, dissolving obscurations such as fear or mistrust that govern historical material civilization. In the state of complete trust, each person will be as transparent crystals, communicating without fear and having their needs met in a harmonious way.

There is no government in telepathic civilization. Instead, there is all-pervading attunement to higher-dimensional frequencies that establish self-organizing, self-regulating councils. In other words, people will know they are in resonance and that they have a particular aim they are going toward and everyone will know which council or group they are working with to accomplish a particular end. When something is needed, people naturally come together and when a project is complete, they disperse. This is just some idea of how this process works.

TELEPATHY AND UTOPIA

Utopia implies a sense of perfection. Utopias were invented because the mind knew things could be more perfect. Even in the myth of progress, machines could always get more perfect, but the self-sabotaging nature of the humans is such that no matter how hard we try to make it perfect it always becomes even more imperfect! So at the end stage it is almost impossible to perceive clearly. All our ways and methods become even more imperfect until we reach the final close-out of the 12:60 civilization.

In the 13:20 frequency everything is in perfect time. That is, everything happens right on time. As people live more and more by synchronicity they realize that everything is perfect. In that understanding where everything happens for a reason, we realize we are part of a larger plan. The more we trust this larger plan, the more perfect we become. This is the process of syntropy, we are always getting better. Our way of life becomes ever more dynamic and harmonic, leading us to increasing levels of perfection and entering us into new gradations of spiritual/mental evolution. This is the mechanism of cosmic evolution—a dynamic, syntropic harmony.

ALL IN ONE AND ONE IN ALL

In the unobstructed unification of mind, which is the nature of telepathic civilization, the One is recognized as the All and the All is recognized as the One. This does not mean that there are not many different types of beings, but at our core we are one. In telepathic civilization, each being is aware of its capacity to engage the mental layers and levels of thought, perception and feelings that are available to all beings. At this level, we gain access to different states of consciousness that distinguish every type of being that exists. In other words, there is a microcosm and macrocosm to each being that is holographically consistent for all beings.

One being is all beings. The evolution of the human from the aboriginal stage of the unconscious noosphere, embedded in the symbolic structures that contain the components of the future, then enters into the future being, the being of the telepathic tomorrow. This is the unification of one being as all beings. This is also the meaning of psychic compression, the chief quality of the future timespace.

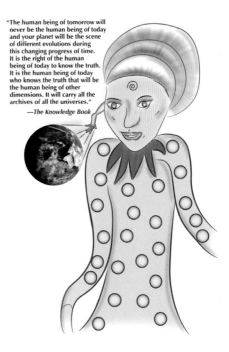

"The human being of tomorrow will never be the human being of today and your planet will be the scene of different evolutions during this changing progress of time. It is the right of the human being of today to know the truth. It is the human being of today who knows the truth that will be the human being of other dimensions. It will carry all the archives of all the universes."

—*The Knowledge Book*

These are visions to reflect on in considering the coming timespace. The being of tomorrow is so because s/he has absorbed and incorporated the structures and mathematical language into the function of his/her total being: physical, etheric, mental, emotional, psychic, etc. This mathematical language is integrated into an operating structure that extends the being into the universe while simultaneously maintaining the form that is projected by the physical structure.

Telepathic civilization has always existed; this is why there have always been visitations from other worlds. Telepathic civilization occupies a multidimensional thought space (which we call universe or cosmos). By superior mathematical constructs of mind, telepathic entities traverse different dimensions due to the common factor of resonance of form constants that are scattered through the different dimensions.

In other words, there is form that remains constant in different dimensions and as we pass through the different dimensions we translate a particular resonance and frequency from one mental layer or dimension to another according to a common form constant. This is due to fractal consistency that remains constant throughout the dimensions.

Superior mathematical constructs of mind may take on similar form configurations through different dimensions in which the telepathic thought construct might be directed. In telepathic civilization, new superior mathematical thought form constructs, through different interdimensional episodes, may appear at specific time event horizons in third-dimensional reality. What is passed to the third dimension may be a future present event in telepathic civilization.

Telepathic contacts with civilizations can also be viewed as interventions that modify mental constructs within the collective unconscious of the planet; the noosphere. These interventions can come from any (past, present or future) time event in telepathic civilization which in the third dimension represents the spiritual power of "a word returned to its source."

The *word* originates from a pre-existing point within a light universe outside this universe. The word enters this universe as a resonance that may go through any number of dimensions until it reaches the physical: 28 to 42 dimensions down. Here it hits the noosphere and according to the higher mind science that is generating the "word", it multiplies itself into a great number of structures which we call "language".

This "word" that originated at a point outside the universe goes through various form constructs before reaching the planetary noosphere. According to the need of group or tribe, the "word" manifests itself into different constructs that we call Spanish, Japanese or Hebrew. These language structures are then channelled by elders of those particular tribes so all children learn that particular language by the time they are three or four years old. By the time they are seven, most children will have learned the grammatical structure and all of the nuances associated with that particular language. This is due to a cosmically disposed capacity of mind that is engineered into the human from a higher dimension.

There are many different ways of conceiving of the universal timespace of cosmic telepathic civilization. This particular one represents the imprint of a modular interdimensional transfer unit. What we see in this graphic is the archetypal structure of a nine-storied pyramid beneath which is the sarcophagus of the tomb with the remnants of a particular entity, Pacal Votan inside of it.

The whole structure is embedded in a hyperelectrical field. Because of this modular harmonic archetypal configuration, the entity can use the surrounding resonant fourth-fifth-dimensional electrical field and ascend through the vibrating structure of the nine-storied pyramid to a higher dimensional configuration of the same structure. The entity can then return to that point in the higher dimension and continue operating as a citizen of telepathic civilization—or return at will by the same means and methods.

The form structure of the sarcophagus lid is actually the resonance of a higher-dimensional archetypal

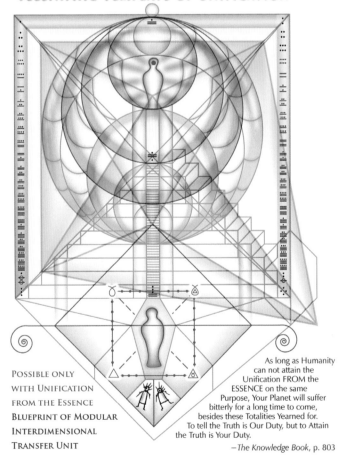

MESSAGE FROM THE STAR MASTERS
TELEPATHIC TEMPLATE OF UNIFICATION

POSSIBLE ONLY
WITH UNIFICATION
FROM THE ESSENCE
BLUEPRINT OF MODULAR
INTERDIMENSIONAL
TRANSFER UNIT

As long as Humanity can not attain the Unification FROM the ESSENCE on the same Purpose, Your Planet will suffer bitterly for a long time to come, besides these Totalities Yearned for. To tell the Truth is Our Duty, but to Attain the Truth is Your Duty.

—*The Knowledge Book*, p. 803

construct. This provides a modular transference to different dimensions. This is an example of how what we call time travel is accomplished in the telepathic civilization. In the telepathic civilization meditation is the principal mode of being. This is why there is such an emphasis on Zen or Dzogchen practice, clearing the mind of the conditioned aspects and habitual tendencies of the civilization that is passing, arriving at a clear state where higher mind may assume control.

OM NAMAH SIVAYA

PRIMAL
TIMESPACE
MEDITATION OF KALI YUGA ARCHETYPE

MANIFEST PROJECTION OF MEDITATION OF KALI YUGA ARCHETYPE

The mind has been conditioned to think that if it is not thinking then there is something wrong. We don't have to be compulsive or engage our thoughts or think we can solve anything by conceptualizing or thinking about it. In telepathic civilization it is understood, because of the unobstructed unification of mind that we don't need to fill our mind with conceptual mental constructs of trying to figure things out. We just remain receptive and open and whatever thought that arises is probably an accurate resonance of a particular path or mode of action or perception that needs to be followed through. This is also how we might experience transference of thought.

Here there is a primal timespace meditation of a Kali Yuga archetype and also a manifest projection of the meditation of the Kali Yuga archetype. The Kali Yuga archetype took form in a mind construct that was then projected into a third-dimensional entitization that can be visualized.

NOOSPHERE
TIMESPACE
OF
NON-EGO

Yogi Milarepa was a well grounded mathematician who had attuned his mental state to the unchanging level of non-ego, while most clearly knowing all the inmost secrets and deepest recesses of the minds of others.

"He was a well-grounded mathematician who had attuned his own mental state to the unchanging level of non-ego, while most clearly knowing all the inmost secrets and deepest recesses of the minds of others."
Tibet's Great Yogi Milarepa
P. 38 [W.Y. Evans-Wentz]

$33 \times 33 \times 12$
$= 13068 =$
112×108

$21^2 \times 2$	882
$+12^2 \times 2$	288
-9^2	81
$=33^2$	1089

$=33^3$	35977
$=1,3,3,1 V$	8154
$=BMU$	216

Where did this image of Shiva come from and who dreamed that up? These are projections of telepathic thought forms. In their original form they are highly abstracted geometries, but appear modified in the third-dimensional time space point to take on a particular appearance, like the meditating Shiva. This is the basis—the ground floor of telepathic civilization.

Mathematicians may experience states of mind that are utterly clear, logical and focused that they are transported into another world. This conforms to the popular image of mathematicians being ungrounded in reality. To enter into the mathematical world of number there has to be some level of non-ego, whether they know it or not. However, most mathematicians don't have the spiritual sensibility to connect the world of number with mental spiritual evolution.

In telepathic civilization, numbers are coordinates in a vast cosmic lattice of unification signals. The universe is meaningful and certain numbers and combinations of permutations spell out telepathic code languages that define the trajectory of spiritual-mental evolution into the supermental field of creation. This is a definition of mathematics from the fourth dimension.

Telepathy—the Value of 21

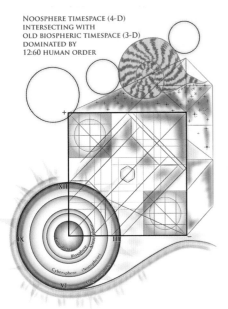

NOOSPHERE TIMESPACE (4-D)
INTERSECTING WITH
OLD BIOSPHERIC TIMESPACE (3-D)
DOMINATED BY
12:60 HUMAN ORDER

Telepathy is the function of a self-existing frequency structure by which the universe remains in resonance with itself. In the mind of non-ego we can tune into this telepathic frequency structure of the universal order. This is why it says of Milarepa he was "a mathematician attuned to the unchanging level of non-ego". This is because he was thoroughly telepathic: "Knowing all the inmost secrets and deepest recesses of the minds of others." This is 100 percent telepathic. Follow the logic.

Highly developed telepaths must function at a level of non-ego all the time. Obviously the nature of telepathic civilization is non-egoic. This is very different from the post-modern civilization.

The sea shell represents the structure of mathematics in nature, the logarithmic spiral and the golden mean as it is incorporated into a snail. Different structures of mathematical orders are impacting the noosphere. This is the structure of the triangular of 21 which equals 231, and then when we take the cubes of 1-21 they are 231 squared. 21 is the eighth value in the Fibonacci sequence. In the Law of Time, 21 is the value of the Hunab Ku and the basis of the 441 matrix, 21 squared.

Even the Balinese calendar is a matrix of 21:210 or 21 × 10, or 7 × 30, this is the key number.

Within the 441 cube matrix of 21 squared, there are various other coded matrices. Keep in mind that we are dealing with a "fractal frequency chip" that also conforms to a program latent in the corpus callosum. This program, the complement and extension of the 64

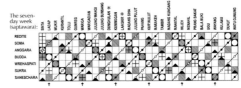

UR runes, is called the *Telepathic Talking Tree of Life* (see graphic, page 204-205). It contains the keys of the code language of the Second Creation. Here we are dealing with the six octaves of the rune strands of the Second Creation. The rune strands account for six octaves or $6 \times 8 = 48$ notes or tones. This six octave range is the span of what the human ear can hear.

The six octaves and the 48 runes—the octave keys of the Second Creation—occur in three sets. The first two octaves describe the actual second creation of the cosmic timespace. The first AC upper left octave is called the Octave of the Divine Decree. This describes the formal creation of the timespace and the firmament, division of day and night, until the "Timespace establishes Cosmos as the one Universal Mind."

The second CA strand, lower right, takes the fiery element of creation, metaphorically described as the Cosmic Creation realized as the Tree of Cosmic Fire, representing the principle of active creation. The tree is the principle of the creation of life. The tree of fire is the principle of the tree that grows in the mind and conducts the creation process of the second creation. Here, the cosmic tree of fire further defines the processes of day and night, and universal order in its process of alternation, concluding with the creation of the planet mind (noosphere) and the star mind.

The next set of runes is the two center octaves: the upper one, AC, is the creation of life as a Galactic Life Whole; and the lower one, CA, is the creation of art as the Galactic Art Whole. So we have the creation of the cosmos and then the principle of how the cosmos creates the internal aspects of itself. This involves the creation of life as the galactic life whole, the galaxy being the unit that contains all the possible permutations of the order of existence that we call life.

From this galactic life process comes the secondary stage where life creates art. So we have 1) the creation of cosmos, 2) cosmos creates consciousness, 3) consciousness creates galactic life, and 4) life creates galaxy as art including the expansion of cosmic consciousness into the universal creation domain.

CONSCIOUSNESS AS CREATOR OF THE GALACTIC LIFE WHOLE

The eight runes of the Galactic Life Whole create or define the possibility of cosmic consciousness which, in turn, creates the possibility of the galactic art whole. The eight UR runes of the Galactic Art Whole then define feedback units of the universe, creating the universe as an art form. When we talk about creating the planet as a work of art, we are actually talking about evolving a reflection of the galactic art whole that enters our system, attuning us to the galaxy as the medium of cosmic life expansion and evolution.

The last two rune strands relate to consciousness and mind. The fifth rune strand (lower left) is the Union of Ascent and Descent. This refers to the higher tantric principle of masculine and feminine operating as a unified force: the tendency of spirit (feminine) to descend and of matter (masculine) to evolve. This is another way to look at it.

The mind creates its opening to the channel of higher or hierarchical command. In opening to the higher command, the mind receives systematic orders of organization. This process of channelling becomes the way we restructure the very nature of reality and how we create cosmic order. The art whole shows us how to shape cosmic reality, but the union of ascent and descent takes us into the heart of the creation of cosmic order—the commands and the ordinances. In this way we are cosmic scientists operating in a vast universal telepathic field.

The sixth and final rune strand (upper right) is the infinite mind wave. This is the higher telepathic galactic Dzogchen where we rest in the infinite mind wave and learn to create time through this mind wave. In the final stage we realize the infinite mind wave evolving infinitely. These six octaves build on the 64 UR runes that have already been established.

The 64 UR runes reflect the evolvement of the life codes understood as the 64 codons of the DNA up to the highest stages of the biological or physical evolutionary process.

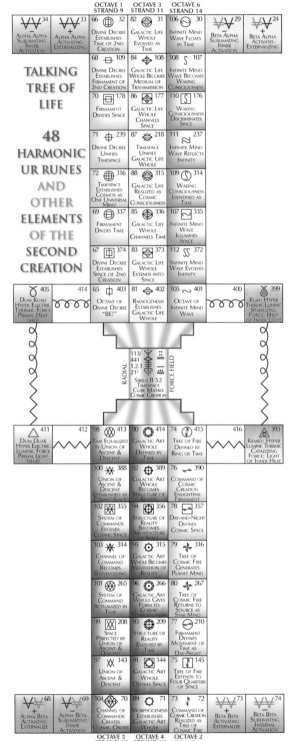

This includes its possibility to evolve into the noosphere and evolve into a perception of the galactic order. The 48 rune keys and six octaves of the second creation build on the 64 UR runes to describe how we become co-creators of our evolutionary process. The UR rune tones are keys of attunement to those processes of creation.

The second aspect that holds the 441 telepathic infrastructure together is the hyperparton of the six plus one units that coordinate the form structure of the six octaves. The *dum kuali*, the hyperelectrical thermic force, is the primal heat, and the *dum duar* the hyperelectrical luminic force, is the primal light. These two partons are balanced by the secondary forces of the heat of inner light (kum) and the light of inner heat (kemio). They create four parton force fields that connect the octaves.

The generator of the galactic life forms (UR rune 81) is the *hyper neutron*. The generator of the galactic art whole is UR rune 90, the generator is the hyper electron. The parton structure holds the two sets of octaves together. Where does this structure exist? It exists in a telepathic mental layer which is meant to be embedded into the corpus callosum of the brain and this then becomes the core of the seventh mental sphere.

At the very center of the hyper particle holding the telepathic structure all together, we encounter the Sirius 52-B hyperplasma or element 113. This is an etheric transgalactic psychoelectric quantum particle that is a telepathically unifying element: Its origin is Sirius B.

In addition to the 64 UR runes, located in the upper part of the corpus callosum, there are 6 octave strands of the second creation with 48 runes. 48 + 64 = 112 UR runes. The center hyperplasma holds the 113th element. Element 113 also corresponds to the center unit of the 441 matrix.

These six harmonic rune strands line either side of the axis of the corpus callosum. This is the core channel of the 441 timespace cube matrix, the basis of the new telepathic form language that is imprinting the noosphere. This creates the radial force field which will allow the mind and brain, as it evolves in the telepathic civilization, to become radialized, resulting in radial perception. Right now it seems we cannot see behind us, but with a fully developed holomind perceiver we will have genuinely panoramic vision and a wrap-around sense field (see *CHC Vol. II*, p. 185 and *CHC Vol. III*, p. 120).

This telepathic element 113 creates hypersensitivity in the brain, radializing and equalizing perceptual functions. This is what creates "radial experiences." This possibility already exists in certain biological forms such as the starfish, which is a radiolarian with purely radial structures. In these biological types, their forms of perception are inherently radial.

The evolutionary line that developed up to the human became bilateral. For this reason, the human perceptual field is bilateral, organized by right and left; back and front; top and bottom. These six primary orientations establish the six sides of the cube. Once we have become cubed, then we may become radialized on our path to perfection.

As we enter telepathic civilization we will experience a perceptual shift into a hyper radial state.

As we enter telepathic civilization we will experience a perceptual shift into a hyper radial state, that is, we will unify all three binary orientations. In the final stages of biological evolution our whole neuro-anatomy will become increasingly radialized. Once perceptions are radialized then we can reform the rest of the biological apparatus. This is the function of the Sirius B element.

In addition, there are four hyperplasmic flows: the alpha-alpha flow, the alpha-beta flow, the beta-beta flow, and the beta-alpha flow—which each have two components: the activating and the sublimating. The activating component externalizes and the sublimating component internalizes. There are eight component possibilities of terminals and generators, accommodating the activating and sublimating pairs.

The whole of this structure consists of 65 units. Just as the 64 units of the DNA code, there are 48 octave runes plus 16 outer units (generators and terminals). There are 64 units like the DNA code. The 65th unit at the center is the Sirius B, the hyper radial plasma coordinating unit. This is a 65-unit structure that forms the core of the 441 matrix. The 441 matrix is the mathematical array which is the channel of the noosphere. Every one of these 65 units is coordinated with a number frequency from the 441 matrix.

With these numbers, we can determine where each UR rune fits into the 441 matrix. In the matrix, the number 441 occurs at V. 11, H.11, and is loaded into the noosphere. Because the 441 matrices are loaded into a particular instrument or agent of transmission, they are then available as structural information units conforming to different dimensions and permutations within the larger telepathic order.

The following is as an example of telepathic language and grammar in the 441 rune triplet. The following is an example of two rune triplet sequences: 144 – 414 – 441, and 117 – 171 – 711.

---

441 AS FREQUENCY TRIPLET INTEGERS

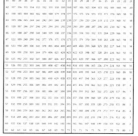

441 is a set of integers with three recombinant possibilities: 144, 414, 441. The difference between 441-414 is 27 or 3 cubed. The difference between 414 and 144, is 270 (27 × 10). The difference between 144 and 441, is 27 plus 270 which is 297 or 11 × 27. This means there are three recombinant frequencies all based on an interval difference of 27. 441 + 414 + 144 = 999. 999 = 27 × 37. Also, if we add 1 + 4 + 4 + 4 + 1 + 4 + 4 + 4 + 1, the sum is 27. This is one rune triplet.

The other frequency triplet example is 117 (9 × 13), which also has three possibilities: 117 (9 × 13); 171 (9 × 19); 711 (9 × 79). The difference between 117 and 171 is 54 (27 × 2). The difference between 171 and 711 is 540 (27 × 20); and the difference between 117 and 711 is 594 (27 × 22).

1 + 1 + 7 + 1 + 7 + 1 + 1 = 27, and, 117 + 171 + 711 = 999, same sum as the three integers of 441. 441 + 414 + 144 = 117 + 171 + 711 =999

These are two base frequency triplet keys. We get a charge out of this because we are dealing with telepathic information. The fundamental formula is 4:7::7:13. 4 + 7 = 11. Then, 11 × 13 = 143. If we multiply 999 × 143 = 142857. This number is a pure cyclic sequence, the reciprocal of seven.

If we divide 1 by 7, we get a fraction whose whole number equivalent is 142857, or 13 × 11 × 999. As we saw in Chapter 3, the reciprocal of 7 is a cyclic number. Any number from 1-6 multiplied by 142857, yields a number that is the same digits in a different order but always in sequence.

When we get to the factor of six, 857 142, we see it is a perfect reverse of the two triplet sets of 142 857. When we get to 7 × the reciprocal, we get 999 999! 999 999 divided by 999 is 1001 (143 × 7), this is a pure cyclic sequence that encodes the power of 7 which is the base of the 441 (note 999 and 1001 are reciprocals of each other).

There are two main points to consider in the examples of recombinant frequencies: 1) Number combination forms a type of grammar that triggers telepathic recognition and 2) All numbers connect with each other to form a larger recombinant matrix of possibilities cued to the numbers, 4, 7, 11, 13, 27, and 37. These numbers have aspects that refer both to the 441 matrix and to the reciprocal of seven. We see a deeper structure of meaning coded into the cube and the 13:20 formulations. Through these two rune triplets, we discover a basis of understanding seven and the reciprocal of seven. For instance, when 142 857 is reduced to its base matrix unit, it is 414—the middle unit of the 144 – 414 – 441 triplet! This is an example of the telepathic form language that exists in different mathematical whole number formulas. Because of the structure and meaning of 441 we can begin to see how it establishes a particular working system. We look forward to telepathic civilization!

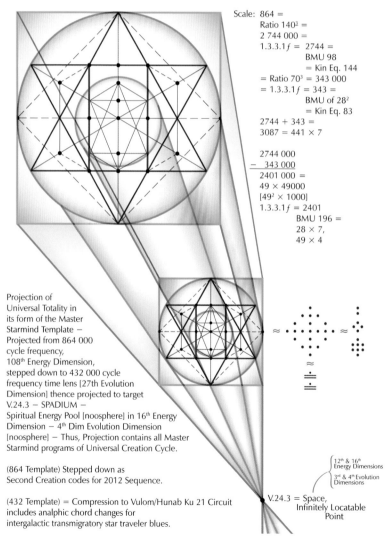

Scale: $864 =$
Ratio $140^3 =$
$2\,744\,000 =$
$1.3.3.1f = 2744 =$
$\qquad$ BMU 98
$\qquad$ $=$ Kin Eq. 144
$= $ Ratio $70^3 = 343\,000$
$= 1.3.3.1f = 343 =$
$\qquad$ BMU of 28^2
$\qquad$ $=$ Kin Eq. 83

$2744 + 343 =$
$3087 = 441 \times 7$

$\begin{array}{r} 2744\,000 \\ -\ \ 343\,000 \\ \hline 2401\,000 = \end{array}$
49×49000
$[49^2 \times 1000]$
$1.3.3.1f = 2401$
$\qquad$ BMU 196 $=$
$\qquad$ $28 \times 7,$
$\qquad$ 49×4

Projection of
Universal Totality in
its form of the Master
Starmind Template –
Projected from 864 000
cycle frequency,
108th Energy Dimension,
stepped down to 432 000 cycle
frequency time lens [27th Evolution
Dimension] thence projected to target
V.24.3 – SPADIUM –
Spiritual Energy Pool [noosphere] in 16th Energy
Dimension – 4th Dim Evolution Dimension
[noosphere] – Thus, Projection contains all Master
Starmind programs of Universal Creation Cycle.

(864 Template) Stepped down as
Second Creation codes for 2012 Sequence.

(432 Template) = Compression to Vulom/Hunab Ku 21 Circuit
includes analphic chord changes for
intergalactic transmigratory star traveler blues.

$\left\{ \begin{array}{l} 12\text{th \& }16\text{th} \\ \text{Energy Dimensions} \\ 3\text{rd \& }4\text{th Evolution} \\ \text{Dimensions} \end{array} \right.$

V.24.3 = Space,
Infinitely Locatable
Point

CHANNEL **13**

ALPHABETS OF THE NEW TIMESPACE

A timespace is a matrix for the creative organization of intelligence according to specific stages of cosmic evolution. The noosphere of the new timespace opens to the cosmic reality of synchronicity. The study and understanding of the experience of synchronicity is enhanced by the presentation of the synchronic codes as whole system information tables.

All codes in some way are symbolic language systems. All languages conform to certain set rules and forms of order. Understanding and placing the elements of the symbolic language system in different tables to facilitate their learning and application has been an approach utilized by alchemists, sages and people of learning throughout the different stages of the historical evolution.

The codes of the synchronic order are no exception. Our understanding is enriched and enlivened when the elements of the vocabulary and grammar of synchronicity—the alphabets of the new timespace—are broken down into discrete templates demonstrating the various correspondences for each component. It is the systematic tables of correspondences that show us the universal character of the synchronic codes.

In this concluding channel of the *Book of the Timespace*, we present some of the principle elements of the synchronic codes as different whole system information tables, the easier for study and application. These elements may be presented in the following categories:

1. The 20 Solar Seals
2. The Thirteen Galactic Tones
3. The Seven Radial Plasmas and Heptad Gates
4. The 64 UR Runes and Codons
5. The 48 Harmonic Runes of the Second Creation
6. Time of Prophecy: The 26 Years of the Harmonic Convergence

1. **The 20 Solar Seals.**
   The 20 Solar Seals form the base multi-dimensional language units for identifying yourself within the synchronic order and providing you access to other elements and levels of the cosmic spectrum of experience. They are called Solar Seals because they represent a fourth-dimensional solar frequency cycle. The Seals hold the keys to your archetypal persona. By studying the correspondences and aspects of the 20 Solar Seals and experiencing them on a daily basis as well—the whole purpose and meaning of the synchronic order—your entry into the noosphere as a galactic archetype will greatly assist in establishing the normative level of the new humanity.

2. **The Thirteen Galactic Tones**
    Organized into their pulsar groups, the thirteen tones constitute the cosmo-galactic language of the movement of time. The correspondences of the galactic tones unify and establish the body as a cosmic vehicle extending through time into the cosmos. The thirteen tones are a whole system fractal order, and can be applied at different time levels—13 days, 13 moons, 13 years, 13 baktuns, etc. The point is that the thirteen tones code the frequencies of the endless cycles of time with a common language, which, once mastered, becomes essential for successful sensory teleportation and time travel through the different dimensions.

3. **The Seven Radial Plasmas and Heptad Gates**
    Between the 20 and the 13, mathematically speaking, there is the interval of seven. In the coding of the seven days of the week—a heptad—the seven is accounted for by the seven radial plasmas. These are micro-quantum particles that carry electro-telepathic charges and are the building blocks underlying the electro-plasmic universe. Each day of the week is coded by one of these charges. The first three plasmas establish a sensory quantum, the last three charges, establish a telepathic quantum. Between them is the connecting catalytic charge. All together, the weekly recapitulation of the plasmas bonds you to the ever-recurring primal creation process.

4. **The 64 UR Runes and Codons**
    Coding the AC and CA templates of the noosphere psi bank are the 64 UR Runes and Codons. In the cosmic science of the Law of Time the 64 UR Runes are the information units governing the permutation sequences of the 64 codons coding all living matter. In the 20 Tablets of the Law of Time the 832 permutation sequences run one codon per week for sixteen years, 1997-2013, while one of the 64 UR Runes codes each of the 64 quarters of this 16-year cycle. In the advanced synchronic sequence of the 13 Moon/28-day cycle as it runs through the 441 matrix, these 64 sequences repeat four times every 260 days. By making telepathically available these psychogenetic life codes on a daily basis, you can participate in the creation of your own galactic life renewal program.

5. **The 48 Harmonic Runes of the Second Creation**
    While there are eight strands of UR Runes that code the psi bank, governing the evolutionary sequences of planetary life, there are six strands of UR harmonic runes that govern the sequence of the "Second Creation." Since the genetic base of physical biological life is already established with the 64 UR Runes, the 48 UR harmonic runes are more like musical tones, and the six UR strands are referred to as Octaves. Within their six-octave range these 48 tones define the frequencies of cosmic evolution as a function of telepathic resonances. These harmonic runes are to be imprinted on the axis of the corpus callosum. Three octaves

of 24 runes define the AC psychogenetic template, and the same for the CA psychogenetic template. These runes are fully activated after 2012.

6. **Time of Prophecy: The 26 Years of the Harmonic Convergence**
   The *Cosmic History Chronicles* are a function of the "time of prophecy, the 26 years of the Harmonic Convergence." In this time map we can see the dispensation of the Law of Time in relation to the stages of prophetic fulfillment. Without the Law of Time it would not be possible to even conceive of the Cosmic History Chronicles. As a process, the Chronicles are completely a function of the sixteen-year Cube of the Law, 1997-2013: Stage of preparing the transmitter-receiver vehicles, 1997-2001; activation stage, 2001-2005; production stage 2005-2011; realization stage, 2011-2013+. In this way, the Cosmic History Chronicles constitute a superconscious transmission exemplifying the evolvement of the noosphere as a program of the synchronic codes.

THE 20 SOLAR SEALS

Name	Color	Chakra	Family	Clan	Direction	Planet & Bode #	Key Characteristic	Radial Plasma & action	7 Major Arcanum	Body	Time Cell		Archetype
Dragon	Red (initiates)	Throat	Cardinal	Fire	East	Neptune G/K (300)	Memory	Alpha releases	Time-space	Right index finger	Time Cell 1 Input	INFORM	Primal Force
Wind	White (refines)	Heart	Core	Fire	North	Uranus G/K (196)	Spirit	Silio discharges	Cube	Right middle finger	Time Cell 1 Input	INFORM	High Priestess
Night	Blue (transforms)	Solar Plexus	Signal	Fire	West	Saturn G/K (100)	Abundance	Limi purifies	Transcendence	Right ring finger	Time Cell 1 Input	INFORM	Dreamer
Seed	Yellow (ripens)	Root	Gateway	Fire	South	Jupiter G/K (52)	Flowering	Seli flows	Avatar	Right pinky finger	Time Cell 1 Input	INFORM	The Innocent
Serpent	Red (initiates)	Crown	Polar	Blood	East	Maldek G/K (28)	Sex	Dali targets	Throne	Right big toe	Time Cell 2 Store	REMEMBER	Serpent Initiate
World-bridger	White (refines)	Throat	Cardinal	Blood	North	Mars G/K (16)	Death	Alpha releases	Time-space	Right index toe	Time Cell 2 Store	REMEMBER	Hierophant
Hand	Blue (transforms)	Heart	Core	Blood	West	Earth G/K (10)	Accomplishment	Silio discharges	Cube	Right middle toe	Time Cell 2 Store	REMEMBER	Avatar
Star	Yellow (ripens)	Solar Plexus	Signal	Blood	South	Venus G/K (7)	Art	Limi purifies	Transcendence	Right ring toe	Time Cell 2 Store	REMEMBER	Artist
Moon	Red (initiates)	Root	Gateway	Blood	East	Mercury G/K (4)	Purification	Seli flows	Avatar	Right pinky toe	Time Cell 3 Process	FORMULATE	Healer
Dog	White (refines)	Crown	Polar	Truth	North	Mercury S/P (4)	Love	Dali targets	Throne	Left thumb	Time Cell 3 Process	FORMULATE	Compassionate One
Monkey	Blue (transforms)	Throat	Cardinal	Truth	West	Venus S/P (7)	Magic	Alpha releases	Time-space	Left index finger	Time Cell 3 Process	FORMULATE	Magician
Human	Yellow (ripens)	Heart	Core	Truth	South	Earth S/P (10)	Free Will	Silio discharges	Cube	Left middle finger	Time Cell 3 Process	FORMULATE	Sage
Sky-walker	Red (initiates)	Solar Plexus	Signal	Truth	East	Mars S/P (16)	Prophecy	Limi purifies	Transcendence	Left ring finger	Time Cell 4 Output	EXPRESS	Prophet
Wizard	White (refines)	Root	Gateway	Truth	North	Maldek S/P (28)	Timelessness	Seli flows	Avatar	Left pinky finger	Time Cell 4 Output	INFORM	Wizard
Eagle	Blue (transforms)	Crown	Polar	Sky	West	Jupiter S/P (52)	Vision	Dali targets	Throne	Left big toe	Time Cell 4 Output	EXPRESS	Seer
Warrior	Yellow (ripens)	Throat	Cardinal	Sky	South	Saturn S/P (100)	Intelligence	Alpha releases	Time-space	Left index toe	Time Cell 4 Output	EXPRESS	Pathfinder
Earth	Red (initiates)	Heart	Core	Sky	East	Uranus S/P (196)	Navigation	Silio discharges	Cube	Left middle toe	Time Cell 5 Matrix	SELF-REG.	Navigator
Mirror	White (refines)	Solar Plexus	Signal	Sky	North	Neptune S/P (300)	Meditation	Limi purifies	Transcendence	Left ring toe	Time Cell 5 Matrix	SELF-REG.	Yogi/Yogini
Storm	Blue (transforms)	Root	Gateway	Sky	West	Pluto S/P (388)	Self-generation	Seli flows	Avatar	Left pinky toe	Time Cell 5 Matrix	SELF-REG.	World-Changer
Sun	Yellow (ripens)	Crown	Polar	Fire	South	Pluto G/K (388)	Enlightenment	Dali targets	Throne	Right thumb	Time Cell 5 Matrix	SELF-REG.	Enlightened One

THE THIRTEEN GALACTIC TONES

Tone	Name	Creative Power	Action	Function	Pulsar	Overtone Pulsar	Body Part	Time Lens	Template	Tonal Value	Frequency
•	Magnetic	Unify	Attract	Purpose	4-D Time Pulsar	Magnetic Time overtone pulsar	Right ankle	108	Star Mind Template	108 (1 × 108)	Magnetic frequency Power of Attraction
••	Lunar	Polarize	Stabilize	Challenge	1-D Life Pulsar	Lunar Life overtone pulsar	Right knee	144	Template of Tollan (New Jerusalem)	288 (2 × 144)	Polar frequency Power of Stabilization
•••	Electric	Activate	Bond	Service	2-D Sense Pulsar	Electric Sense overtone pulsar	Right hip	216	Template of the Cosmic Cube	648 (3 × 216)	Electric frequency Power of Bonding
••••	Self-Existing	Define	Measure	Form	3-D Mind Pulsar	Mind-Time overtone pulsar	Right wrist	288	Template of the Sphere of Polar Harmonic	1152 (4 × 288)	Self-existing frequency Power of Morphogenesis
—	Overtone	Empower	Command	Radiance	4-D Time Pulsar	Time-Life overtone pulsar	Right elbow	108	Star Mind Template	540 (5 × 108)	Magnetic frequency Power of Attraction
•̄	Rhythmic	Organize	Balance	Equality	1-D Life Pulsar	Magnetic Time overtone pulsar	Right shoulder	144	Template of Tollan (New Jerusalem)	864 (6 × 144)	Rhythmic frequency Power of Balance
••̄	Resonant	Channel	Inspire	Attunement	2-D Sense Pulsar	Lunar Life overtone pulsar	Neck	216	Template of the Cosmic Cube	1512 (7 × 216)	Resonant frequency Power of Attunement
•••̄	Galactic	Harmonize	Model	Integrity	3-D Mind Pulsar	Electric Sense overtone pulsar	Left shoulder	288	Template of the Sphere of Polar Harmonic	2304 (8 × 288)	Galactic frequency Power of Holonomy
••••̄	Solar	Pulse	Realize	Intention	4-D Time Pulsar	Mind-Time overtone pulsar	Left elbow	108	Star Mind Template	972 (9 × 108)	Solar frequency Power of Pulsation
═	Planetary	Perfect	Produce	Manifest	1-D Life Pulsar	Time-Life overtone pulsar	Left wrist	144	Template of Tollan (New Jerusalem)	1440 (10 × 144)	Planetary frequency Power of Manifestation
•═	Spectral	Dissolve	Release	Liberate	2-D Sense Pulsar	Magnetic Time overtone pulsar	Left hip	216	Template of the Cosmic Cube	2376 (11 × 216)	Spectral frequency Power of Dissolving
••═	Crystal	Dedicate	Universalize	Cooperate	3-D Mind Pulsar	Lunar Life overtone pulsar	Left knee	288	Template of the Sphere of Polar Harmonic	3456 (12 × 288)	Crystal frequency Power of Universalization
•••═	Cosmic	Endure	Transcend	Presence	4-D Time Pulsar	Electric Sense overtone pulsar	Left ankle	108	Star Mind Template	1404 (13 × 108)	Cosmic frequency Power of Endurance

THE SEVEN RADIAL PLASMAS AND HEPTAD GATES

	DALI	SELI	GAMMA	KALI	ALPHA	LIMI	SILIO
Chakra	Crown	Root	Third Eye	Secret Center	Throat	Solar Plexus	Heart
Force	Thermic Force (litmio & dalmi)	Luminic Force (sigma & sigma)	Thermic-Luminic Force (dalton & nemur)	Luminic-thermic Static distension (kappa & kappa)	Double-extended Electron (dual & dual)	Mental Electron (naur & naur)	Mental Electron Neutron (seldi & disle)
Action	Target	Flow	Pacify	Catalyze	Release	Purify	Discharge
Major Arcanum (days)	Throne (1, 8, 15, 22)	Avatar (2, 9, 16, 23)	Mystery (3, 10, 17, 24)	Initiation (4, 11, 18, 25)	Timespace (5, 12, 19, 26)	Transcendence (6, 13, 20, 27)	Cube (7, 14, 21, 28)
Patron	Christ	Muhammad	Pacal Votan	Quetzalcoatl	St. John of Patmos	Padmasambhava	Buddha
Interdim. Star Map	Omnigalactic Source	Crystal Earth	Hunab Ku	Ahau Kin (Sun)	Sirius	AA Midway Station	Pleiades
Heptad	108 (1)	291 (2)	144 (3)	315 (4)	414 (5)	402 (6)	441 (7)
Gate	∀∀ Alpha Alpha	∀∀ Alpha Beta	∀∀ Beta Beta	∀∀ Beta Alpha	Ⓔ Hyperelectron	Ⓝ Hyperneutron	Sirius Beta 52 Element 113
Lattice #	V.11–H.2	V.11–H.5	V.11–H.20	V.11–H.17	V.11–H.14	V.11–H.8	V.11–H.11
Body	Base of skull	Middle back of head	Third eye	Just above 3rd eye to left	Front center of skull	Back top of skull	Center of skull
Function	Profound Samadhi	Informative Samadhi	Conscious Waking Mediumship	Higher Mind Control	Hyperelectronic Superconscious	Hyperneutronic Subliminal Conscious	Hyperplasmic Enlightenment
Time Dim.	7th Time Dim. GM108X forcefield Cosmic Command Descending	7th Time Dim. GM108X forcefield Cosmic Command Descending	8th Time Dim. Arcturus forcefield Harmonic Command Ascending	8th Time Dim. Arcturus forcefield Harmonic Command Ascending	9th Time Dim. Universal Cosmic Cube	9th Time Dim. Universal Cosmic Cube	9th Time Dim. Inner Core Time
Circuits	Circuit 2 1st Time Dim. Cosmic Creation (opens Circuit 2)	Circuit 5 3rd Time Dim. Cosmic Synchronization (opens Circuit 5)	Circuit 2 4th Time Dim. Cosmic Cube (closes Circuit 2)	Circuit 5 2nd Time Dim. Cosmic Ascension (closes Circuit 5)	Circuit 8 5th Time Dim. Red Kuali forcefield right-handed time (opens Circuit 8)	Circuit 8 6th Time Dim. Blue Duar forcefield left-handed time (closes Circuit 8)	Center
Mental Sphere	1st Mental Sphere Preconscious (Rear right hemisphere)	2nd Mental Sphere Subconscious (Front right hemisphere)	3rd Mental Sphere Waking Consciousness (Front left hemisphere)	4th Mental Sphere Continuing Consciousness (Rear left hemisphere)	5th Mental Sphere Superconscious (connects front back right hemisphere)	6th Mental Sphere Subliminal Conscious (connects front back left hemisphere)	7th Mental Sphere Holomind Perceiver (Connects all time dimensions)
UR Rune	84 Galactic Life Whole Becomes Medium of Transmission	88 Galactic Life Whole Realized as Cosmic Consciousness	91 Galactic Art Whole Defines Space	95 Galactic Art Whole Becomes Meditation of Reality	90 Galactic Art Whole Defined by Time	81 Radiogenesis Establishes Galactic Life Whole	441 Tonality of Sirius-Beta Encodes 7 Days of Creation as Interval of Lost Time

THE 64 UR RUNES AND CODONS

WAY OF THE TREE •	WAY OF CONDUCT ••	WAY OF WIELDING POWER •••	WAY OF THE TRANSCENDENT FOURTH ••••	WAY OF THE IRRESISTIBLE FIFTH —	WAY OF DYNAMIC CONSTRUCTION ·—·	WAY OF THE TELEPATH ··—	WAY OF THE GALACTIC OCTAVE ···
1 Time Generates Tree / Creative Genesis	9 Genesis of Conduct / Discipline	17 Time Evolves Way of Wielding Power / Arousing Joy	25 Time Concentrates Cosmic Awareness / Synchronicity	33 Time Meditates Cosmic Order / Devotion	41 Principle of Dynamic Construction / Temple of Joy	49 Revolution of Telepathy / Revolution of Time	57 Penetration of Galactic Octave / Mind of Breath
2 Tree Informed / Primal Matrix	10 Conduct Treads the Way / Practice	18 Way of Wielding Power Informs Mind / Taming Mind	26 Cosmic Awareness Informed / Temple of Time	34 Mind Informed by Cosmic Order / Prayer	42 Principle of Dynamic Construction Evolves Mind / Radiosonic Way	50 Telepathy Transforms / Transformation of Time	58 Song of the Galactic Octave / Radiance of Joy
3 Tree Holds Form of Space / Fresh Start	11 Way of Conduct Shapes Space / Dynamizing	19 Way of Wielding Power Shapes Space / Wizard's Aspiration	27 Cosmic Awareness Empowers Space / Temple of Being	35 Cosmic Order Enlightens Space / Mind Expanding	43 Principle of Dynamic Construction Evolves Space / Indomitable	51 Telepathy Arouses Energy of Space / Thunder/Arousing Being	59 Galactic Octave Sounds Mind of Space / Dissolving
4 Tree Shapes Space / Listen Again	12 Way of Conduct Informed by Truth / Stabilizing	20 Way of Wielding Power Tames Itself / Wizard's Contemplation	28 Cosmic Awareness Transcends Space / Time of Bursting	36 Cosmic Order Becomes Self-Enlightening / Inner Radiance	44 Principle of Dynamic Construction Empowered by Time / Time Penetrating	52 Telepathy Establishes the Temple / Meditation/The Temple	60 Galactic Octave Limits Space / Measuring
5 Tree Evolves Space / People Together	13 Truth Evolves Way of Conduct / People Organized	21 Way of Wielding Power Conforms to Truth / Arousing Vision	29 Space Flows as Cosmic Awareness / Heart/Moon Crystal	37 Cosmic Order Informs Time / Power of the Home	45 Principle of Dynamic Construction Released into Time / Ocean of Presence	53 Telepathy Evolves the Temple / Evolving	61 Galactic Octave Resounds as Mind / Inner Space
6 Tree Defines Life / People Apart	14 Conduct Defines the Way / Wisdom of the People	22 Way of Wielding Power Defines Radiance of Space / Temple of Vision	30 Radiance of Space Defines Cosmic Awareness / Vision/Sun Crystal	38 Cosmic Order Holds Radiance of Space / Discrim-inating	46 Dynamic Construction Becomes Creative Space / Radiant Emptiness	54 Temple Incorporates Telepathy / Transcending	62 Galactic Octave Defines Evolution / Inner Time
7 Tree of Time Turns the Earth / Power of the People	15 All Points Unify in Conduct / Way of the People	23 Way of Wielding Power Descends to Earth / Mind's Release	31 Cosmic Awareness Establishes Binary Order / Mind Attracting	39 Cosmic Order Returns to Heart of Heaven / Heart's Discipline	47 Dynamism Resolved as Architectonics / Calling the Source	55 Telepathy Becomes Time Travel / Wisdom Arousing	63 Galactic Octave Universalizes Space / Accomplished
8 Tree of Time Turns Heaven / Unity of the People	16 Conduct Unifies the Way / The People Triumph	24 Way of Wielding Power Ascends to Heaven / Radiant Return	32 Binary Order Defines Movement of Space / Mind Enduring	40 Cosmic Order Returns to Heart of Earth / Heart's Release	48 Archi-tectonics Releases Order of Whole / Reaching the Source	56 Time Travel Unifies the Mind / Voyaging	64 Galactic Octave Unifies the Dimensions / Prepared

CA

AC

THE 48 HARMONIC RUNES OF THE SECOND CREATION

OCTAVE 1 STRAND 9	OCTAVE 2 STRAND 10	OCTAVE 3 STRAND 11	OCTAVE 4 STRAND 12	OCTAVE 5 STRAND 13	OCTAVE 6 STRAND 14
65 Octave of Divine Decree "BE!"	**73** Command of Cosmic Creation Realized as Tree of Cosmic Fire	**81** Radiogenesis Establishes Galactic Life Whole	**89** Morphogenesis Establishes Galactic Art Whole	**97** Union of Ascent and Descent	**105** Octave of Infinite Mind Wave
66 Divine Decree Establishes Time of Second Creation	**74** Tree of Fire Defined by Ring of Time	**82** Galactic Life Whole Evolved as Time	**90** Galactic Art Whole Defined by Time	**98** Time Equalized by Union of Ascent and Descent	**106** Infinite Mind Wave Floats in Time
67 Divine Decree Establishes Space of Second Creation	**75** Tree of Fire Extends to Four Quarters of Space	**83** Galactic Life Whole Extends into Space	**91** Galactic Art Whole Defines Space	**99** Space Perfected by Union of Ascent and Descent	**107** Infinite Mind Wave Illumines Space
68 Divine Decree Establishes Firmament of Second Creation	**76** Command of Cosmic Creation Enlightens Firmament	**84** Galactic Life Whole Becomes Medium of Transmission	**92** Galactic Art Whole Becomes Structure of Reality	**100** Union of Ascent and Descent Established as Cosmic Space	**108** Infinite Mind Wave Becomes Waking Consciousness
69 Firmament Divides Time	**77** Firmament Defines Movement of Time as Day-Night	**85** Galactic Life Whole Channels Time	**93** Structure of Reality Evolved by Time	**101** System of Command Actualized in Time	**109** Waking Consciousness Identified as Time
70 Firmament Divides Space	**78** Day-and-Night Defines Cosmic Space	**86** Galactic Life Whole Channels Space	**94** Structure of Reality Becomes Architecture of Space	**102** System of Commands Evolves Cosmic Space	**110** Waking Consciousness Discriminates Space
71 Divine Decree Unifies Timespace	**79** Tree of Cosmic Fire Generates Planet Mind	**87** Timespace Unifies Galactic Life Whole	**95** Galactic Art Whole Becomes Meditation of Reality	**103** Channel of Command Becomes Self-evolving	**111** Infinite Mind Wave Reflects Infinity
72 Timespace Establishes Cosmos as One Universal Mind	**80** Tree of Cosmic Fire Returns to Source as Star Mind	**88** Galactic Life Realized as Cosmic Consciousness	**96** Galactic Art Whole Gives Form to Cosmic Consciousness	**104** Channel of Commands Creates Cosmic Order	**112** Infinite Mind Wave Evolves Infinity

Time of Prophecy: The 26 Years of Harmonic Convergence

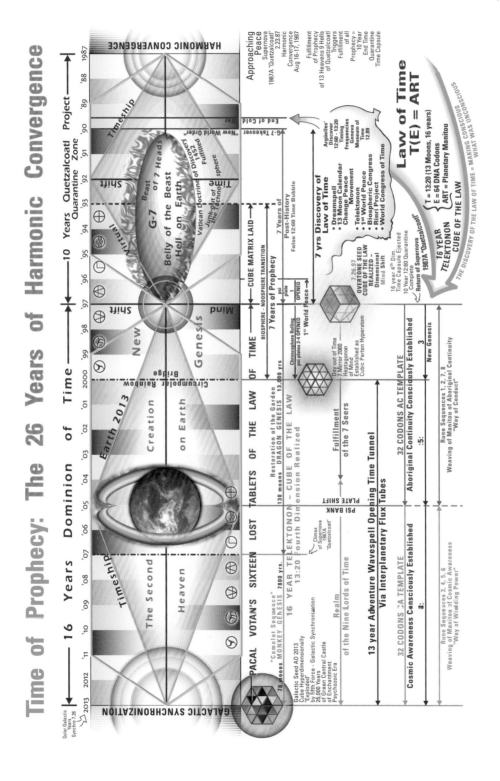

APPENDIX

ORIGINS OF THE TIMESPACE OF COSMIC HISTORY

The voice of Cosmic History is multiple. When it first found its channel for the *Book of the Timespace* some seven years ago, it spoke with an aboriginal clarity from somewhere in what is now called the New World, the American landmass, the Western hemisphere.

This is because it spoke from the channel Tollan—Tula—the origin of the Galactic Maya who were able to locate Tula on this planet among the peoples of the New World. This was for a reason. These peoples were distinct from those of the Old World, with their horses, their cattle, their camels, their evolved metallurgy, and their decimal and duodecimal numerology, astrology and mathematics.

The situation in the New World was radically different in its circumstances for what is usually referred to as the "rise of civilization." These differences gave rise to a totally different perception of life in the universe—a cosmo-shamanic world view, or what is called in cosmic history, "sorcerer's whole body perception." (See *CHC Vol. I*, Chapter 5).

Within the context of this perception, the Galactic Maya were able to expand their civilization and evolve their prophetic (vigesimal) mathematics and numerology based on a system and lineage of the transmission of knowledge known as GM108X. *Cosmic History Chronicles* is fully an exfoliation of this lineage of transmission. It flows from a galactic mind stream with multiple voices—one of these being the voice of the primal timespace Tollan. That is the voice that speaks in this early transcript of the *Cosmic History Chronicles*.

We present this early transcript as Appendix so that the reader might appreciate the pure voice and vision that underlies the present volume, the fifth in the series of *Chronicles: Book of the Timespace*. This voice and vision are actually from the purified stream of consciousness that comes from the future, from the Sixth Sun of Consciousness. Listen to it.

Note: *We are painting a picture here, creating a vision. This is not a linear, or even a factual story, and there are in it several voices that speak. But it is true. It is a picture painted from a mind that is not bound by space or time as they are now defined.*

Tollan is the cultural zone and civilization of the Maya. The name Tollan or Tula also appears within Nahuatl speaking languages and cultures. In the rise of

Alpha Seal: Begins the telepathic quantum. The horizontal line divides the fourth-dimensional world from the third dimension below. The point of union occurs on the third-dimensional plane and diverges to the fourth dimension. Timespace is the point of manifestation. The Timespace is the fifth of the Seven Major Arcana and corresponds to Tollan, an archetypal codeword of the original city in the heavenly realms that manifests in the third dimension.

The shaman invoked the spirit animal in him/herself. The shaman knew which plants were helpful, which were harmful, and which would bring visions.

civilization came the development of agriculture—cultivation of seeds for the creation of food crops. When agriculture develops, society becomes sedentary. Nomadic society subsists on hunting and gathering.

What animals did they hunt in the New World? Deer, small game, Elk, rabbits, crocodiles in swampy area, some wild pigs, fish, etc. There were also jaguars and mountain lions. The New World had far less domesticated animals—there were no cows, camels, horses or goats. There were no chickens, but there were pheasants and turkeys. Farther north there were bears. The New World had all sorts of berries, fruit and nuts. It was an easy place for a nomad to travel through.

The program shifted when the people started to cultivate seed plants around 7000-8000 BC. People in Central America began to augment their hunting, gathering and fishing with planting different seeds—primarily corn, tomatoes, squash, pumpkins, peppers. Think of the cultural effects when there is a hunting/gathering society as opposed to an agrarian society. (When society becomes totally agrarian that's when civilization begins). This is important to understand. They used simple spears to hunt. They didn't have big sophisticated weapons. They did have atlatl (spear) thrower—a stick with a groove in it so you can launch it.

Most people say that during the Ice Age the American Indians came across the Bering Strait from Asia around 25,000 BC. The hunting/gathering society was divided into different stages: Paleolithic, Mesolithic and Neolithic. Paleolithic—Old Stone Age—was characterized by simple stone work. Mesolithic—Middle Stone Age—was characterized by more chipping in the stonework. Neolithic— New Stone Age, they polished the stone. The farther north one traveled, the more fur clothes were required—that is why there are more bears in the north. They also made ceremonial things like drums and rattles.

Much of biblical society had a pastoral culture— intermediate between hunter and gathering and agriculture. This is also reflected in the Quran with suras like "The Cow" or "Livestock". Pastoral culture didn't exist in Central America. It was a dramatic shift when they transitioned from a hunting and gathering society to an agrarian society. Lots of people lived in caves, partook in sweat lodges and went on vision quests. Petroglyphs exist throughout North and South America. These are images or symbols engraved or chipped into rock or stone. Petroglyphs can also be found in places such as Australia, Africa, Altai and Central Asia, etc.

The New World also had lots of hallucinogenic plants and they made ceramics and wove baskets as well as yarn painting. Imagine what kind of life and belief system they had then, when the world was wide open and as large as the sky.

When agrarian society kicks in civilization follows, then come houses, sedentary villages and towns. Different tools are made in agrarian society like for weaving, planting or cutting down trees. Everything always had a meaning; the origin of things, even tools, always came from some vision. People depended on creatures—deer, bear, elk. They talked to the animals who they knew as their benefactors. The shamans were very involved in the spirit life of the animals. Shamans would dress up like the animals—the Balams or the Olmecs seem to have evolved from shamanism whose main nagual was a jaguar. Jaguar babies were known as the initiates.

The shaman invoked the spirit animal in him/herself. The shaman knew which plants were helpful, which were harmful, and which would bring visions. The shaman is the one who can converse with the animals. The society of the shaman is always on the lookout for the successor/the apprentice. The ones who were usually chosen were the ones who were weird—many had suffered a great deal in their life.

The apprentice was put through rigorous practice—like being dropped into icy water where he/she had to find a small hole to wriggle through. The apprentice was sometimes blindfolded and dropped into the woods for a vision quest. That quality or state of mind was very important in the formation of the civilization in the New World.

The civilization of Sumeria and Egypt had a vastly different pastoral culture and were without a strong sense of shamanism. Joseph and Abraham were from the gentle pastoral societies. The civilizations of the New World never had the pastoral stage. They phased in from hunting and gathering to the rise of civilization, and the shamanic experience was strong the whole way through.

The Huichol Indians in northwest Mexico became agrarian but the center of the culture is peyote. This gives a clue of the strong shamanic influence throughout Mexico. The agrarian brings ceramics, basket weaving, houses and is the beginning of making sculptures out of stone. In Central and South America there are large sculptures of jaguars and mountain lions. The funerary ceremonies also became more elaborate.

Chinese civilization was similar to Mesoamerica in that they had a strong shamanic influence. In the New World there was not much development of metallurgy, nor were there any beasts of burden or the wheel. As the sedentary culture becomes civilization (highly centralized order) there has to be more administration of the daily life. The shaman evolves more into a priest or political figure. It's important to understand all the background. Maya were galactic in origin but they had to land and find a place to develop culture. They used many hallucinogenic substances that put them in a very psychedelic state.

Both the shamanic and psychedelic visions create cosmic states of mind. Mind at large suddenly becomes available and the cosmic tapestry can be entered into.

By 2000 BC civilization or a relatively centralized agrarian society developed a high level of art and architecture and mathematics and types of symbolic script like hieroglyphs. The developments of math and writing show a whole other level of mental development or cultivation. A good question is: Why would any people develop math and invent a system of number? Just for accounting? Or is there a higher knowledge bestowed?

By the time we arrive at baktun 9, the Classic period, there is a very high level of mathematical/geometrical ways of thinking. The lines are clean, representing a high stage of mental development. We have to put our empathy and emotional body into being the first to have discovered new territory. If we do not tune into this then we cannot have a complete sense of what Cosmic History is. We have to feel in our heart and being the lives that have gone before us. In this regard, we are just late hybrid beings squatting on the land. Generations and generations of people have been here and had a vision of themselves and the land. The vision is the most important thing. It doesn't matter how insignificant we might think the animal, insect or voice is because anything can speak.

The civilization of the New World has a mix of spirit animals/animism with a mathematical/geometric order. The mental order of the society remains integrated with the spiritual animal order of nature. It did not get separated.

Cosmic History comes out of this cultural cradle and embraces everything. Americans are now taught Babylonian values.

It is important to balance the perception of the anthropologist with the voice of the indigenous, original people. We must develop the sorcerer's perception which is the cultivation of the empathy body to see, experience and feel what it was like 10 or 30 thousand years ago or 500 years ago. We have to see all the different points. What would have changed 500 years ago to 10 thousand years ago? This is the only way we can be in touch with the different levels and stages of human cultural development. From the point of view of Cosmic History nothing ever died. Magic never died, God is still alive. There is a place where everything that ever was is still living. At the very least it is available in a storage vault in the psi bank.

Cosmic History is the reawakening and recognition of all values, especially those that have been displaced by erroneous Babylonian values. Part of our work is to recognize and elevate into our perception the values that have been dismissed by Babylonian thinking and realize they are still alive and we can tune into them because part of our work is the cultivation of the sorcerer's whole body knowing.

All those values were originally a part of our own psychobiology. We are awakening ourselves completely through yogic/meditative practices so we can remember how to speak with the spiritual voice of nature. The study of Mesoamerican culture is very helpful in this process. We have to understand the whole planetary order, and then return to the simple to see what quality or value it has.

In the land of earthly Tollan, there were no beasts of burden. There was no wheel, no chariots and no development of metallurgy. There was no reason to develop these. So this is easily understood in this way. Gold and silver were the only metallurgy. Basically the technological level was very simple but then there was a highly developed agriculture. Since there were no beasts of burden or livestock in the New World, there was never what we refer to as the pastoral phase.

The continuum of culture went from a highly developed shamanism into a civilization phase without that intermediate interval. Compounding that to make it more unique, there were plenty of hallucinogenic plants in the New World giving a heightened vibrancy to shamanism. The use of these substances, particularly mushrooms and peyote, continued into a high civilizational phase.

Only Chinese civilization, to some degree in its early stages, approximates the shamanism of civilizations in the New World. This is interesting because the phenomenon of shamanism as we know it today extends far out to the East, quite apart from the three other centers: Egypt, Mesopotamia and India. Shamanism is a phenomenon that moves across the Arctic Circle and spreads into Siberia, Mongolia and Tibet and into ancient China and across into North and South America.

There are many common characteristics between Siberia and East Asian shamanism and North American shamanism. It appears that the roots of the shamanism were in both Siberia and North America. So the Chinese civilization in its earliest stages had some characteristics in common with the New World civilizations. Though China had beasts of burden and livestock, it was clear that there was a strong shamanic element.

One other factor is that from the rise of high civilization beginning around 2,000-1,500 BC until the time of the Spanish Conquest—for more than 3,000 years there was continued development of high civilization in Mesoamerica—the New World. A continuation of shamanism was highlighted in the Nagualism, which is like a totem or spirit animal. The shamans could take different substances and have communication with the different animals. This animal as an ally is referred to as a nagual. This belief still persists up until the present time.

We have to feel in our heart and being the lives that have gone before us.

The chief spirit animals that characterized Mesoamerican civilization are the eagle, the jaguar and the serpent. In Mesoamerican civilization there are two main languages: Nahuatl and the Mayan language. In the following passages we will speak of things in multiple ways with single words from different languages.

Ocelotl and ix is jaguar. The serpent is coatl, chicchan. These animals represent different powers—both in an animalistic sense and in a more abstract sense. To the serpent was attributed wisdom and lifeforce—Cauhtli, eagle was attributed vision and higher mind.

There was a Mayan named Jose Dias Bolillo, who, in 1942, began to publish many works that he said showed that all the Mayan mathematics came from the serpent, specifically the rattlesnake. The rattlesnake gets new fangs precisely every 20 days. So according to him this is where the 20 comes from.

The rattlesnake has 13 labial scales, a skin with a type of diamond pattern that makes a cross, each point with 13 scales. So we have 20, the 13 and the 52. Bolillo wrote a book based on the rattlesnake as the foundation of Mayan mathematics. $20 \times 18 = 360$. He says that the measure of time is not all based on the Sun and the Moon but on the serpent and the rattlesnake. So every 360 days the rattlesnake changes its fangs 18 times.

If we look at the Aztec Sunstone there are two fire serpents that create the outer form. The two main teams in the ballgames are the eagle knights and the jaguar knights. The same warriors too: the eagle warriors and the jaguar warriors. They would wear headdresses of each animal. The last emperor of the Aztecs was Cuauhtémoc the Fallen Eagle. The tradition of the prophets of Chilam Balam is the jaguar priests, while the serpent was associated with wisdom, knowledge and mathematics. It was said Pacal Votan used a ladder of 13 serpents to ascend and descend from the Rock of Heaven. So the serpent is very powerful and goes back to the origins of Maldek.

Quetzalcoatl is also the serpent, the feathered serpent. This is of esoteric significance, the serpent that learns how to fly. This means that something that was crawling on the ground that has the wisdom of the earth acquires the knowledge and the wisdom to actually fly. This is an interesting and powerful type of metaphor. But in general the fact that is that Quetzalcoatl as feathered serpent shows he has the reptilian serpent, the mammalian jaguar and then the bird. So we have the crawling, the four legged and the wind. The jaguar is the representative of nocturnal, prophetic, esoteric wisdom of the wizards or night seers. These are words of power. They are spoken from the trance of cosmic memory.

The origins of the serpent are with Maldek. Another book with this theme is by a Mayan named Manik Zek Balam. He is a genuine Mayan doctor and practitioner of Mayan acupuncture. His book is called the "End of Planet T" (*Note: Manik Zek Balam was presented the Dreamspell presentation at the house of Elijah Muhammad in Cuernavaca, Mexico, 1992*).

Manik Zek Balam says in his book that a spherical geometry and trigonometry was able to establish the form of the pyramids. He says that the pyramids were centers of transmission and reception and were constructed as resonators to receive and transmit vibrational frequencies. This goes with the very nature, form and structure of the pyramid. He said the pyramids were transmitter/

receptors for the bioenergy of the earth—"the temporary home of the human beings who before them had come from the planet which is now found in the Asteroid belt and which gave origin to these."

He speaks of another planet, Ixtloxiquey—which passed near the Moon and the Earth modifying its geological structure and creating floods—which is remembered as Atlantis and later became known as the star Venus. This indicates that Venus was at one point like a huge parent planet that had something to do with the breakup of Maldek and creating the floods on Earth. Venus always turns in a counter clockwise direction; a day in Venus is longer than a year on Earth. The time it takes Venus to go around the Sun is less than the time it takes for it turn once on its axis.

So Balam talks about the human beings coming from a planet that is now the Asteroid Belt. Since planet "T" (Tollan) is the abode of the original man fallen to Earth, the human must now be reconstituted. For this reason from shamanic times, there was ancient yogic integration with the nagual or nagualism which persisted into high civilization (particularly chief nagualism: eagle, serpent and jaguar). This gave unique character to the Mesoamerican civilization.

We see a counterpoint or balance between hieratical geometrical sensibility in the development of the architectural forms in a structure that is very orderly. In the Temple of Inscriptions in Palenque, Chiapas, Mexico, it is very orderly and elegant. It is evident why the Mayans were called the Greeks of the New World with their architectural sensibility. This clean, clear harmonic geometry of structure is contrasted with the nagualism of the eagle, serpent and jaguar. This creates a dynamic and vibrant quality between the architectonic aspect and the animal aspect.

We also spoke of the diffusionist theories of the origin of man and civilization in the New World, i.e. the diffusion across the Bering Strait before the end of the last Ice Age and possibly the diffusion through the South Pacific particularly to South America by the Polynesian navigators who were some of the most incredible navigators throughout all of history. The

He speaks of another planet, Ixtloxiquey—which passed near the Moon and the Earth modifying its geological structure.

generally accepted theory is that culture came across the Bering Strait during the last Ice Age, the Ice Bridge.

By around 10,000 BC sometime about the end of the Dragon Genesis that Ice Bridge was gone, which slowed the migrations across the Bering Strait. It was believed that from that point at 10,000 BC up to the present the civilization that cultures had developed independent from the rest of the world and were very strongly isolated by the Atlantic and the Pacific Oceans; whereas the landmass of the Old World like Africa, Europe, Eurasia and even down into Indonesia toward Australia is all one big continuum so there is vast pollination of these cultures.

The main track of culture and civilization in the New World was pretty much set by 10,000 BC or sometime at the beginning of the Monkey Genesis, according to the Dreamspell cosmology. The first of the people coming across the Bering Strait seem to have been no earlier than 50,000 BC. There is a strong similarity between Siberian and New World shamanism. In Hopi prophecy there is the coming timespace of the fifth world and Sixth Sun.

If we look at the origin myths or the creation myths, where do the New World people come from? Basically they are saying that they come from within the Earth to where they were not or they came from some other place. It is hard to tell whether they mean they came from across the water or across the sky. The structure of the origin myths is very interesting because it demonstrates a relatively cosmic vision of how the people came to be.

Hopi Creation Story

In the Book of Hopi Prophecies by Dan Katchongva, it tells about the beginning of life according to the Hopi; it illustrates a native creation story that starts like this:

Somewhere down in the underworld we were created by the Great Spirit, the Creator, we were created first one, then two then three. We were created equal of oneness living in a spiritual way where the life is everlasting. We were happy and at peace with our fellow men. All things were plentiful provided by our Mother Earth upon which we were placed. We did not need to plant or work to get food. Illness and troubles were unknown.

For many years we lived happily and increased to great numbers. When the Great Spirit created us he also gave us instructions or laws to live by. We promised to live by his laws so that we would remain peaceful using them as a guidance for living happily upon that land where he created and placed us. From the beginning he warned us that we must not be tempted by certain things by which we might lose this perfect way of life.

The way the materialist historians and anthropologists describe it, the life of early human beings was one of constant struggle for survival. Whereas when we read stories such as Native American stories like the Hopi, it wasn't like that at all. Everyone understood that they had everything they needed.

The Hopi story continues: "We have the advantage of many good things in this life so by and by we broke the creative command by doing what he told us not to do. So he punished us by making us as we are now—both soul and body—he said from now on you'll have to go on your own, and the length of your life will be limited."

This story is similar to the creation story of Adam and Eve in the Quran where it says once they "fell" for temptation that their bodies became visible to them. Does this refer to a fourth-dimensional existence? This is a very different approach from the Darwinian anthropologists. What was the existence on Maldek like? Was the body visible? And if so, how was it perceived and used by the soul? Can we understand it today?

The Book of Hopi says: "He made our bodies of two principles: good and evil. The left side is good where it contains the heart; the right side is evil where it has no heart. The left side is awkward but wise the right side is clever and strong but lacks wisdom. There will be a constant struggle between the two sides and by our actions we will have to decide which one is stronger, the evil or the good. We lived in good ways for many years, but eventually evil proved to be stronger.

Some of the people forgot or ignored the Great Spirit's laws and once again began to do things that went against his instructions. They became materialistic inventing many things for their own gain and not sharing things as they had in the past. This resulted in a great division for some still wanted to follow the original instructions and live simply. Inventive ones clever but lacking wisdom made many destructive things by which their lives were disrupted and which threatened to destroy all the people.

Many things we see today existed at that time. Finally immorality flourished, the life of the people became corrupted with social and sexual license which swiftly involved the chief's wife and daughters who rarely came home to take care of their household duties. Not only the *kikmongvi* but also the high religious leaders were having the same problem. Soon the leaders and others with good hearts were worried that the life of the people was getting out of control.

The kikmongvi gathered the high priests; they smoked and prayed for guidance for a way to solve the corruption. Many times they gathered until finally someone suggested they move, find a new place and start a new life."

This was the previous world. Then comes the emergence into the present world. The story tells how they slip between worlds and pass into the next world. And in the next world they have the first meeting with the Great Spirit.

"… It was here that the Great Spirit first appeared to them on this earth to give them instructions by which they were to live and travel. They divided into groups, each with its selected leader. Before them he laid ears of corn of various lengths. They were instructed to pick one ear of corn to take with them on their journey for their subsistence and their livelihood. One by one they greedily picked out the longest and most perfect

looking ears until only the shortest was left. They did not realize that this was a test of wisdom. The shortest ear was picked by the humblest leader."

Then the Great Spirit gave them their names and the languages by which they would be recognized. The last taker of short corn was named Hopi. Hopi not only means peaceful but "to obey and have faith" in the instructions of the Great Spirit and not to distort teachings or in any way to corrupt the Hopi way of life, otherwise the name will be taken away. Islam has a similar meaning to Hopi, Islam means peace and submission.

The UR—the universal aspect of this teaching totally corresponds with the Quran. He then gave them instructions of which they were to migrate for a certain purpose to the four corners of the new land leaving many footprints, rock writings and runes. For in time many would forget that they were all one united by a single purpose and coming up through the reed, the sipapu.

When they come up from the previous worlds they use the reed which is the meaning of the root word for Tollan. They use the reed to poke away through one world into the next world and the reed also becomes the basis for the sipapu or the tunnel. So the reed, which is the same meaning as Tula, is how they get from one world to the next.

"Now that they were on top we were each to follow our own leaders but so long as we did not forget the instructions of the Great Spirit we would be able to survive. We were now bound by a vow to live by these instructions and to complete our pattern of migration. Ma'asaw told us that whoever would be the first to find him would be the leader of those who were to follow and he disappeared."

This is a traditional Hopi creation story. There are two things we should comment on. One is how highly spiritual their understanding of the origin is and the other is that you are dealing with a passage between different worlds. These are actually what we refer to as emergence myths and throughout the Americas we mind people with many different names, and we might ask: "What does that mean?" The Navajo, for instance, call themselves *Dinay* which means *the people*. When people ask where they come from they say, "We come from the Earth." So this is very interesting.

Of course materialist diffusionist theories dismiss all of this and say it is all just poetic stuff. But it seems that there is a deeper truth to it which has to do with the understanding of the origin of things. The origin is fundamentally spiritual and that the spirituality that is described is a universal spirituality which is the same as the teachings of the Quran.

This universal spiritual nature among the Native American and Mesoamerican people is a powerful attribute or quality of their understanding of their own origin and they say at the end that everything will be known by the different signs or pictographs that are left. For the Hopi the key point of this is Prophecy Rock. Here, the Hopi prophecy shows a trail—then some steps and then a line above which represent civilization and a straight line that represents the path of the original people.

Toward the end of the path of civilization, two signs appeared: the swastika and a circle with eight rays—a sun sign. Then there is a third sign which is like a gourd. The Hopi interpreted the swastika and the sun signs as the First and Second World Wars. The third sign is referred to as the gourd of ashes and is interpreted as the final event—either the Third World War or how everything will come to an end.

At that point the rising line breaks off and the road continues down below. We see the people on the high road whose heads are detached from their bodies. This represents the people of civilization. The people shown at the lower part, their heads are still attached to their bodies but at the other end they have two ears of corn growing, signifying the renewal of the world. This is the prophecy, a pictograph inscribed in rock, which was shown and revealed at Prophecy Rock in 1948.

This image at Prophecy Rock tells the whole story. It is like a pictographic image of the 13 baktun Great Cycle of history. It is what is foretold in the Quran and the Book of Revelations. It is Cosmic History inscribed as the prophecy of history. The image at Prophecy Rock gives us a mythic configuration of the evolution of the timespace of history. Now, at the end of history, the Red Road, the straight road, is all that remains. The renewal of the world is at hand and with it the new timespace, the fifth world, the Sixth Sun.